Cognitive Behavioural Th
Adolescents and Young A

Cognitive Behavioural Therapy for Adolescents and Young Adults: An Emotion Regulation Approach provides a unique focus on therapeutic practice with adolescents and young adults, covering everything from psychological theories of adolescence to the treatment of common emotional difficulties.

Beginning with a review of development through adolescence into adulthood, and the principles of CBT, this book highlights problems with traditional models of CBT for adolescents and young adults. In a fresh approach, this book separates CBT from diagnosis and grounds it instead in emotion science. Adolescents and young adults learn not about disorders and symptoms, but about emotions, emotional 'traps', and how they can use CBT to bring about change. There are chapters on fear, sadness, anger, emotion dysregulation, and happiness. Each chapter provides an outline of emotion science, a clear cognitive behavioural formulation ('trap'), and evidence-based interventions. Clinicians are walked through the process using case illustrations.

Cognitive Behavioural Therapy for Adolescents and Young Adults represents a transformation of CBT practice, and will become a valuable treatment manual to training and practising mental health professionals, especially psychotherapists specialising in CBT.

Dr Lawrence Howells is a clinical psychologist specialising in work with adolescents and young adults. He has previously worked as clinical lead for a youth psychology team and currently works in a multidisciplinary youth mental health team.

"Dr Howells's new book, and method, reimagines CBT for the next generation. Grounded in fine-grain, intelligent clinical practice and expertise, the innovative techniques described here focus on developing a can-do mentality in young people – crucially, helping them reframe their 'symptoms' as normal responses to the developmental challenges of life. On the basis of cutting-edge psychological science, and with many clear case examples, Dr Howells tilts CBT on its axis to show how young people can understand their feelings, harness their latent abilities, and take back control of their futures. At a time when young people are facing unprecedented emotional challenges, Dr Howells's powerful new re-reading of CBT is a priceless gift to give them, their families, and the professionals with whom they work."

Dr Roger Kingerlee, *Consultant Clinical Psychologist, Norfolk and Suffolk Foundation Trust*

"This book offers a practical and refreshingly different approach to doing cognitive behaviour therapy (CBT) with adolescents and young adults. It is an ideal text for the therapist who is starting out in offering CBT for adolescents, as well as for the more experienced clinician who wants to refresh their knowledge and to review and reflect on their applied skills. The evidence base and theory driving the approach blends seamlessly into each chapter. A great addition to the existing CBT practitioner texts for those working with adolescents and young adults!"

Dr Maria Loades, *Senior Lecturer/Senior Clinical Psychologist/NIHR Research Fellow, University of Bath*

"As health care restructures to respond in a more timely way to the mental health needs of young people in transition from childhood to adulthood, we urgently need psychosocial interventions that are fit for purpose and transcend our artificial diagnostic frameworks. Dr Howells offers a developmentally attuned approach which is transdiagnostic and, with its primary focus on emotions, is better targeted than traditional CBT for young people. Novel therapies like this are needed as the new 12–25 system of youth mental health care takes shape in many countries. They can be enhanced through new technologies like virtual reality and online platforms but the theoretical and practical building blocks mesh well with the experience and needs of young people. This approach is likely to evolve further with feedback from young people themselves and experienced therapists."

Professor Patrick McGorry, *Professor of Youth Mental Health at the University of Melbourne, and President of the International Association for Youth Mental Health*

"The term 'paradigm shift' is often overused. However, in the case of Lawrence Howells' new book I believe that we are witnessing exactly that. This book gives us a really fresh approach to CBT with adolescents and young adults, at a time where effective psychological therapy approaches with this age group are more crucial than ever. Howells' approach will help adolescents and young adults to understand a range of emotions – fear, sadness, anger, and shame – and to learn methods of bringing about change, aiming at a desired outcome of happiness and wellbeing."

Professor Jamie Hacker Hughes, *Consultant Clinical Psychologist, Psychotherapist and Supervisor, and Past President of the British Psychological Society (2015–2016)*

"An excellent, stimulating and at times challenging addition to the literature, this book is highly recommended for both novice and experienced therapists or indeed anyone working with young people who feel that simple yet powerful models would be useful in helping them to connect with and help young people experiencing a variety of emotional issues. Highly recommended."

Dr Jon Wilson, *Consultant Psychiatrist and Medical Psychotherapist at the Norfolk Youth Service. Clinical Senior Lecturer at the University of East Anglia*

Cognitive Behavioural Therapy for Adolescents and Young Adults

An Emotion Regulation Approach

Lawrence Howells

Routledge
Taylor & Francis Group

LONDON AND NEW YORK

First published 2018
by Routledge
2 Park Square, Milton Park, Abingdon, Oxon OX14 4RN

and by Routledge
711 Third Avenue, New York, NY 10017

Routledge is an imprint of the Taylor & Francis Group, an informa business

British Library Cataloguing in Publication Data
A catalogue record for this book is available from the British Library

Library of Congress Cataloging in Publication Data
Names: Howells, Lawrence, author.
Title: Cognitive behavioural therapy for adolescents and young adults :
an emotion regulation approach / Lawrence Howells.
Description: Milton Park, Abingdon, Oxon ; New York, NY :
Routledge, 2018. | Includes bibliographical references.
Identifiers: LCCN 2017059367| ISBN 9781138707467 (hbk) |
ISBN 9781138707474 (pbk) | ISBN 9781315201382 (ebk) |
ISBN 9781351781848 (web) | ISBN 9781351781831 (epub) |
ISBN 9781351781824 (mobipocket)
Subjects: LCSH: Cognitive therapy for teenagers. | Adolescent psychotherapy.
Classification: LCC RJ505.C63 H69 2018 | DDC 616.89/14250835 – dc23
LC record available at https://lccn.loc.gov/2017059367

ISBN: 978-1-138-70746-7 (hbk)
ISBN: 978-1-138-70747-4 (pbk)
ISBN: 978-1-315-20138-2 (ebk)

Typeset in Times New Roman and Gill Sans
by Florence Production Ltd, Stoodleigh, Devon, UK

Printed and bound in Great Britain by
TJ International Ltd, Padstow, Cornwall

For Lucy, Taliesin, Tegan, Cassidy, and Seren

Contents

Acknowledgements

I would like to thank the staff of the Youth Mental Health service in Norfolk for all of their support and encouragement. I would especially like to thank Dr Nicky Martin, Glyn Bannon-Ryder, and Dr Peter Cairns, whose contributions and support over the years have made this book possible. I would also like to thank the staff of the Youth Wellbeing Team in Norfolk for their dedication in taking on and furthering the ideas outlined in this book.

I am grateful to the adolescents and young adults who have sought the help of these various services whose courage, resilience, hard work, and feedback has driven the process of development and clarification of this work.

Finally, I would like to thank my family for putting up with me while I put this book together, and also for their critiquing and proof-reading along the way.

Chapter 1

Introduction

There is increasing recognition that the transition from childhood to adulthood is a period with an increasingly widening timeframe. Children are beginning adolescence earlier, whether defined biologically, psychologically, or societally. Adults are emerging later, as defined by psychological, intellectual, or financial independence, or indeed brain development. Adolescence, previously often thought of as the 'teen' phase, is now more frequently defined as the period between around 10 until 25 years of age (see Chapter 2).

There is also increasing recognition that this decade and a half is a time of intense difficulty and a time when young people frequently require help. As a result, specialist youth mental health projects and services are beginning to develop across the world; programmes and international conferences are flourishing.

Despite growth in this area and increasing provision of services specifically for adolescents and young adults, there is a relative lack of literature tailored to this age range. The majority of literature categorises itself as either for adults or for children and their families.

This treatment manual aims to provide clinicians with a guide to CBT targeted specifically at those aged between 10 and 25. The book begins with a detailed outline of adolescent and early adult development and provides a context for the remainder of the book (Chapter 2).

Cognitive behavioural therapy (CBT) is an intervention that has developed over the past 50–60 years with a clear foundation in empiricism and testing out each new development. As a result of this, CBT is now the psychological therapy with most evidence for the widest variety of difficulties (Chapter 3). The evidence base for CBT across the age range is also strong. As a result of this, demand for CBT is high and clinical services across the world are stretched. Clinicians are working within settings that place a high value on turnover and have high expectations of the numbers of sessions that can be undertaken. The space for stopping and thinking, reading and learning is squeezed. As a result, clinicians find it difficult to keep up with the evidence and to provide treatment in a manner most consistent with what is most effective (see Chapter 4).

Alongside this, the evidence base for CBT is growing and there are ever-increasing numbers of models for different presenting problems or problems with slightly different foci, depending on their authors. For obsessive-compulsive difficulties, for example, clinicians can choose between five different models (see Chapter 4).

Working as a clinician in everyday practice has therefore become increasingly difficult, and there is little time to research the evidence base for each slightly different presentation, or to effectively keep up with the vast array of different models that are provided within the discipline of CBT. The risk of this situation is that, while the models, when implemented by their proponents in specific populations, might be increasing in effectiveness, the practice of CBT on the ground suffers and its effectiveness declines (see Chapter 4).

This treatment manual aims to provide clinicians with a limited number of discrete, simple, models that they can use to cover the majority of presentations seen in everyday practice with adolescents and young people. It brings together research and evidence in ways that are designed to be clear and easy to understand, so that clinicians can become experts in a few models that they can tailor and apply to the majority of their clients, directing them towards clear, evidence-based interventions.

Increased recognition of difficulty for adolescents and young adults has produced a wide variety of response. Schools, colleges, employers, and other institutions are increasingly providing information about psychiatric disorders as part of 'mental health' or 'emotional wellbeing' programmes and there are national programmes designed to increase awareness of mental health difficulties.

These kinds of programme are often thought of as unquestionably helpful and yet the evidence is not so positive. The diagnostic model is not as valid or reliable as is often assumed, it tends to decontextualize difficulties, increase stigma, reduce agency, and has a negative impact on identity development (Chapter 4). That the predominant model offered to adolescents and young adults to understand their emotions is an illness model, may well be an important contributory factor to the apparent increase in 'illness' in this population. One of the main aims of this book is to provide an alternative framework through which adolescents and young adults can understand their emotions and their difficulties with emotions.

This fresh approach is outlined in Chapter 5, where adolescents and young adults are given the opportunity to understand their difficulties and receive intervention without having to view themselves as 'disordered' or 'ill'. CBT is separated from the diagnostic model and is grounded instead in emotion science. The chapter outlines the theoretical basis before detailing the five principles of the approach: what emotions are, what emotions are for, how emotions are regulated, adolescent development, and the hand brain. Each of these principles is based on evidence from a variety of different disciplines, including academic psychology, neuroscience, and applied psychology. These five principles inform the rest of the book, which is a practical treatment guide for clinicians working with adolescents, young adults, and their families.

Subsequent chapters look at specific emotions: Fear (Chapter 6), Sadness (Chapter 7), Anger (Chapter 8), and Emotion dysregulation (Chapter 9). Each of these chapters explores the emotion in detail, looking at its causes, the impact it has on different aspects of the emotional experience, and then outlines a trap that provides a detailed understanding of what can go wrong. Each chapter contains an intervention section, taking clinicians through exactly what to do and how to do it, with illustrative material. There is a section outlining how these treatment models relate to the evidence base at the end of each chapter. There are two brief chapters on Disgust (Chapter 10) and Guilt and shame (Chapter 11), which look at how these emotions might interact with the traps outlined earlier.

The last chapter is Happiness (Chapter 12). Happiness is not usually included in treatment manuals, but is often a desired outcome for treatment. This chapter outlines what causes happiness, what it is (and isn't), and its functions. It then outlines the happiness wheel and brings together the interventions, the majority of which are already covered in other parts of the book, that are shown to help adolescents and young adults move towards a life characterised by happiness, wellbeing, and flourishing.

While broad, this book does not aim to cover everything. It specifically neglects:

- Psychosis. This book does not specifically cover psychosis or psychotic phenomena. However, the book does cover many of the difficulties experienced alongside psychosis, for example sadness or social fears.
- Trauma work. This book begins predominantly from a here-and-now perspective. Trauma is included in longitudinal formulations and informs the traps and difficulties in this book, but work designed to support the processing of trauma memories using techniques such as reliving or rescripting is not covered.
- Medication. This is a psychological volume designed for psychologically training clinicians and so medication is not covered.

In summary, this book aims to achieve a number of related objectives:

- Provide a detailed guide to treatment tailored specifically for adolescents and young adults, rather than children or adults.
- Ground treatment in models of psychological development and emotion rather than disorders and illness.
- Provide clinicians with clear, concise CBT formulations and evidence-based treatment plans, all illustrated with case material.
- Cover the full range of different presentations seen in 'everyday' clinical practice.

Throughout the book, example case material is used to illustrate the concepts and ideas. In addition, a number of different adolescents and young adults whose therapy has been based on the ideas of this book have provided quotes that are used at the beginning of the chapters. Each individual involved has provided consent for their words to be used for this purpose.

Chapter 2

Adolescent development

I feel like a person of value and I have certain expectations of people. I want to achieve things in my life; I'm still young.

(21-year-old male)

Adolescence is a phase of life which is often negatively perceived by society at large. A survey in 1999, for example, found that members of the general public tended to use words such as 'rude', 'irresponsible', and 'wild' to describe adolescents, and that fewer than half the respondents expected that adolescents would have a positive impact on society (Farkas et al., 1997). This same survey found that people tended to cite a lack of basic values such as honesty, respect, and responsibility as adolescents' biggest failings. These negative perceptions of adolescence appear to be longstanding; Arnett (1999) cites Aristotle's quote that youth "are heated by nature as drunken men by wine" and Shakespeare's a Winter's Tale:

I would that there were no age between ten and three-and-twenty, or that youth would sleep out the rest . . . for there is nothing in between but getting wenches with child, wronging the ancientry, stealing, fighting. . . .

(Act III scene 3)

As well as these societal beliefs, parents tend to perceive adolescence as the most difficult stage of their children's development (Buchanan et al., 1990).

Despite these negative stereotypes, adolescents themselves report a much more positive experience. The majority of adolescents report good relationships with their parents, other adults, and friends, as well as fairly good levels of wellbeing (Farkas et al., 1997, Laursen, Coy, and Collins, 1998).

The developmental processes taking place during adolescence and early adulthood provide the backdrop to all our work with individuals in this stage of life. It is important that we understand, and can explain these developmental processes to adolescents, young adults, and their families. This chapter therefore outlines the changes taking place during adolescence, in a range of areas, and looks at the theoretical frameworks that have been used to understand this period of life.

What and when is adolescence?

Adolescence is a period of transition. It is the passage between childhood and adulthood and involves accelerated growth in a variety of different areas.

Given that adolescence is a phase of life, it is difficult to define in terms of distinct age ranges. For many, adolescence is synonymous with teenagerhood, suggesting an age range of between 13 and 19. For others, adolescence ends earlier, somewhere around society's legal age limits relating to the transition to adulthood, for example at 16, the age of sexual consent in many countries, or at 18, the age of the vote. Interestingly, Shakespeare in his quote above chooses the wider definition of 10 to 23, and other early authors have chosen similarly wide definitions, for example 12 to 25 (Hall, 1904).

In today's society, there are good reasons to adopt a broader age range. Firstly, many of the changes associated with adolescence are beginning earlier; children appear to be entering puberty at a younger age than they did previously (see below) and many other aspects of adolescence (such as sexual exploration) are beginning earlier, fuelled by changes in society and access to information (Bloch, 1995). Other aspects of adolescence, however, are delayed and are occurring later than in previous generations. Across the developed world, for example, young people are spending increasing amounts of time in education and are also financially dependent on their families for longer. These societal changes do not impact equally across society and there is general consensus that the process of adolescent transition has become extended, pluralised, and fragmented (Coleman, 2011). Finally, research into brain development has found that the brain continues to evolve and develop in quite fundamental ways all the way through into the late 20s and early 30s (see below). Given this widening age range, some authors have tended to break down the period into smaller timeframes, for example early adolescence, later adolescence, and emerging adulthood (Patton et al., 2016).

Given the level of individual difference in the rate of transition, it is perhaps imprudent to adopt rigid age ranges to define adolescence. However, to give a rough idea about the population we are considering, adolescence is considered in this book to cover the period between the ages of 10 and 25 years.

It is important to outline this idea to clients, families, and other clinicians. Adolescence is not a phase of life that ceases abruptly upon turning 18, but is a more nuanced and gradual phase lasting into the twenties and often longer. Reference to brain research in relation to this explanation often adds significant weight to the argument! As individuals in their twenties tend not to identify themselves as adolescents, the term "adolescents and young adults" is used throughout this book.

Physical development

Puberty is a period of physical development characterised by rapid changes in body size, shape, and composition. It produces the most rapid rate of linear growth since infancy and the greatest sexual differentiation since foetal life (Rogol, Roemmich, and Clark, 2002).

Sexual maturation occurs during puberty under the influence of gonadal steroid hormones; primarily testosterone in boys and oestradiol in girls. The early stages of sexual maturation often involve the appearance of pubic hair, adult-type body odour, and occasionally acne. In boys, the first signs of formal sexual maturation are the thinning and reddening of the scrotum and the enlargement of the testes. This occurs on average around 111/2 to 12 years, although is considered normal between 9 and 14. Sperm production and ejaculatory capacity are present during early sexual development (on average around 131/2 years).

In girls, the first evidence of formal sexual maturation is the appearance of breast buds. This occurs on average at 11 years, usually between 8 and 13 years. Menarche usually follows the onset on breast development by about 21/2 years, at an average age of around 13 years. More than half of girls have irregular inter-menstrual intervals for the first two years (Rogol, Roemmich, and Clark, 2002).

Interestingly, puberty appears to begin, on average, around four years earlier than a century ago, a fact that is thought to be related primarily to environmental factors such as improved sanitation, health, and nutrition (e.g. Bloch, 1995).

Brain development

Physical changes in the body are accompanied by physical changes in the brain. Early brain research found that environmental stimulation was necessary during very early life in order for development to occur in the sensory regions of the brain (Hubel and Wiesel, 1962). It was widely agreed that the brain was an organ which required appropriate environmental stimulation at specific 'sensitive periods' in infancy in order to properly develop.

Later research using human autopsy found substantial changes occurring later in development as well; both qualitative and quantitative differences were found pre- and post-adolescence in the areas of the brain such as the prefrontal cortex. Subsequent studies have found similar differences using imaging techniques in brains pre- and post-adolescence (Blakemore and Choudhury, 2006).

Research now suggests that, rather than a single period of sensitivity in early infancy, the brain has an extended period of development into adolescence. What appears to be a second period of rapid brain development occurs particularly in the frontal and the parietal cortices (Sowell et al., 2001). These regions of the brain are implicated in tasks of executive function, including working memory, and the ability to direct attention, to make decisions, and to inhibit otherwise automatic responses. Imaging studies have found links between development, brain activation in these areas, and performance on tasks requiring executive function (Blakemore and Choudhury, 2006).

Overall, it seems that the changes taking place during adolescence in the internal structure of the brain, particularly in the frontal and parietal cortices, might be as dramatic as those taking place in the body.

Cognitive development

These structural changes in the brain parallel changes in terms of brain function, and there are important developments in cognitive ability during adolescence, particularly in relation to executive function.

Piaget was one of the first psychologists to systematically study cognitive ability, outlining a stage model in which individuals move through four discrete stages of cognitive development. The key shift during adolescence in Piaget's model is that between the third 'concrete operational stage' and the fourth 'formal operational stage', a process that is thought to begin around 11 years and continue until 15–20 years (Inhelder and Piaget, 1958). In Piaget's stage model, 'formal operations' is a stage of thought characterised by the ability to conduct operations on operations; to think about thinking. This second order level of thought enables a shift from thinking about the world in a concrete manner (the 'real'), to a more abstract manner (the 'possible'). In developing this theory, Piaget and his colleagues developed a host of different tasks they presented to children and adolescents of increasing age to determine the process of development of thought. A number of these nicely illustrate the qualitative difference in thought between childhood and adulthood.

Elkind (1966) presented individuals with a series of pairs of images. Choosing the correct image caused a light to flash, the task being to find the property of the image that was linked to the flashing light. There were a number of possibilities, including vehicles versus non-vehicles, or wheeled objects or non-wheeled objects. Children tended to persevere with inaccurate strategies and struggle to accurately determine the characteristic associated with the light, whereas adolescents tended to adjust their strategy in light of contrary evidence.

In the pendulum test (Inhelder and Piaget, 1958), individuals were asked which factor, or combination of factors, determined the rate of the swing of the pendulum. Formal operational thinkers approached the problem systematically by varying one factor at a time, for example the length of the string, the heaviness of the weight, or the size of the swing. Those who had not yet acquired these abilities (who remained in the third 'concrete operational stage') tended to be less systematic in their approach, varying different factors at once, or changing things at random.

A final task used by Piaget was one in which children and adolescents were asked to imagine where they would put a third eye (Inhelder and Piaget, 1958). Concrete operational thinkers tended to place the third eye in the centre of their forehead, while formal operational thinkers were able to play with the idea and put it in the back of their head so they could see behind them, or on their hand so they could see around corners.

These tasks illustrate the differences thought to exist between concrete and formal operational thinkers. Firstly, there are important differences in the way in which individuals think about the real and the possible. A concrete operational thinker tends to start with the real to determine the possible, whereas the formal operational thinker can begin with the possible – an idea or a hypothesis – and test it against reality. This is an exhibition of abstract thought and can be seen in a strategic approach to the three tests outlined above. Secondly, formal operational thinkers tend to use hypothetico-deductive thought in which they can use an idea about the world to make predictions they can subsequently test. Thirdly, formal operational thought is characterised by the ability to coordinate several dimensions; for example in the pendulum task there are a variety of different interacting dimensions that need to be considered. Fourthly, formal operational thinkers can disregard aspects of situations that are not relevant to the problem at hand and can reason on the basis of illogical premises (e.g. having a third eye).

Piaget's work has subsequently been criticised for focusing too heavily on the concept of discrete stages that are thought to develop in a generalised manner, as it appears that, while individuals might be capable of thinking in a systematic manner, they do not always do so (Ward and Overton, 1990). Subsequent research has found a much wider age range where the abilities associated with the formal operational stage emerge, noting that some individuals never reach this stage of thought (Shayer and Wylam, 1978).

Other theorists have suggested alternatives to a stage-based model, focusing instead on information-processing models suggesting more gradually developing capability, which results in an increasing tendency to such styles of thought. These models tend to focus on development in five areas of ability, namely attention, working memory, processing speed, organisation, and meta-cognition (Casteel, 1993).

Whatever the model used to describe the process, it does appear that, during the process of adolescence, there is a fairly rapid cognitive advancement which takes the individual from a predominantly responsive concrete thinking style towards a more fully conscious, self-directed, and self-regulating mind (Keating, Lerner, and Steinberg, 2004). This allows adolescents and young adults to gradually consider their worlds in a more abstract and principled way and leads to dramatic shifts in the ways in which they view morals, politics, and the social world in general.

These processes of cognitive development are important to hold in mind when working with adolescents and young adults, given the reliance of many of the interventions of CBT on formal operational abilities. It is also important to remember that this development, like the development in the areas of biology and the brain already discussed, takes place in an environmental, social, and educational context. Where there are difficulties in these contexts, there may well be an impact on the quality and the rate of the development of these skills.

Social cognitive development

The ability to engage in more abstract processes of thought enables adolescents to begin to think about the less concrete aspects of their social worlds. Young children, when asked to describe people, tend to focus on physical character-istics such as sex, height, and hair colour, whereas adolescents begin to describe others in terms of their interests, attitudes, and personality (Keating, Lerner, and Steinberg, 2004). The movement towards thinking in more abstract terms about the social world parallels overall cognitive development.

For Selman (1980) a key aspect in social development is the ability to adapt to another's perspective by taking their point of view. He called this ability 'role taking' and outlined a staged model, akin to Piaget's model, in which the achievement of Piaget's stages is seen as necessary but not sufficient for the development of these role-taking stages.

The role-taking stages overlap, and children up to the ages of around 6 are considered to be in Level 0 where they tend to conflate or confuse their own thoughts and feelings with those of others. At Level 1 (between the ages of 4 and 9 years), children understand that individuals may have different perspectives to their own. At Level 2 (7–12 years) children begin to understand that others have a different perspective to their own, and also that others might think about the child's perspective – they can begin to see themselves from another's point of view. At Level 3 (ages 10–15 years), children can take a more complex viewpoint and begin to imagine how both self and others might be viewed from a third-person perspective. Finally, at Level 4 (ages 14 to adult), the individual may move to a higher, more abstract level of inter-personal perspective examining the interactions between broad systems of societal values and individuals or groups.

There is evidence to support the increasing ability of role taking and social understanding with age (Selman, 1971). Further, role-taking ability has been shown to be associated with cooperation, empathy, social functioning, and conflict resolution (Underwood and Moore, 1982). Interestingly, there is work demonstrating that young people can be encouraged to develop their role-taking abilities, and that this leads to changes (and improvements) in the ways in which they relate to others (Chalmers and Townsend, 1990).

Identity development

Given the development outlined so far – the ability to think in the abstract, to view the self from other points of view, and to consider the impact of the environment on the self – the stage is set for the development of a more complex and subtle sense of self.

There are a number of ways in which this sense of the self develops through adolescence. The first is in terms of the degree of differentiation. Adolescents are more able to understand that they might be different from other people, or that they might exhibit different characteristics depending on the situation. They are also more likely to notice or begin to consider the degree of organisation or coherence among different personality traits.

Erikson's psychosocial model: fidelity versus role confusion

Erikson's model of psychosocial development separates the process into eight discrete stages (1968). A healthy developing individual is expected to master and overcome the challenges of each stage. Each stage builds upon the previous stages, but individuals do not have to successfully navigate each stage in order to progress to the next. Unsuccessful navigation, however, may well lead to problems in the future. Each stage is characterised by a particular challenge and Erikson labelled each with a pair of opposing forces, for example "trust versus mis-trust" which is the first stage in which the individual has to learn to trust that they will receive love and care.

Erikson's stage of adolescence was labelled "Fidelity: identity versus role confusion" in which the challenge is to create a coherent sense of self; to battle against a sense of identity diffusion and confusion. This stage was the first in which successful development was more dependent upon the actions of the individual rather than the actions of others; Erikson believed young people needed to experiment and try out different identities, to discard or move through identities in a process of diffusion or identity crisis, in order to reach a point of more stable identity. Erikson (1968) noted that it was important for societies to tolerate this experimentation rather than labelling it as deviant behaviour.

Marcia (1966) attempted to operationalise these ideas using a four-category model of this stage of personality development.

- *Identity diffusion*: the individual has not yet experienced an identity crisis and has made no commitment to a strong sense of identity.
- *Identity foreclosure*: the individual has settled on a sense of self without experimentation or crisis and therefore largely as a result of others' opinions and choices.
- *Moratorium*: the individual is in the process of searching among alternatives for a sense of identity.
- *Identity achievement*: the individual is considered to have arrived at a largely stable sense of identity through a process of crisis and moratorium.

Marcia's work has led to a vast array of research using various instruments to assign individuals to one of the four categories and look at trends across individuals and across time. Kroger, Martinussen, and Marcia (2010) provide a summary of this research and conclude that individuals in the identity achievement category exhibit the highest levels of achievement, moral reasoning, career maturity, and social skills. Those in the identity diffusion category are most socially withdrawn and most likely to struggle with psychological and interpersonal problems. Those in the foreclosure category are most likely to require high levels of approval from others and those in the moratorium category are most likely to struggle with those in authority.

Some (e.g. Cote 2009) have criticised Marcia's model on the basis that it seems that the majority of individuals do not appear to successfully reach identity achievement (between 20–40% in cited studies) and so Marcia may be describing what individuals ought to do rather than what they actually do. This is further supported by the sense that there does not appear to be a common developmental sequence for these stages (Lavoie 1994). Given that Erikson's model was an attempt to describe normative development, Marcia's stages are perhaps less useful than they might be.

Self esteem

Rosenberg's (1965) concept of self-esteem has had a massive impact on society's understanding of the self. Self-esteem is considered the totality of an individual's thoughts and feelings about themselves as an object, i.e. as seen from the outside. Taking this position requires many of the abilities outlined earlier in this chapter, including the ability to think in the abstract and coordinate multiple dimensions, social abilities such as the ability to take different roles outlined, and also, potentially, some sense of coherence in terms of the identity, as outlined by Erikson. Rosenberg's early study focused on a group of adolescents with 'low self-esteem', a construct that was linked, among other things, to depression, anxiety, poor school performance, poor social performance, and isolation (Rosenberg, Schooler, and Schoenbach, 1989).

While this model is a simple and powerful way of thinking about the self, research has tended to find that individuals tend to think about themselves in potentially less abstract terms and tend to have multiple, more specific concepts of themselves. Shavelson et al. (1976), outline a model and associated research which breaks down a general self-concept, for example into academic self-concept, then a subject-specific self-concept. This kind of model appears to have a stronger association with achievement (Coleman, 2011).

This is important to remember when considering our work with adolescents and young adults, where the phrase 'low self-esteem' might be used. It appears that breaking this construct down into specifically problematic core beliefs might be a better way to proceed rather than working with the generalised term of 'self-esteem' (see Chapter 3).

Emotion and emotion regulation development

Later chapters in this book will cover theories of emotion more broadly (e.g. Chapters 5 and 9). In terms of adolescence, however, it is important to consider the development of emotions and emotion regulation.

Defining emotion and emotion regulation

Emotion, as will be later covered, is believed to be a universal human phenomenon. Emotions consist of changes in the conscious experience, the physiology of the body, the face, the thought processes, and behavioural urges. In evolutionary terms, emotions serve to coordinate and synchronise a number of diverse bodily systems to ensure a coherent response when required, which aids longer-term survival.

Emotion regulation is the ability to consciously adjust and respond to emotional states. It does not involve the control or restraint of emotion, nor its suppression, but can be defined as the ability to attenuate and curtail the intensity and duration of emotions as needed, as well as amplify and extend emotion states when necessary (Thompson, 1994). Emotions and their regulation, while different processes, tend to interact continuously and almost seamlessly so that they are difficult to separate. Emotions can be regulated by the individual themselves (internal regulation), or by another individual (external regulation). There is an interaction between these two processes that is important in terms of learning emotion regulation.

Emotion and emotion regulation are linked with performance in many areas of life: the well-adjusted individual is usually emotionally well regulated, and will tend to have access to the full range of emotions, will be able to modulate the intensity and duration of emotions, make fluid changes between emotions, conform to cultural display rules, and will be able to use words to regulate emotion processes (Thompson, 1994).

Emotion and emotion regulation through childhood and adolescence

Infants begin life with an array of emotion behaviours and facial expressions that signal to others to provide nurture and soothing. Over the first years of life, infants develop differentiated emotional states that are connected to specific occurrences; they also develop the language to label these emotional states (Izard, 1991). The primary emotion regulation strategy of the first two years is the regulation of emotional arousal; increasing, decreasing, or maintaining emotional arousal depending on context. This is important for three reasons: to maintain a comfortable emotional state, to establish and maintain social relationships, and to facilitate learning (Kopp, 2003).

During the course of toddlerhood, the 'self-conscious' or 'social' emotions develop (e.g. shame, embarrassment, and pride) and by the end of this period, there is an extensive emotional vocabulary that can be used to describe and regulate the emotional states. During the course of the next few years, children begin to regulate their emotions (and their emotional expressions) on the basis of cultural display rules. These are rules about how individuals 'should' act to fit in with culturally acceptable norms. Modification might include an increase in emotional state (e.g. exaggeration of pain to get sympathy, as often seen on the football pitch!), a decrease in emotional state (e.g. toning down anger when speaking to a teacher), or substitution of emotion (e.g. disappointment at another pair of Christmas socks substituted for happiness and gratitude). These aims of emotion regulation can be achieved through techniques such as self-soothing, distraction, controlling the environment, using a parent or caregiver, avoiding unpleasant situations, and using language to describe feelings or upsetting situations (Kopp, 2003). It appears that children of 6 years, and sometimes as young as 4 years, can understand cultural display rules (Harris et al., 1986) and during the next years the use of display rules and their flexibility increases so that children become adept at modifying emotional expression on the basis of the interpersonal context (Zeman and Garber, 1996).

During adolescence, these abilities continue to develop and there appear to be two age-related trends. With increasing age, there is increasing capacity for emotional regulation resulting from deeper emotional understanding, as well as broader and more sophisticated regulatory strategies. In addition, during adolescence, there is an increasing ability to tailor the regulatory strategy to the particular situation, for example distraction to cope with situations over which there is little control (e.g. parental illness) versus problem-solving to manage situations over which the individual can have an influence (e.g. school) (Zimmer-Gembeck and Skinner, 2011). These age-related trends appear to continue right into adulthood (Garnefski et al., 2002).

It is important to note that these developments are not necessarily linear and that the situations faced during the course of adolescence and early adulthood vary in terms of the degree of emotional regulation required.

Adolescent emotional 'difficulty'

One of the most enduring assumptions about adolescence is the link between adolescence and extremes of negative emotion (Arnett, 1999). Adolescents are characterised or perhaps caricatured as moody, gloomy and victims of raging hormones (Buchanan, Eccles, and Becker, 1992). It does appear that adolescents report experiencing extremes of emotion more frequently than their parents, report feeling 'self-conscious' and 'embarrassed' two to three times more often, and are more likely to feel awkward, lonely, nervous, and ignored (Larson, Csikszentmihalyi, and Graef, 1980).

However, these emotional experiences do not necessarily translate into ongoing emotional problems and adolescence is not found to be a time of life characterised by emotional difficulty more so than any other (Hendry and Kloep, 2012). A study covering half a million individuals across Europe and America (Blanchflower and Oswald, 2008) found that "wellbeing is u-shaped across the lifecycle"; that is, while emotional difficulties do increase through adolescence, they continue to increase up to middle age and then decline. It is also worth noting that suicide rates follow the same pattern and that adolescents do not die by suicide more often than adults (Scowcroft, 2016).

This suggests that, while adolescents do experience emotions more intensely, this experience does not translate into increases in emotional difficulties when compared to other times of life.

Influences on development of emotion regulation

The processes of emotion regulation, whose developing outcomes we have described above, can take place through a variety of means. Saarni (1999) outlines eight skills she considers necessary to achieve emotional competence:

1. awareness of own emotions;
2. ability to discern and understand other's emotions;
3. ability to use vocabulary of emotion and expression;
4. capacity for empathic involvement;
5. ability to differentiate internal subjective emotional experience from; external emotional expression;
6. capacity for adaptive coping with aversive emotions and distressing circumstances;
7. awareness of emotional communication within relationships;
8. capacity for emotional self-efficacy.

Interestingly, the ability to regulate emotions appears to develop in an emotion-specific manner, with different patterns of development for, for example, fear, sadness, and anger (Zimmermann and Iwanski, 2014). There are a variety of different influences on these developing abilities during the course of adolescence and early adulthood. Two are of particular importance: brain and cognitive development, and family and peer relationships.

Brain and cognitive development

The skills and abilities outlined above that are thought necessary for the development of emotion regulation relate to many of the other skill sets that are developing during the course of adolescence and early adulthood, and are outlined in this chapter.

The brain developments occurring during adolescence, for example in the prefrontal cortex, are associated with the ability to exert cognitive control and hence direct behaviour towards particular goals (Dahl, 2004). These regions of the brain are implicated in emotion regulation and increased working memory capacity, and have been associated with improved emotion regulation (Schmeichel, Volokov, and Demaree, 2008). Other abilities, such as the ability to think in the abstract, to take the perspective of another, and to empathise are all key abilities in emotion regulation, as outlined above.

Given the fairly linear development of the prefrontal cortex and abilities such as working memory and cognitive control, it might be expected that emotion regulation would follow a similarly linear pattern. However, the twenties appear to be the point of highest prevalence of a variety of different types of risk behaviour, including criminal behaviour, use of substances, risky driving, and risky sexual behaviour (see Arnett, 1999), which is potentially attributable to difficulties in emotion regulation. One possible explanation is that there are differential processes of maturation in different regions of the brain, and in the ways in which they link together, which results in a non-linear and, at times, disjunctive process of development (Steinberg, 2008).

Family and interpersonal context

The development of emotion regulation skills occurs in an interpersonal context and the interaction between individuals and their families and peers informs this process. This is thought to occur via three routes: observational learning, parenting practices and explicit instruction around emotion, and the emotional climate of the family.

Excessive parental negative emotion appears to have a negative impact on emotion regulation and aggression (Chang et al., 2003). Experiencing parental punishment or minimisation upon expressing emotion is associated with a tendency to refrain from discussing emotions and seeking help with difficult situations (Fabes et al., 2001). Maternal dampening of positive affect is also associated with poorer emotion regulation (indicated by measures of depression) (Yap et al., 2008). Conversely, maternal emotion coaching – in which mothers approached upset adolescents to talk about the situation and associated emotions – resulted in fewer problems for adolescents both at the time and at three-year follow-up (Shortt et al., 2010). The frequency and content of parent–child emotional talk is related to various aspects of emotion regulation including the ability to identify emotions (Dunn et al., 1991), and to regulate negative affect (Denham et al., 1994). There are significant gender effects apparent here, with mothers and fathers responding differently to boys and girls in terms of the way in which they speak about emotion (Denham et al., 1994).

It is important to note, as in other parts of this chapter, the limitations of the cross-sectional research upon which these findings are based. There will clearly be an interaction between the behaviour of children and the behaviour of their parents. As a result, we cannot and must not infer simple causality in terms of a certain parenting style producing different child outcomes. Nevertheless, it does make sense that emotion regulation will be influenced and shaped by the family context.

Summary

Emotion and emotion regulation develop in tandem during the course of childhood, adolescence, and early adulthood. Individuals are increasingly able to remain aware of their emotions, and curtail, attenuate, or magnify them dependent on context. Clearly not all adults achieve this level of regulation, but there is an increasing tendency towards regulation during the course of early life. Emotion regulation abilities are heavily influenced by the development of other aspects of life, as outlined in this chapter, and also on the interpersonal context of the individual. Chapter 5 develops these ideas, which are important foundations for the approach outlined in this book.

Relations with families and peers

So far, we have focused on the development of adolescents as individuals, but this development obviously occurs within the context of family and peer relationships and is affected by and affects these relationships.

Growing independence and separation from family

Traditional theories of adolescence (for example storm and stress, see later in this chapter) viewed conflict between adolescents and their parents or carers as inevitable and instrumental in the process of developing autonomy. This view invited a view of adolescent separation as tumultuous and resulting in an almost complete separation between parents and children. Psychodynamic thinkers applied a similar concept of emotional autonomy to adolescent development in which adolescents were thought to separate psychologically from their parents, to view them in a different way, and to rely less upon them emotionally.

Evidence relating to adolescent development supports a much more gradual and cohesive approach to growing autonomy and separation. There is support for the notion that there is conflict between adolescents and their parents that rises and falls during the course of adolescence (Laursen et al., 1998). However, the idea that adolescence is the time of life most characterised by this conflict is disputed by other evidence which suggests that fewer than 10% of adolescents experience serious difficulties with their parents (Holmbeck, 1996) and conflict with parents does not figure as a major concern of adolescents (Kloep, 1999). Indeed, when compared with the 3–15 conflicts per hour that have been recorded between parents and toddlers (Klimes-Dougan and Kopp, 1999), adolescence appears a period of relative harmony!

In relation to autonomy and independence in decision-making, increasing input into the decisions of life is associated with good outcomes for adolescents (Silverberg and Gondoli, 1996). Importantly, though, this tends to work best through negotiation and joint decision-making between adolescents and families; unilateral adolescent decision-making tends to be related to poorer adjustment and greater involvement in harmful activities (Dornbusch et al., 1990). Interestingly, unilateral parental decision-making has been linked with negative outcomes in European and American samples, but with more positive outcomes in African-American populations (Lamborn et al., 1996).

Finally, in terms of emotional autonomy, research has found that high levels of emotional autonomy are linked with increased parental rejection and higher degrees of conflict within the family as well as poorer outcomes for the individual themselves (see Silverberg and Gondoli, 1996).

All of this suggests that while adolescence is a period of increasing independence and autonomy, this is best achieved through negotiation and continued connection; conflict and emotional separation are associated with poor outcomes for adolescents.

Parenting style

Other research has looked at different aspects of family context such as parenting style. Maccoby and Martin (1983) outlined a construct of two orthogonal axes of parenting style: responsiveness and control. This results in four categories of parenting: authoritative (responsive and controlling), authoritarian (non-responsive and controlling), permissive (responsive and non-controlling), and indifferent (non-responsive and non-controlling). In looking at associations between measures of this construct and outcome in 10,000 adolescents, the study found that the positive correlates of authoritative parenting transcended demographic factors such as ethnicity, socioeconomic status, and family structure (Lamborn et al., 1991). In a later book, Steinberg (2008) suggests that the power of authoritative parenting style is due to the presence of three important elements: warmth (love, care, and nurture), structure (clear expectations, limits, and boundaries), and support of autonomy (accept and encourage individuality and movement towards independence).

It is important here to remember the limits of cross-sectional research and to notice that it would be much easier for parents to adopt an authoritative style at certain times or with a cooperative adolescent. Thus, the finding that the parenting style is linked to good outcomes for adolescents might have more to do with the nature of the reciprocal relationship between parent and adolescent than the qualities of the individual parents themselves. To account for this, families have been conceptualised as systems in which each part of the system has an impact on, and is influenced by, the other parts of the system (e.g. Olson, 2000). In this context, it is the qualities of the system that are most important in terms of outcome. The model suggests, and is supported by research (Olson, 2000), that there is an optimal amount of cohesion (not emotionally over-involved or detached) and an optimum amount of flexibility (not chaotic or rigid) that is negotiated via good communication that can lead to 'balanced' systems that are sustainable and functional over time. Conceiving of families in this way can help to take account of some of the difficulties of the uni-directional models outlined above.

Peers

A number of the theories outlined so far in this chapter refer to a gradual shift of relative importance placed by adolescents on their relationships, moving from the family towards friends and peers. Friendships and peer networks are central to the process of experimenting with an acceptable identity and are key to the concept of autonomy. Friendships have a different quality to parental relationships, being more equal and reciprocal, and tend to evolve during the course of adolescence. With increasing age, adolescents tend to spend more time away from the family and with friends and peers.

That peers are an important factor in adolescent development has been established; friends provide an important context for the development of self-worth and provide security and emotional support (Newcomb and Bagwell, 1995). The presence of friends compared to its absence has been repeatedly linked to positive effects on the psychological, social, and emotional adjustment of adolescents (Hartup, 1993).

While friendships tend to be perceived positively, there has been a trend to view broader peer relationships in adolescence negatively. Some authors have suggested that adolescents turn so far away from their parents and towards their peers that parents matter little during adolescence (Harris, 1998), or even that adolescents have a separate society that is organised in an anti-adult fashion (Coleman, 1961). In fact, empirical evidence suggests that, while adolescents do place increasing levels of importance on their peers during the course of adolescence, parents remain important sources of support (Coleman, 2011). It is interesting to note, in the context of some of the discussion about families and the uni-directional assumptions made here, that the question of whether peers or parents are more important is somewhat artificial given that the reality is likely to be a complex systemic interaction between adolescent, peers, and family.

Peer influence or 'peer pressure' is something that has been studied extensively, and research suggests that, when the need for social acceptance is high, peer influence tends also to be high. It seems that the need for acceptance appears higher at lower ages, and is also linked with individual difference. Peer influence seems strongest earlier in adolescence (i.e. 12 to 15) and wanes as the individual gains confidence in their identity; those who receive greater support from their family are also likely to be less influenced by peer pressure (Coleman, 2011).

One of the stereotypes of adolescence is that it is a time of 'invincibility' and engagement in risk behaviour (Hall, 1904). This risk behaviour has been linked by many to peer influence (Gardner and Steinberg, 2005). While there is evidence that the twenties are the point of highest prevalence of a variety of different types of risk behaviour (see Arnett, 1999), the notion that normal adolescent development is associated with increased risk behaviour is not supported by the evidence. It is consistently noted that the vast majority of young people do not engage in any form of criminal behaviour (Roe and Ashe, 2008), do not take drugs (Lader, 2015), and that unintentional injury is the single leading cause of death not just in adolescence but across age ranges (e.g. 1 to 44 years in the US, Heron, 2013). In addition, peer influence is not always negative and most adolescent peer groups share values with adult groups (Youniss, McLellan, and Strouse, 1994), although some do value anti-social behaviour.

While lots of research has been conducted to examine the impact of being in contact with friends and peers, other research has looked at the impact of rejection or bullying by peers. In examining those who are rejected or isolated from peers a distinction is ordinarily made between those who are withdrawn and those who are aggressive. Given what we have said about the importance of the peer group in terms of the formation of an identity as an acceptable and successful person, rejection and bullying represent significant threats to this. Indeed, research does support the notion that being the victim of bullying is associated with depression, loneliness, lower self-esteem, and more limited social skills (Hawker and Boulton, 2000). Likewise, engaging in bullying behaviour is associated with longer-term difficulties (Olweus, 1993). Research suggests that bullying is a significant problem: in a European survey, it was found (with high levels of variation between countries) that 17% of all adolescents were bullies, 26% were victims, and 20% were both (Eslea et al., 2004).

An important part of peer relating in adolescence is sexual development and exploration. It is integral to Erikson's model (e.g. 1968), as the ability to relate intimately to others involves openness, sharing, trust, and commitment. Experiences of intimacy therefore signify a sense of identity, acceptability, and maturity. Sexual development is an extremely important part of adolescent development and represents a significant part of the lives of adolescents and young adults. This is important to consider in clinical work and we need to ensure that we allow space to talk and consider sexual development, experimentation, and difficulty in our work with adolescents and young adults.

Bringing it all together: theories of adolescent development

There are a number of theories that have attempted to explain the findings outlined above and to provide a broad framework within which to study adolescent development.

Storm and stress: the 'first' theory of adolescence

One of the most influential models of adolescent development is that of Granville Stanley-Hall. Stanley-Hall was a pioneer of early psychology in the 1900s in America and the first president of the American Psychological Association. His work of 1904 entitled "Adolescence: its psychology and its relations to physiology, anthropology, sociology, sex, crime, religion, and education" was the first contemporary account dedicated to the study of adolescence. Hall suggested that adolescence was a period of 'storm and stress' in which all young people go through a period of instability and upheaval before establishing relative equilibrium in adulthood. He suggested that this period was characterised by three areas of instability: behavioural risk-taking, conflict with parents, and emotional disturbance (Arnett, 1999).

One of the main issues with Stanley-Hall's theory of adolescence is that it pathologises adolescence; it defines the period as inevitably and inherently problematic and difficult, both for adolescents and their families, and perhaps for the wider population. This negativity is evident in society's perceptions of adolescence as we outlined in the introduction to this chapter. The evidence relating to this theory has been explored in various parts of this chapter already and the conclusion is that, while there is some evidence at a population view to support these assertions, the storm and stress of adolescence appears to represent the exception rather than the rule.

The question for those of us wanting to support adolescents through their development from childhood into adulthood is what it is that makes a successful transition to adulthood most likely and how can we work towards supporting adolescents to move through it in this way?

Staging theories of adolescence

Staging models suggest that individuals move through certain stages during the course of their development (e.g. Piaget, Erikson, Marcia mentioned earlier). Each of these models has stood the test of time, partly because they are easy to understand and they capture something of the developmental process. However, research tends to find more fluid boundaries between stages than the theory suggests, and that, particularly moving towards the final stage of development they appear to become idealistic, setting out positions of development that many individuals never reach or do not always maintain (see Piaget, Erikson, or Marcia mentioned earlier). In addition, these models tend to place a great deal more weight on an individual's development over the environment they inhabit.

Contextual theories of adolescence

Contextual theories build on Bronfenbrenner's ecological theory (1979). In this theory, Bronfenbrenner outlines a number of different behavioural systems that impact upon individuals and their development, including Microsystems, which are those directly relating to adolescents (e.g. family, school, friendship network) up to Macrosystems, which are things such as the cultural milieu or the current national political processes. Individual development proceeds via the interactions between individuals and these different systems in a person-process-context-time specific manner.

A development of this theory, known as the life-course theory, looks at the specific interactions that might take place between individuals and their context. It is based on longitudinal research across the life-course undertaken by Elder (1998), who outlines some principles of these interactions. He notes that historical events have a significant impact on individuals' lives and highlight the importance of the timing of these events, relative to stage of life. From Elder's research, he noted that one group (born in 1929) experienced the great depression as children, whereas another group (born in 1920) experienced it as adolescents; their ages during World War II were obviously also different. The timing of these events relative to their life course had a dramatic impact on the course of the development of the two groups (those born in 1929 developed into better functioning adults). The life course theory also places importance on the interdependence of individuals and individual active construction of their lives through the choices and actions they make.

Another contextual theory, known as developmental contextualism (Lerner and Castellino, 2002), outlines a framework in which there are whole patterns of dynamic person-context interactions that are the background to individual development. A key idea following from this theory is that of 'goodness-of-fit' between an individual and their context, which has been investigated from an educational and a parenting point of view (Eccles, Lord, and Roeser, 1996; Reitz, Deković, and Meijer, 2006).

Focal model

A final model by Coleman (2011), provides a blend of the easy-to-understand nature of the stage models, with the more nuanced and ecologically valid nature of contextual models. The idea is that there are a multitude of different tasks and transitions to be navigated during the course of adolescence. The evidence above shows that, while some adolescents struggle, most adolescents tend to manage this process fairly well. The focal model suggests that adolescents tend to focus on one issue at a time, specifically the issue that fits best in terms of timing and goodness-of-fit with the environment. For example, adolescents might tackle their exams as a priority at one point, and postpone grieving for a grandparent until after the exams, before managing a break-up with a partner after that. In this manner, most individuals manage adolescence fairly well, but are likely to struggle with the transition if they a) have been struggling already, or b) have too many transitions to manage at once. The model was borne out of longitudinal studies with developing adolescents and research suggests that adolescents do appear to deal with relationship concerns one at a time (Goossens and Marcoen, 1999, Kloep, 1999). Further, there is evidence to support the notion that those facing lots of transitions tend to struggle, for example with poor self-esteem and school performance (Simmons and Blyth, 1987).

This model is perhaps the most clinically useful of those described above. Firstly, it is based on an understanding of successful adolescent transition, to which most adolescents, young adults, and their families aspire. Secondly, it is simple and relatively easy to understand and explain. Thirdly, it relates clearly and directly to clinical practice.

Summary

Adolescence is a widening phase of life, now considered to span from around 10 until around 25 years of age. It involves changes in the body, the brain, cognitive ability, social ability, identity, emotional regulation, family relationships and relationships with peers.

Importantly, adolescence is not, inevitably, a time of strife, difficulty, and conflict. The majority of adolescents and young adults manage the transitions fairly well and maintain good relationships with family and friends throughout. The focal theory suggests that this is made possible by a tendency to approach transitions one at a time. Adolescence and early adulthood are more problematic where there are pre-existing difficulties, or where there are too many transitions to navigate at once.

All clinical work with adolescents and young adults takes place against this background of rapid and dramatic change. As clinicians, we need to be mindful of this context, which has many implications for clinical work, for example in considering when to provide intervention, what the goals of intervention might be, how best to achieve these goals, and at what point to end.

These ideas are further developed in Chapter 5, which outlines the approach taken in this book.

References

Arnett, J.J., 1999. Adolescent storm and stress, reconsidered. *American Psychologist*, *54*(5), pp. 317.

Blakemore, S.J. and Choudhury, S., 2006. Development of the adolescent brain: implications for executive function and social cognition. *Journal of Child Psychology and Psychiatry*, *47*(3–4), pp. 296–312.

Blanchflower, D. G. and Oswald, A. J., 2008. Is well-being U-shaped over the life cycle? *Social Science & Medicine*, *66*(8), pp. 1733–1749.

Bloch, H. S. 1995. *Adolescent development, psychopathology, and treatment*. Madison, CT: International Universities Press.

Bronfenbrenner, U., 1979. *The ecology of human development: experiments by nature and design*. Cambridge, MA: Harvard University Press.

Buchanan, C. M., Eccles, J. S., Flanagan, C, Midgley, C, Feldlaufer, H., and Harold, R. D., 1990. Parents' and teachers' beliefs about adolescents: effects of sex and experience. *Journal of Youth & Adolescence*, *19*, pp. 363–394.

Buchanan, C.M., Eccles, J.S., and Becker, J.B., 1992. Are adolescents the victims of raging hormones? Evidence for activational effects of hormones on moods and behavior at adolescence. *Psychological Bulletin*, *111*(1), pp. 62.

Casteel, M.A., 1993. Effects of inference necessity and reading goal on children's inferential generation. *Developmental Psychology*, *29*(2), pp. 346.

Chalmers, J.B. and Townsend, M.A., 1990. The effects of training in social perspective taking on socially maladjusted girls. *Child Development*, *61*, pp. 178–190.

Chang, L., Schwartz, D., Dodge, K.A., and McBride-Chang, C., 2003. Harsh parenting in relation to child emotion regulation and aggression. *Journal of Family Psychology*, *17*(4), pp. 598.

Coleman, J.C., 2011. *The nature of adolescence*. Hove, UK: Routledge.

Coleman, J.S., 1961. *The adolescent society: the social life of the teenager and its impact on education*. Oxford: Free Press of Glencoe.

Côté, J.E., 2009. Identity formation and self-development in adolescence. In R.M. Lerner, and L. Steinberg (eds) *Handbook of adolescent psychology*. New Jersey, CT: John Wiley & Sons, pp. 266–304.

Dahl, R.E., 2004. Adolescent brain development: a period of vulnerabilities and opportunities. Keynote address. *Annals of the New York Academy of Sciences*, *1021*(1), pp. 1–22.

Denham, S.A., Zoller, D., and Couchoud, E.A., 1994. Socialization of preschoolers' emotion understanding. *Developmental Psychology*, *30*(6), pp. 928–936.

Dornbusch, S.M., Ritter, P.L., Mont-Reynaud, R., and Chen, Z.Y., 1990. Family decision making and academic performance in a diverse high school population. *Journal of Adolescent Research*, *5*(2), pp. 143–160.

Dunn, J., Brown, J., and Beardsall, L., 1991. Family talk about feeling states and children's later understanding of others' emotions. *Developmental Psychology*, *27*(3), pp. 448–455.

Eccles, J.S., Lord, S.E., and Roeser, R.W., 1996. Round holes, square pegs, rocky roads, and sore feet: the impact of stage-environment fit on young adolescents' experiences in schools. *Adolescence: Opportunities and Challenges*, pp. 47–92.

Elder, G.H., 1998. The life course as developmental theory. *Child Development*, *69*(1), pp. 1–12.

Elkind, D., 1966. Conceptual orientation shifts in children and adolescents. *Child Development*, pp. 493–498.

Erikson, E.H. 1968. *Identity, youth, and crisis*. New York: Norton.

Eslea, M., Menesini, E., Morita, Y., O'Moore, M., Mora-Merchán, J.A., Pereira, B., and Smith, P.K., 2004. Friendship and loneliness among bullies and victims: data from seven countries. *Aggressive Behavior*, *30*(1), pp. 71–83.

Fabes, R.A., Leonard, S.A., Kupanoff, K., and Martin, C.L., 2001. Parental coping with children's negative emotions: relations with children's emotional and social responding. *Child Development*, *72*(3), pp. 907–920.

Farkas, S., Johnson, J., Duffett, A., and Bers, A., 1997. *Kids these days: what Americans really think about the next generation*. New York: Public Agenda.

Gardner, M. and Steinberg, L., 2005. Peer influence on risk taking, risk preference, and risky decision making in adolescence and adulthood: an experimental study. *Developmental Psychology*, *41*(4), pp. 625–635.

Garnefski, N., Legerstee, J., Kraaij, V., van den Kommer, T., and Teerds, J.A.N., 2002. Cognitive coping strategies and symptoms of depression and anxiety: a comparison between adolescents and adults. *Journal of Adolescence*, *25*(6), pp. 603–611.

Goossens, L. and Marcoen, A., 1999. Relationships during adolescence: constructive *vs.* negative themes and relational dissatisfaction. *Journal of Adolescence*, *22*(1), pp. 65–79.

Hall, G.S., 1904. *Adolescence*. 2 vols. New York: Appleton.

Harris, J.R., 1998. *The nurture assumption. Why children turn out the way they do*. New York: Free Press.

Harris, P.L., Donnelly, K., Guz, G.R., and Pitt-Watson, R., 1986. Children's understanding of the distinction between real and apparent emotion. *Child Development*, pp. 895–909.

Hartup, W.W., 1993. Adolescents and their friends. *New Directions for Child and Adolescent Development*, *1993*(60), pp. 3–22.

Hawker, D.S. and Boulton, M.J., 2000. Twenty years' research on peer victimization and psychosocial maladjustment: a meta-analytic review of cross-sectional studies. *Journal of Child Psychology and Psychiatry*, *41*(4), pp. 441–455.

Hendry, L., and Kloep, M., 2012. *Adolescence and adulthood: Transitions and transformations*. Basingstoke, UK: Palgrave Macmillan.

Heron, M., 2013. Deaths: leading causes for 2010. *National Vital Statistics Reports: from the Centers for Disease Control and Prevention, National Center for Health Statistics, National Vital Statistics System*, *62*(6), pp. 1–96.

Holmbeck, G.N., 1996. A model of family relational transformations during the transition to adolescence: parent–adolescent conflict and adaptation. In J. Graber, J. Brooks-Gunn, and A.C. Pedersen (eds) *Transitions through adolescence: interpersonal domains and context*. Mahwah, NJ: Erlbaum, pp. 167–199.

Hubel, D.H. and Wiesel, T.N., 1962. Receptive fields, binocular interaction and functional architecture in the cat's visual cortex. *The Journal of Physiology*, *160*(1), pp. 106–154.

Inhelder, B. and Piaget, J., 1958. *The growth of logical thinking from childhood to adolescence*. London: Routledge and Kegan Paul.

Izard, C.E., 1991. *The psychology of emotions*. New York: Plenum Press.

Keating, D.P., 2004. Cognitive and brain development. In R.M. Lerner and L. Steinberg (eds) *Handbook of adolescent psychology*. Hoboken, NJ: John Wiley & Sons, pp. 45–84.

Klimes-Dougan, B. and Kopp, C.B., 1999. Children's conflict tactics with mothers: a longitudinal investigation of the toddler and preschool years. *Merrill-Palmer Quarterly, 45*(2), 226–241.

Kloep, M., 1999. Love is all you need? Focusing on adolescents' life concerns from an ecological point of view. *Journal of Adolescence, 22*(1), pp. 49–63.

Kopp, C.B. and Neufeld, S.J., 2003. Emotional development during infancy. In R.J. Davidson, K.R. Scherer, and H.H. Goldsmith (eds) *Handbook of Affective Sciences*. New York: Oxford University Press, pp. 347–374.

Kroger, J., Martinussen, M., and Marcia, J.E., 2010. Identity status change during adolescence and young adulthood: a meta-analysis. *Journal of Adolescence, 33*(5), pp. 683–698.

Lamborn, S.D., Mounts, N.S., Steinberg, L., and Dornbusch, S.M., 1991. Patterns of competence and adjustment among adolescents from authoritative, authoritarian, indulgent, and neglectful families. *Child Development, 62*(5), pp. 1049–1065.

Lamborn, S.D., Dornbusch, S.M., and Steinberg, L., 1996. Ethnicity and community context as moderators of the relations between family decision making and adolescent adjustment. *Child Development, 67*(2), pp. 283–301.

Lader, D. 2015. *Drug misuse: findings from the 2014/15 Crime Survey for England and Wales*. London: Crown.

Larson, R., Csikszentmihalyi, M., and Graef, R., 1980. Mood variability and the psychosocial adjustment of adolescents. *Journal of Youth and Adolescence, 9*(6), pp. 469–490.

Laursen, B., Coy, K.C., and Collins, W.A., 1998. Reconsidering changes in parent-child conflict across adolescence: a meta-analysis. *Child Development, 69*(3), pp. 817–832.

Lavoie, J.C., 1994. Identity in adolescence: issues of theory, structure and transition. *Journal of Adolescence, 17*(1), pp. 17–28.

Lerner, R.M. and Castellino, D.R., 2002. Contemporary developmental theory and adolescence: developmental systems and applied developmental science. *Journal of Adolescent Health, 31*(6), pp. 122–135.

Maccoby, E.E. and Martin, J.A., 1983. Socialization in the context of the family: parent–child interaction. In P.H. Mussen and E.M. Hetherington (eds) *Handbook of child psychology: formerly Carmichael's manual of child psychology*. New York: John Wiley & Sons, pp. 1–101.

Marcia, J.E., 1966. Development and validation of ego-identity status. *Journal of Personality and Social Psychology, 3*(5), pp. 551–558.

Newcomb, A.F. and Bagwell, C.L., 1995. Children's friendship relations: a meta-analytic review. *Psychological Bulletin, 117*(2), pp. 306–347.

Olson, D.H., 2000. Circumplex model of marital and family systems. *Journal of Family Therapy, 22*(2), pp. 144–167.

Olweus, D., 1993. Victimization by peers: antecedents and long-term outcomes. In K.H. Rubin and J.B. Asendorf (eds) *Social withdrawal, inhibition, and shyness in childhood*. Hillsdale, NJ: Erlbaum, pp. 315–341.

Patton, G.C., Sawyer, S.M., Santelli, J.S., Ross, D.A., Afifi, R., Allen, N.B., Arora, M., Azzopardi, P., Baldwin, W., Bonell, C., and Kakuma, R., 2016. Our future:

a Lancet commission on adolescent health and wellbeing. *The Lancet, 387,* pp. 2423–2478.

Reitz, E., Deković, M., and Meijer, A.M., 2006. Relations between parenting and externalizing and internalizing problem behaviour in early adolescence: child behaviour as moderator and predictor. *Journal of Adolescence, 29*(3), pp. 419–436.

Roe, S. and Ashe, J., 2008. *Young people and crime: findings from the 2006 Offending, Crime and Justice survey.* London: Crown.

Rogol, A. D., Roemmich, J. N., and Clark, P. A., 2002. Growth at puberty. *Journal of Adolescent Health, 31*(6), pp. 192–200.

Rosenberg, M., 1965. *Society and the adolescent self-image.* New York: Princeton University Press.

Rosenberg, M., Schooler, C., and Schoenbach, C., 1989. Self-esteem and adolescent problems: modeling reciprocal effects. *American Sociological Review,* pp. 1004–1018.

Saarni, C., 1999. *The development of emotional competence.* London: Guilford Press.

Schmeichel, B.J., Volokhov, R.N., and Demaree, H.A., 2008. Working memory capacity and the self-regulation of emotional expression and experience. *Journal of Personality and Social Psychology, 95*(6), pp. 1526–1540.

Scowcroft, E., 2016. *Suicide Statistics Report 2016: Including Data for 2012–2014.* UK: Samaritans.

Selman, R.L., 1971. Taking another's perspective: role-taking development in early childhood. *Child Development, 42*(6), pp. 1721–1734.

Selman, R.L., 1980. *The growth of interpersonal understanding: developmental and clinical analyses.* London: Academic Press.

Shavelson, R.J., Hubner, J.J., and Stanton, G.C., 1976. Self-concept: validation of construct interpretations. *Review of Educational Research, 46*(3), pp. 407–441.

Shayer, M., and Wylam, H., 1978. The distribution of Piagetian stages of thinking in British middle and secondary school children II–14- to 16-year-olds and sex differentials. *British Journal of Educational Psychology, 48*(1), 62–70.

Shortt, J.W., Stoolmiller, M., Smith-Shine, J.N., Mark Eddy, J., and Sheeber, L., 2010. Maternal emotion coaching, adolescent anger regulation, and siblings' externalizing symptoms. *Journal of Child Psychology and Psychiatry, 51*(7), pp. 799–808.

Silverberg, S.B. and Gondoli, D.M., 1996. Autonomy in adolescence: a contextualized perspective. *Psychosocial Development During Adolescence, 8,* pp. 12–61.

Simmons, R.G. and Blyth, D.A., 1987. *Moving into adolescence: the impact of pubertal change and school context.* New York: Aldine Transaction.

Sowell, E.R., Thompson, P.M., Tessner, K.D., and Toga, A.W., 2001. Mapping continued brain growth and gray matter density reduction in dorsal frontal cortex: inverse relationships during postadolescent brain maturation. *Journal of Neuroscience, 21,* pp. 8819–8829.

Steinberg, L. 2008. *Adolescence* (8th edn). New York: McGraw-Hill.

Thompson, R.A., 1994. Emotion regulation: a theme in search of definition. *Monographs of the Society for Research in Child Development, 59*(2–3), pp. 25–52.

Underwood, B. and Moore, B., 1982. Perspective-taking and altruism. *Psychological Bulletin, 91,* pp. 143–173.

Ward, S. and Overton, W, 1990. Semantic familiarity, relevance, and the development of deductive reasoning. *Developmental Psychology*, *26*, pp. 488–493.

Yap, M.B., Allen, N.B., and Ladouceur, C.D., 2008. Maternal socialization of positive affect: the impact of invalidation on adolescent emotion regulation and depressive symptomatology. *Child Development*, *79*(5), pp. 1415–1431.

Youniss, J., McLellan, J.A., and Strouse, D., 1994. "We're popular, but we're not snobs": adolescents describe their crowds. In R. Montemayor, G.R. Adams, and T.P. Gullotta (eds) *Personal relationships during adolescents*. Thousand Oaks, CA: Sage, pp. 101–122.

Zeman, J. and Garber, J., 1996. Display rules for anger, sadness, and pain: it depends on who is watching. *Child Development*, *67*(3), pp. 957–973.

Zimmer-Gembeck, M.J. and Skinner, E.A., 2011. The development of coping across childhood and adolescence: an integrative review and critique of research. *International Journal of Behavioral Development*, *35*(1), pp. 1–17.

Zimmermann, P. and Iwanski, A., 2014. Emotion regulation from early adolescence to emerging adulthood and middle adulthood: age differences, gender differences, and emotion-specific developmental variations. *International Journal of Behavioral Development*, *38*(2), pp. 182–194.

Chapter 3

Principles of cognitive behavioural therapy (CBT)

There's no magic bullet cure, you have to work at it, plough away at it.

(21-year-old male)

It felt helpful to lay a foundation in my past experience [genogram]. Seeing it all written out like that really does help.

(22-year-old male)

It is important to hold in mind the principles of CBT and the components of the approach associated with its efficacy. This chapter provides an outline of the historical context of CBT, before looking in more detail at the theoretical principles underpinning its practice today. It then considers the practical constructs of CBT and the evidence base upon which CBT has been built.

History of CBT

Freudian psychoanalysis dominated psychotherapy for the early part of the twentieth century. It is characterised by an emphasis on early events that are thought to continue to influence current attitude, mannerisms, emotion and thought via irrational and unconscious drives. With the growth of psychology as a rigorous scientific discipline, psychoanalysis came under increasing criticism due to its focus on constructs that could neither be observed nor measured, and a lack of empirical evidence to support either its theory or its effectiveness (Eysenck, 1952).

Behaviourism, a powerful movement in experimental psychology, took a different view, working with only what was observable and measurable, the assumption being that what went on inside the mind was not observable and therefore not amenable to scientific study. Behavioural therapy followed from this movement and provided a compelling alternative to the prevailing psychoanalytic view. Founded in scientific research, behavioural therapy quickly began to test its effectiveness and to build an evidence base.

Behavioural therapy (Wolpe, 1958) began with basic behavioural principles such as classical and operant conditioning, which maintain that stimuli in the environment can become associated with other stimuli (classical conditioning) or with the behaviour of individuals (operant conditioning). The theory is that this process can be manipulated to encourage or to remove associations. Early studies in behavioural therapy focused on the fear response and quickly demonstrated that approaches such as systematic desensitisation, the process of reducing associations between fear and environmental stimuli, were effective in reducing difficulties seen in anxiety disorders.

Despite this success there was some discomfort in behaviourism's notion that everything inside the head is unimportant, given that it is such an obvious and fundamental part of human existence. As a result, a cognitive revolution began in the late 1960s and early 1970s that incorporated the brain's capacity for cognition, interpretation and evaluation of the world into the model, while still remaining grounded in the scientific discipline and holding on to the empiricism that had led to the rapid growth of behavioural therapy.

While many thinkers of the time were involved in this process, the main proponent was Aaron Beck who developed a cognitive therapy treatment for depression (Beck et al., 1979). The core concept was that depression was caused and maintained by dysfunctional cognitions about the self, the world, and the future, and that therapy designed to target these cognitions would bring about a change in presentation. Indeed, Beck and his colleagues (Rush et al., 1977) found that cognitive therapy was as effective as antidepressant medication for depression.

Theoretical principles of cognitive behavioural therapy

Over time, the cognitive and the behavioural models have converged to lead to a multiplicity of cognitive behavioural models, all of which share a number of different principles. The next part of this chapter will outline these principles. It is adapted from a similar introduction outlined by Westbrook, Kennerley, and Kirk (2011).

Cognitive principle

The cognitive principle holds that our cognitions – our thoughts, beliefs, attributions, and values – are all central to our experience of the world. Stated differently, the way in which we see the world and the meaning we attach to the events within it, has a powerful impact on the way that we feel and behave.

For example, if an adolescent messages a friend and they do not reply, they can make a number of different causal attributions for this behaviour. They could, for example, think:

1. "Their device has run out of battery";
2. "They're bored of me";

3. "I've done something to offend them"; or
4. "Something terrible has happened to them."

Each of these interpretations has a different impact on the way in which they might feel and they might choose to respond.

Behavioural principle

The behavioural principle holds that behaviours are crucial in learning about the world. Behaviours are also seen as learnt responses to past events.

Human beings are adaptive

Both the cognitive and behavioural positions are consistent with evolutionary theory in holding that human beings, like other creatures, adapt to respond in the best way possible to their environments. Humans will therefore do certain things because this behaviour has been reinforced in the past. In addition, humans will exhibit particular patterns of thought because this way of thinking has been reinforced or learned in some earlier situation.

Interactions between different aspects of human experience

The integration of the cognitive and behavioural models has led to a general principle in CBT that these different aspects of human experience interact. Different models may emphasise some of these aspects over others, as will become evident during the course of this book, but the general principle holds: cognitions, feelings, behaviours, and physiology (bodily responses), all interact with each other and with the environment to produce the overall human experience.

Here-and-now principle

The majority of cognitive behavioural models assert that maintenance is different from cause: the factors that keep a problem going are not necessarily the same factors that initially caused the problem. Therefore, in order to bring about relief or improvement from a particular situation, it is not always necessary to find the initial cause. This principle is at odds with Freudian psychoanalysis.

Almost all CBT approaches advocate starting with a here-and-now process focusing on what it is that is keeping the problem going, rather than starting with what it is that might have initially caused the problem.

Empiricism

Modern CBT has held on to the importance of scientific rigour evident in early behavioural therapy, which has led to a vast and growing evidence base in terms of efficacy and mechanism. This principle is also evident within the model: many of the metaphors and concepts used in CBT, for example behavioural experiments, are drawn from the scientific arena.

It is perhaps this principle that is primarily responsible for the success of CBT as compared with other therapies, as it has been able to compete with and demonstrate efficacy alongside other interventions such as medication (see later in this chapter and also Chapter 4 for more information).

Collaboration

A final principle of importance in modern CBT is that of collaboration. In a move away from the psychoanalytic world in which the clinician holds the answers but says little, CBT is based on sharing and collaborating to work towards shared goals or objectives. In practice, this often involves using paper and worksheets or diagrams so that clinicians can work things out together with those seeking their help.

Practical constructs of CBT

There are a number of different constructs that are used to deliver these principles in practice, ranging from generic interpersonal and therapeutic skills to specific CBT concepts. These different constructs are detailed next.

Therapeutic relationship

CBT is a therapeutic process and we need to establish a working therapeutic alliance with the individual seeking help. This is not a task or a phase of intervention in itself, but takes place alongside other processes of therapy. Without a sufficient therapeutic alliance, it is unlikely that anybody will be willing to engage in the often difficult and challenging processes of therapy.

The relationship in CBT is collaborative, based on the active participation of both parties. It involves working together in the pursuit of new knowledge and new ideas. Techniques such as summarising, feeding back, and Socratic questioning/guided discovery are all important in maintaining this active collaboration between clinician and the individual seeking help. Summarising and feeding back are both designed to demonstrate understanding and empathy, as well as inviting further curiosity about the situation. Socratic questioning/ guided discovery is a particular style of questioning that aims to deepen knowledge and understanding. There is a great deal of material available about Socratic questioning in CBT (e.g. Padesky, 1993).

Goal-oriented, time-limited, focused interventions

CBT is a focused, time-limited therapy. Establishing and agreeing the aims of the work is an important early stage of therapy. This provides a framework within which to measure and assess progress (often using psychometric instruments) and to keep a focus for the work. CBT is premised on the idea of a limited number of sessions targeted towards bringing about the change specified in these early sessions. This structure is also evident within individual sessions and techniques such as agendas and summarising aim to support the focus of the work.

Here-and-now formulation

Formulation is defined by Gillian Butler (1998, p2) as "the tool used by clinicians to relate theory to practice . . . It is the lynchpin that holds theory and practice together." A formulation should bring together the understanding we have about people in general with the experience of the individual seeking help. The formulation should provide an understanding of what is going on and begin the process of thinking about what might help.

An important aspect of the formulation in CBT is the here-and-now or maintenance formulation. This aspect of the formulation highlights the aspects of the situation that are keeping it going, rather than those that initially brought it about.

Often the first model of formulation encountered in CBT is the 'five-part model' (Padesky and Mooney, 1990), which helps to identify the different elements on which the practice of CBT is based. Padesky's model includes five

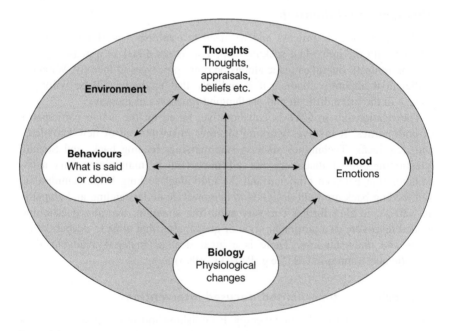

Figure 3.1 Here-and-now formulation

parts: biology, mood, behaviour, thoughts, and environment, and highlights the interactions between these different parts. Variations on these five aspects and the ways in which they are arranged form the basis of the majority of CBT formulations. A here-and-now formulation using the elements as defined in this book, is outlined in Figure 3.1.

This formulation highlights how thoughts, feelings, physiology, and behaviour interact with each other and with the environment. The advantage of this kind of formulation is that it is easy to use and understand. Many clinicians will begin the process of learning CBT using these five aspects to deconstruct problems. These ideas have been developed and tailored to specific presentations, enabling increased precision and focus. However, this also makes it more difficult to make decisions about which model to use and to ensure that each model is properly applied (see Chapter 4).

The maintenance formulation in CBT is one of the most important tools at our disposal. Its function is to help us align what we understand about people in general with the problems with which individuals present. This enables us to understand and to explain what is going on and what might help to bring about change.

Historical and schematic formulations

The idea that CBT is not interested in history is a myth. One of the principles of CBT outlined above is that humans adapt to their environments and so any particular combination of thoughts, feelings, physiology and behaviours is a product of history. As we have started this chapter with a history of CBT, understanding individuals within the context of their histories can be just as important.

CBT has a number of concepts that help us to understand how an individual's history might affect them. These can be illustrated in a longitudinal formulation (Figure 3.2)

A longitudinal CBT formulation builds up a picture of the individual's early life and then considers the impact that these experiences have on them, and the ways in which they have then managed these experiences. This informs the maintenance cycle placed at the bottom. While not all of this information might be presented at once, the knowledge contained within it should be sufficient to provide an overall understanding of the presenting difficulty, what maintains it, and its historical context. We consider the elements of this longitudinal formulation in turn.

Early experiences

We begin with the individual's early life. This can be done through discussion or often more helpfully with adolescents and young adults, through a timeline, genogram, or both.

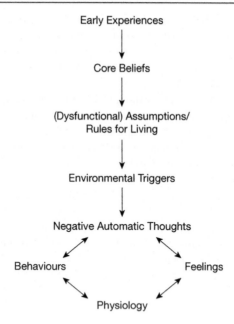

Figure 3.2 Longitudinal CBT formulation

A timeline is a line, either straight or curved, upon which is written significant events in an individual's life. These should include both positive and negative experiences. Sometimes a colour code is used to highlight different aspects of the events, or sometimes positive events are placed above the line and negative ones below (although this leaves a problem where they are perceived as both!). There are also adaptations to this that include using string and objects rather than pens and paper, which can make the process more fun and engaging. Timelines are a good way to get a sense of what has gone on and are good for picking out significant single events. They are less helpful where there is a great deal of trauma, as they can be overwhelming, and they are also not sensitive to acts of omission, for example receiving inadequate care.

Genograms are systematic ways of building family trees, involving established representational practices. Figure 3.3 shows some common symbols and structures to illustrate families. While the process of drawing a genogram is informative, the issue with this is that it can feel as though the individual themselves gets lost in favour of talking about everybody else. To counteract this, we can annotate the genogram with comments about the relational quality between the people on the genogram, focusing in particular on the individual's experience. This can facilitate a detailed exploration of an individual's life and results in the genogram containing descriptions of relationships around a central tree. Colours help to make this look approachable rather than overwhelming. This approach helps capture more of the ongoing quality of relationships in individuals' lives and can

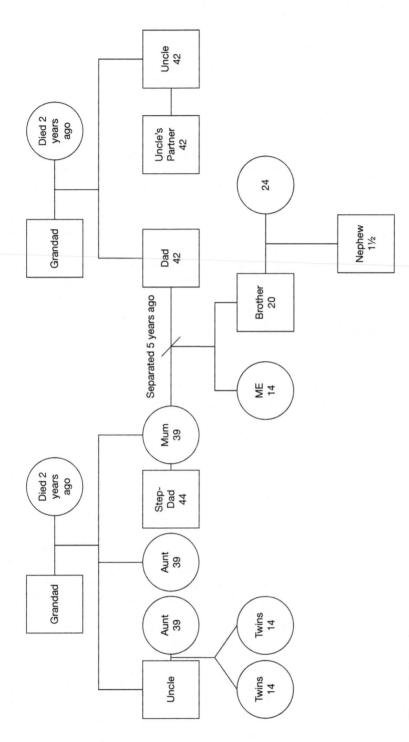

Figure 3.3 Example genogram

capture the omissions that are often missed in timelines. It can also help when relatives or friends are mentioned in therapy and reinforces the link between early experiences and subsequent beliefs and rules.

Of course, it is possible to use both techniques to get a thorough sense of an individual's experience of life.

Core beliefs

In CBT, an individual's early life is seen to influence their learning about the world; learning that is conceptualised as core beliefs. Beck et al. (1979) outlined three types of core beliefs, which have become known as the cognitive triad: beliefs about the self, the world (and others), and the future. Core beliefs are not seen to be necessarily consciously held, but are influential appraisals or expectations of the world: it is 'as if' these beliefs were held. This means that individuals might not go around with the thoughts 'the world is unpredictable' in their heads, but this sense of unpredictability would influence their thoughts, feelings, behaviours, and physiology. Given their assumed development early in life, core beliefs do not tend to be particularly subtle or nuanced – they are usually absolute, particularly when maladaptive – and they are ordinarily written as short statements. Example core beliefs are outlined in Table 3.1.

Dysfunctional assumptions

This second layer of thought is also a model of understanding. We do not assume that individuals operate with these conscious phrases in their heads, but

Table 3.1 Example core beliefs

Domain	Example maladaptive beliefs	Example adaptive beliefs
The self	I am a failure I am useless I am powerless I am bad	I am able I am confident I am helpful I am good at . . . I can have an influence
The world (and others)	The world is unpredictable The world is a horrible place Other people are dangerous Other people have it in for me	The world is generally quite safe Most people are friendly The world is relatively predictable
The future	Nothing good will ever come of anything Everything will always turn out badly Disaster is just around every corner	There are things to look forward to The world is full of opportunity

they can be seen to think, feel, behave, and respond 'as if' they were using these assumptions.

The central idea is that no individual would be able to function in life with a set of core beliefs such as: "I'm powerless," "The world is unpredictable" or "Everything will always turn out badly." It would not be possible to live in accordance with this set of beliefs as the individual would be paralysed by the sense of danger and their inability to do anything to protect themselves. As a result, individuals are seen to build ways of living, or assumptions about the world, to protect themselves from the overwhelming emotions and impossible situations in which they would otherwise find themselves.

Dysfunctional assumptions are usually more complex than core beliefs and are often more difficult to identify. It can take some time to work through this process, but it can reap significant rewards.

A simple way to understand dysfunctional assumptions is that they are protective against core beliefs; a dysfunctional assumption provides a shell under which resides the core belief. This is why each assumption is made up of two parts, one is the attempt at protection and the other is the belief that is protected against. Young, Klosko, and Weishaar (2003) provide a helpful way of thinking about rules for living in their schema work, outlining three basic defences

Table 3.2 Example dysfunctional assumptions

Core belief	Dysfunctional assumptions/rules for living
I am a failure	I may as well not try because I will only fail (surrender) If I work really hard and do everything perfectly then I won't be a failure (over-compensation) If I avoid pushing or challenging myself then I can't fail (avoidance)
I am powerless	I may as well let it all happen because I'm so powerless there's nothing I can do (surrender) If I keep control over everything then I won't be powerless (over-compensation) If I stay at home and never face anything then it won't matter that I'm powerless (avoidance)
The world is unpredictable	I may as will live in chaos as the world is so unpredictable (surrender) I need to ensure that everything is controlled otherwise everything will fall apart (over-compensation) I must hide from the world because it is so scary and unpredictable (avoidance)
The future will be disastrous	I may as well not bother because everything will go wrong anyway (surrender) I must make sure I do everything completely right now, otherwise everything will go wrong tomorrow (over-compensation) I may as well kill myself because my future will be horrible (avoidance/surrender)

against a schema or a core belief: surrender, over-compensation, and avoidance. Table 3.2 provides some examples of core beliefs and associated dysfunctional assumptions.

There are some important things to remember when trying to identify dysfunctional assumptions:

- While not all core beliefs need associated dysfunctional assumptions, the most powerful or distressing beliefs will have the most powerful assumptions associated with them.
- The assumptions should clearly contain two aspects, the protective aspect and the core belief.
- The assumptions are maladaptive or dysfunctional, which means they are usually extreme. For example: 'I must always . . .' or 'I should never. . .'.
- In the same way that core beliefs can come together (for example "I'm powerless" and "The world is unpredictable"), some assumptions can be responses to different core beliefs (e.g. avoiding leaving the house might avoid lots of different beliefs about the world, the self, and others).
- Human beings are adaptive. If individuals had only one or two dysfunctional assumptions, they would have figured out that they do not work! The reason they hang on to dysfunctional assumptions is that they switch between different assumptions as a form of change. The issue is that they are all too extreme. This is particularly important in Chapter 9 on emotion dysregulation.

Environmental triggers

Environmental triggers activate core beliefs and assumptions. A core belief and associated assumption about failure, for example, would be triggered by receiving criticism or getting feedback from others (e.g. a school report or work appraisal). An environmental trigger activates the beliefs and assumptions and the individual experiences the thoughts, feelings, behaviours, and physiology outlined in the maintenance cycle.

Cognitive behavioural interventions

Interventions in CBT can appear complex and it can be difficult to get a sense of which to use and when. Conceptually, however, they are simple. All interventions are designed to target one or two of the different elements of the formulation. Interventions can be grouped into four categories on the basis of their supposed mode of operation: behavioural, cognitive, behavioural experiments, and physiological. Importantly, interventions in CBT are not considered to take place outside the therapy room, but can be conducted in sessions or 'in-vivo'. In this way, clinicians are actively involved throughout the process of formulation and intervention and join with those seeking help in the pursuit of change.

Behavioural interventions

Behavioural interventions bring about change by altering behaviour. Changing behaviour can bring about a change to the entire system outlined above, affecting interactions with the environment, feelings, physiology, and thoughts, and potentially, over time, dysfunctional assumptions and core beliefs. They are derived from behavioural theory and based, usually, on classical or operant conditioning principles, involving repetition and gradual increase in intensity. They are the simplest to explain, the easiest to understand and often the most powerful.

Cognitive interventions

Cognitive interventions bring about change by manipulating or challenging thought processes. They are often combined under the umbrella term 'cognitive restructuring' and involve verbal, logical, reasoning processes designed to help people understand and question the ways in which they see themselves, the world, and the future. They often rely on formal operational abilities (see Chapter 2) such as thinking about thinking, systematic abstract thought, evidence gathering and weighing up alternative hypotheses. They vary considerably in complexity.

Behavioural experiments

Behavioural experiments operate on behaviours and cognitions at once. Behavioural change is placed within the context of an experiment designed to test a particular cognitive prediction. This process involves the formal operational abilities and the ability to make abstract predictions about the world, to weigh up alternative ideas and to systematically evaluate outcomes against these prior predictions. Behavioural experiments can only be used where behavioural intervention is possible, but can accelerate and help generalise change.

Physiological interventions

Physiological interventions tend to be shorter-term than the others and are designed to bring about fairly swift change by manipulating the body's physiology, which then has an influence on the other aspects of the system: thoughts, feelings, and behaviours.

Example CBT formulation

Figure 3.4 shows an example longitudinal formulation with maintenance cycle. Early experiences, core beliefs, dysfunctional assumptions, environmental triggers, and maintenance cycle all fit together to give a sense of the presenting issue, how it developed, and how it is maintained. There are multiple choices of intervention, including targeting the behaviour, challenging the thoughts, undertaking behavioural experiments, and working on the physiology. More will be said about sadness-based presentations such as this one in Chapter 7.

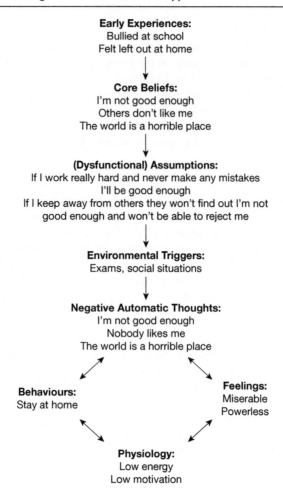

Figure 3.4 Example longitudinal formulation

Evidence base

CBT has a strong evidence base for a variety of different presentations. It has been shown to be effective, when compared to placebo or wait list, for many different presentations, including depression, generalised anxiety disorder, panic disorder, social phobia and post-traumatic stress disorder (Hofmann et al., 2012).

Research traditionally proceeds along child/adolescent and adult lines; research into the effectiveness of CBT for the population at issue here is difficult to delineate. Indeed, for the age group 18–25, there is little specific evidence at all. Despite these limitations, a recent review of meta-analyses in children and adolescents found that, in both anxiety and depression presentations, CBT showed medium to large effect sizes compared to non-active control groups and small to medium effect sizes when compared to active treatments (Crowe and McKay, 2017). CBT has also been shown to be effective for children and adolescents diagnosed with conditions such as chronic pain (Fisher et al., 2014), and conduct problems (Fossum et al., 2016).

In conclusion, CBT has a vast and growing evidence base across presenting difficulty and across the age-range.

Summary

CBT developed during the course of the last four decades and is based on a model of interaction between environment, thoughts, feelings, physiology, and behaviour. There is an emphasis on here-and-now formulations that help us to link what we know about people in general to what individuals experience, and these formulations lead to discrete, focused interventions that are undertaken within and between sessions. CBT also has constructs that can incorporate history into the formulation structure. CBT has a strong evidence base for a variety of different presentations across a variety of different populations.

References

Beck, A.T., Rush, A.J., Shaw, B.F., and Emery, G., 1979. *Cognitive treatment of depression: a treatment manual*. New York: Guilford.

Butler, G., 1998. Clinical formulation. In A.S. Bellack and M. Hersen (eds) *Comprehensive clinical psychology*. Oxford: Pergamon.

Crowe, K. and McKay, D., 2017. Efficacy of cognitive-behavioral therapy for childhood anxiety and depression. *Journal of Anxiety Disorders*, *49*, pp. 76–87.

Eysenck, H.J., 1952. The effects of psychotherapy: an evaluation. *Journal of Consulting Psychology*, *16*(5), pp. 319–324.

Fisher, E., Heathcote, L., Palermo, T.M., de C Williams, A.C., Lau, J., and Eccleston, C., 2014. Systematic review and meta-analysis of psychological therapies for children with chronic pain. *Journal of Pediatric Psychology*, *39*(8), pp. 763–782.

Fossum, S., Handegård, B.H., Adolfsen, F., Vis, S.A., and Wynn, R., 2016. A meta-analysis of long-term outpatient treatment effects for children and adolescents with conduct problems. *Journal of Child and Family Studies*, *25*(1), pp. 15–29.

Hofmann, S.G., Asnaani, A., Vonk, I.J., Sawyer, A.T., and Fang, A., 2012. The efficacy of cognitive behavioral therapy: a review of meta-analyses. *Cognitive Therapy and Research*, *36*(5), pp. 427–440.

Padesky, C.A., 1993, September. Socratic questioning: changing minds or guiding discovery. In: A keynote address delivered at the European Congress of Behavioural and Cognitive Therapies, London (Vol. 24).

Padesky, C.A. and Mooney, K.A., 1990. Clinical tip: presenting the cognitive model to clients. *International Cognitive Therapy Newsletter*, *6*(1), pp. 13–14.

Rush, A.J., Beck, A.T., Kovacs, M., and Hollon, S., 1977. Comparative efficacy of cognitive therapy and pharmacotherapy in the treatment of depressed outpatients. *Cognitive Therapy and Research*, *1*(1), pp. 17–37.

Westbrook, D., Kennerley, H., and Kirk, J., 2011. *An introduction to cognitive behaviour therapy: skills and applications*. London: Sage.

Wolpe, J. (1958). *Psychotherapy by reciprocal inhibition*. Stanford, CA: Stanford University Press.

Young, J.E., Klosko, J.S., and Weishaar, M.E., 2003. *Schema therapy: a practitioner's guide*. New York: Guilford Press.

Chapter 4

Problems with diagnostic-based CBT in adolescents and young adults

I was terrified I would become the diagnosis.

(22-year-old male)

In this chapter, we highlight the difficulties faced by clinicians in routine clinical practice working hard to provide adolescents and young adults with the best possible service. The first issue is with diagnosis-based CBT in the context of adolescent and early adult development. The second issue is the disparity between CBT delivered in university research trials and CBT delivered in routine clinical practice.

This outlines the rationale for the fresh approach taken in this book and detailed in Chapter 5.

Problems with diagnosis

As summarised in Chapter 3, CBT has, throughout its history, had a foundation in empiricism. At its heart is the importance of testing interventions to ensure their effectiveness. Research and the empirical foundation of treatments for emotional distress are grounded, for the most part, within a diagnostic understanding and CBT has grown around this framework.

CBT and diagnosis

This growth of CBT alongside the growth of evidence-based practice has done a great deal for psychological therapy. Despite the fact that it is much more difficult to evaluate psychological intervention in the same way as pharmaceutical intervention, proponents of CBT have been able to emulate enough of the characteristics of pharmaceutical trials to demonstrate that CBT is at least as effective, if not more so, than pharmaceutical intervention (see Chapter 3). As a result, guidelines across the world, for a variety of disorders, routinely recommend psychological therapy (usually CBT) as an alternative or an adjunct to medical intervention.

Strategy and funding has followed in the wake of this evidence and the UK, for example, has seen a massive investment in the provision of psychological interventions over the past decade to the point at which almost one million working age adults now access psychological services each year (NHS England, n.d.). Clearly, embedding empiricism within CBT and embracing the culture of evidence-based practice has meant that CBT is available to more people than ever before.

A second benefit of the diagnostic framework is the clear language in which difficulties can be understood, described, and treated. Having a diagnostic label provides a sense that the difficulty is understandable, that there are other people with similar difficulties, and it provides access to information about the kind of interventions available. In this way, the diagnostic framework has shaped not only the research, but the theories of emotional distress, and the structure and delivery of insurance, benefits, and treatment services. As a result, the diagnostic framework has become accepted by professional groups, the media, and the general public. We often hear people saying such things as "now I know what's wrong with me I can do something about it."

However, alongside these benefits of the diagnostic approach, there are some costs, particularly in relation to adolescents and young adults. There are concerns about the reliability and validity of the diagnostic framework, issues with the individual and biological emphasis of the framework, as well as with the resulting stigma and its impact on individuals and families. Each will be considered in turn.

Reliability, validity, utility

Diagnosis is often spoken about as if it were fact; "I have been diagnosed with . . .," or "I have . . . ." A diagnosis is, however, a clinical judgement based on observation, interpretation of behaviour, and self-report, rendering it subject to variation and bias (Kirk and Kutchins, 1994). This leads to potential issues on two fronts: reliability and validity.

Reliability is the degree to which the same diagnosis is given in different situations, for example by different clinicians. Studies tend to find that reliability is variable across different diagnoses and with differing levels of information; for common diagnoses, some controlled studies have found high levels of reliability across clinicians (Ruskin et al., 1998), but for less common diagnoses it is significantly lower, much closer to chance levels (Matusak and Piasecki, 2012). In addition, the information collected in routine clinical practice, being less than that usually collected in structured diagnostic interviews, often results in extremely low levels of reliability (Saunders et al., 2015). These issues with reliability have led to a growth in the numbers of diagnoses available, but this has had a resultant impact on the validity of diagnoses (McGorry et al., 2007).

The validity of a diagnosis is the degree to which it relates to a valid underlying construct. Many authors highlight psychiatry's failure, relative to other branches of medicine, to isolate or describe the underlying biological cause for the majority of diagnostic categories (e.g. van Os et al., 2003). In addition, there are high levels of overlap between diagnostic categories (Kinderman et al., 2013;

McManus et al., 2016). There is also evidence that diagnostic categories are not particularly stable over time; one study finding that fewer than 20% of individuals meeting criteria for a diagnosis of Obsessive Compulsive Disorder (OCD) at initial interview reported symptoms during their lifetimes that met the same criteria one year later (Nelson and Rice, 1997). In addition, diagnoses have not been found to be particularly good predictors of relevant constructs, such as need for services, quality of life, or treatment outcome (Johnstone et al., 1992; van Os et al., 1999).

Finally, the utility of the diagnostic framework is not supported by evidence. Regular surveys of psychiatric morbidity in England, the most recent of which was conducted during 2014–15 (McManus et al., 2016), use the concept of Common Mental Disorders which is derived via an assessment of 14 clusters of symptoms (for example sleep problems, depression, and worry). While these map on to psychiatric diagnoses, the most common category of disorder was 'common mental disorder – not otherwise specified' rather than any recognised psychiatric diagnosis and only a minority of individuals met criteria for a single diagnosis alone.

All of this has led some authors to conclude that the diagnostic model "struggles to fulfil its key purposes of guiding treatment selection and predicting outcome" and that "understanding of this is crucial in youth mental health" (McGorry et al., 2007: p. S40).

These issues with the reliability, validity and utility of the diagnostic framework, while usually accepted, are rarely incorporated into its use at a clinical level. This means that the majority of individuals believe that psychiatric diagnoses are reliable, valid, useful, and that there is no other way in which difficulties can be understood.

Decontextualisation

Diagnosis is a medical term. It is the process through which an underlying problem is detected by examination of observable symptoms. A psychiatric diagnosis aims to define a mental disorder 'that occurs within the individual' (APA, 2013). This leads to an over-emphasis on certain aspects of difficulties, and an under-emphasis on others. Biology, for example, tends to be over-emphasised, and there is a tendency to neglect the environment in which the individual exists; their social, cultural, familial, and historical contexts.

As outlined in Chapter 2, there is an interaction throughout life between the individual and their context and evidence repeatedly demonstrates the importance of these interactions. Evidence suggests that those meeting criteria for diagnostic categories share many past experiences. For example, those diagnosed with schizophrenia are far more likely to have experienced childhood adversity than those diagnosed with an anxiety disorder (Matheson et al., 2013). Other studies have found significant associations between prevalence of diagnosed depression and characteristics of the built environment (Weich et al., 2002).

While these findings are not necessarily inconsistent with the assumptions of the diagnostic framework, the contextual factors that impact on emotional distress are underplayed by the diagnostic model. Given the importance of the environment in the lives of adolescents and young adults, this relative neglect of their context is a particular problem.

Diagnosis and stigma

Another negative factor associated with the diagnostic model is the stigma of diagnosis. Stigma refers to the negative stereotyped beliefs held by societies about diagnosis and individuals with these labels. These negative beliefs are associated with damaging consequences for those with diagnostic labels in all walks of life, including education, employment, and social functioning (Thornicroft, 2007). That there is significant stigma associated with mental health is almost unrefuted and there is recognition across the world that stigma represents a particular challenge to the mental health of young people (Patel et al., 2007).

As a result, a great deal of money and energy has been spent on attempts to reduce the stigma of mental illness. The theory has been that increasing the awareness of mental illness should reduce the stigma and negative attitudes of the general population. As a result, anti-stigma campaigns have been established across the world, for example 'Time to Change' in the UK, 'One of Us' in Denmark, or 'Bring Change 2 Mind' in the US, all of which have aimed to raise awareness of mental health difficulties. They have educated the populous within a diagnostic framework, using diagnostic labels and symptoms, as well as citing high rates of annual prevalence (e.g. the one in four statistic used by the 'Time to Change' campaign in the UK).

Despite these campaigns and enthusiasm for them at a policy level, the evidence that they are effective is less than compelling. A variety of studies have found that campaigns raising the profile of medical and biological explanations of mental illness tend to increase rather than decrease negative attitudes (Read et al., 2006; Schomerus, Matschinger and Angermeyer, 2014). This is in line with findings that mental health professionals, despite their increased knowledge (again, primarily from a diagnostic viewpoint) relative to the lay population, exhibit similarly high levels or even higher levels of stigma towards those with psychiatric diagnoses (Nordt, Rössler, and Lauber, 2006).

Diagnosis and identity

Diagnosis is clearly associated with negative stereotypes and stigma at a population level. However, the provision of a psychiatric diagnosis to an individual not only has the potential to have an impact on the way that they are perceived by society, but on the way in which the individual perceives themselves.

As outlined in Chapter 2, adolescence and young adulthood is a time in which individuals are forming a sense of themselves as individuals interacting with others and within a wider context. Against this background, there is potentially a greater risk than at other times of life that diagnostic labels will be incorporated into identity and have a dramatic impact on the development of the adolescent and young adult.

Evidence investigating the processes of diagnosis and identity tends to look at two aspects of identity: self-esteem, and self-efficacy.

Self-esteem, as outlined in Chapter 2, refers to the way in which the individual views themselves as an object; the collection of beliefs they hold about themselves. Individuals, being a part of society, also develop a set of beliefs about particular diagnoses or people who have a particular diagnosis, as outlined in the stigma section above. When individuals are given a diagnosis, there is an invitation to apply these beliefs to themselves; a process known as self-stigmatisation.

High levels of self-stigmatisation have been associated with low scores on measures of self-esteem and this is after controlling for other factors such as diagnosis, level of depression, and demographic variables (Corrigan, Watson, and Barr, 2006, Link et al., 2001, Rüsch et al., 2010). Other studies have linked this self-stigmatisation to behaviours such as social withdrawal (Link et al., 2001), which is likely to compound the effects on self-esteem. From a different perspective, those with higher levels of self-stigma tend to tell stories about themselves and their lives with lower social worth (Lysaker et al., 2008).

Self-efficacy, defined as the sense of agency and empowerment of individuals, has also been linked with self-stigmatisation. Evidence has shown that the provision and acceptance of a psychiatric diagnosis is associated with lower levels of self-efficacy and lowered perceived ability to bring about change (Corrigan et al., 2006; Rüsch et al., 2006; Wright, Gronfein, and Owens, 2000).

Psychological formulation: an alternative

Psychological formulation represents an alternative framework in which to understand emotional distress. Psychological formulation can be defined in various ways, but one of the most succinct definitions comes from Butler (1998: p. 2) "A formulation is the tool used by clinicians to relate theory to practice. . . It is the lynchpin that holds theory and practice together. . . Formulations can best be understood as hypotheses to be tested." In this context, a psychological formulation aims to relate an individual's experience or difficulty to what is known more generally about human psychology. This formulation should then suggest a course of action or intervention. According to Johnstone et al. (2011), psychological formulation is:

- grounded in psychological theory and evidence;
- constructed collaboratively, using accessible language;
- constructed reflectively;
- centrally concerned with personal meaning; and
- best understood in terms of usefulness rather than 'truth'.

In this way, a psychological formulation tends towards a narrative account, or a diagrammatic representation of the problem, which tends to be more detailed and comprehensive in comparison to the categorical and more reductionist approach of diagnosis.

Psychological formulation aims to situate human experience in its context and therefore does not include the bias towards a single factor (e.g. biology) as with diagnosis. Given that psychological formulation tends to be grounded in an understanding of human experience and response, it is also less likely to result in stigma and negative prejudice. Indeed, contextualised explanations of difficulties tend to be less stigmatising than biological ones (Read et al., 2006). This emphasis on a shared experience with other humans rather than the differences, is likely to be carried forward into a reduced negative impact on self-esteem and self-efficacy relative to diagnosis.

With regards to the reliability and validity of psychological formulation, the evidence is not so clear. In a review of case formulation using CBT, Bieling and Kukyen (2003) concluded that reliability can be fairly high for the descriptive elements of formulation (i.e. presenting problems), particularly when carried out by experienced clinicians with systematic training, but tends to be lower for the inferential aspects of the formulation (e.g. underlying core beliefs or rules for living). Reliability and quality of formulation is associated with experience and accreditation status (Kuyken et al., 2005).

Many authors argue that neither reliability nor validity are relevant in psychological formulation; what is important is the degree to which it is useful and supports progress towards treatment (Johnstone et al., 2011). Studies looking at the impact of written formulation letters have found that psychological formulation can be experienced as increasing hope, understanding, and deepening the therapeutic relationship; however, it can also be saddening, overwhelming, or lead to hopelessness (Chadwick, Williams and Mackenzie, 2003; Pain, Chadwick and Abba, 2008). One study looking at more traditional diagrammatic CBT formulations found a stronger positive influence, but also noted that distress was caused by formulations perceived to be inaccurate, or to have negative implications for the self (Redhead, Johnstone, and Nightingale, 2015).

Psychological formulation has existed for many decades and many psychological practitioners as well as others (including those seeking help) frequently argue that it represents a better alternative to the diagnostic framework. Despite this, the majority of clinicians, including psychologists, still use a diagnostic framework in their practice. This is most likely because psychological formulation, being individualised, does not provide the easy, simple categorical language afforded by diagnosis; psychological formulation works when speaking about individuals, but its individualised nature makes generalising to population levels difficult. This means, in turn, that psychological formulation does not lend itself to researching interventions for populations of people and does not fit with the evidence-based model. As a result, the diagnostic model remains dominant across services.

Summary

A diagnosis is not a fact, it is a model which attempts to help us understand the difficulties people face. There are significant benefits of using the diagnostic model in CBT, including a demonstration of efficacy at levels similar to medical intervention, which has brought significant advantages in terms of funding and the availability of CBT across the developed world. However, incorporating the diagnostic model into the fabric of CBT results in significant costs for those receiving the intervention. This is because psychiatric diagnosis is associated with negative societal beliefs, as well as negative beliefs in self-concept and self-efficacy. This is of particular concern in adolescents and young adults, given their processes of development. Psychological formulation goes some way to address these issues, but despite its presence for many decades, the diagnostic model remains predominant.

Problems with CBT in routine clinical practice

As outlined in Chapter 3, CBT can be fairly simply understood and the interventions grouped in a fairly broad manner. Formulations can also be fairly simply developed using models such as the five-part model (Padesky and Mooney, 1990). Despite its apparent simplicity, however, the trend in CBT is for a proliferation of different models. This is partly driven by the diagnostic model where each edition of a diagnostic manual invariably includes a greater number of different diagnoses. It is also partly driven by a desire to increase the specificity and the focus of the intervention to target particular presentations.

With this received wisdom, it would be expected that more and more specific models and interventions would lead to better and better treatment over time. However, this position is not supported by the evidence. Studies investigating components of CBT and comparing them to others often bring up surprising results: one study found that cognitive intervention was as effective as behavioural intervention for depression, and that there was no increase in effectiveness for the two combined (Jacobson et al., 1996). Two meta-analytic studies of interventions for social anxiety disorder, including exposure, cognitive restructuring, and social skills training, found no significant difference between the different types of interventions (Gil, Carrillo, and Meca, 2001, Powers et al., 2008). More recent research has found some evidence in support of particular models of CBT for social anxiety disorder, but there are caveats to this finding in terms of a greater quantity of research, and the proponents of the model being those undertaking the trials (Mayo-Wilson et al., 2014). One study directly comparing diagnosis-specific with transdiagnostic models did not find a significant difference between interventions (Norton and Barrera, 2012). In addition, despite increasingly specific models of intervention, and increasing quantities of research evidence, the effectiveness of CBT over time appears to be declining rather than increasing, at least for depression (Johnsen and Friborg, 2015).

Much of the evidence in support of CBT comes from manualised treatments delivered in university settings. CBT delivered in routine clinical environments is less effective, a finding that has been attributed to lower levels of fidelity to treatment manuals, less knowledge of the evidence, beliefs about the relevance of the evidence, and funding issues (Ishikawa et al., 2007; Shafran et al., 2009). Central elements of CBT (e.g. behavioural change) are often omitted in clinical practice; indeed, more often omitted than included (Becker, Zayfert and Anderson, 2004; Stobie et al., 2007). Waller (2009) attributes this 'drift' away from the core elements of CBT to the challenging nature of these interventions for both clinicians and those seeking help. The quality of CBT delivered by those with additional training has been found to be higher, but even clinicians trained to this higher level frequently deliver CBT at levels deemed below competence (Brosan, Reynolds, and Moore, 2007; Kuyken et al., 2005). Clinicians also appear to over-rate their ability to deliver CBT competently; this being particularly the case where practitioners are less experienced (Brosan, Reynolds and Moore, 2008).

That there is a difference between the type of CBT delivered in university settings and in routine clinical practice is hardly surprising. Clinicians on the front-line are expected to work with a broad variety of presentations, with increasing demands on services and decreasing support, supervision, and ongoing training. Over time, the landscape of CBT itself has also become increasingly complex. There are more and more diagnostic categories to understand, and even within categories there are more and more theoretical models to choose between. As an example, there are five different models for obsessive-compulsive disorder (e.g. Franklin and Foa, 2002; Salkovskis, 1985; Rachman, 1997; Salkovskis, Forrester, and Richards, 1998; Wells, 2013). Some models are also complicated to understand and to explain. This makes it difficult, in routine clinical practice, to choose between the different models and to be familiar enough with them to deliver them confidently. Without high levels of confidence, it is hard to maintain a focus on the core elements of CBT: behavioural change and cognitive challenge.

In summary, there is clear evidence that CBT, when delivered competently, is likely to be more effective than many other interventions for a variety of pres-entations. Despite the proliferation of different models for different presentations, there is no strong evidence available to support one model over another. How-ever, there is evidence to suggest that much of the CBT provided in routine clinical practice falls short of the quality of university research trials. This is potentially attributable to an over-emphasis on the development of new models which can be researched and trialled, and an under-emphasis on supporting clinicians in routine practice to make the best possible use of the research knowledge.

Summary

The diagnostic framework has provided a structure in which CBT has grown and flourished. It has provided a way of understanding and a way of treating emotional distress. However, this comes at a cost. There are issues with the reliability and validity of the framework, issues with its bias towards an individualised, biological understanding of the distress, and issues with the stigma produced at both at societal and individual levels.

Psychological formulation has provided an alternative structure, which is more individualised and less likely to produce stigma. However, in spite of its being offered as an alternative to diagnosis for many decades, it has not moved as far forward as might be expected, perhaps as a result of the ease of the categorical approach of diagnosis when compared to the individualised approach of psychological formulation.

Finally, the practice of CBT in routine clinical settings falls dramatically short of the CBT upon which the evidence is based. This is potentially attributable to the increasingly complex landscape of CBT with a proliferation of models and ideas resulting in difficulties choosing between models, insufficient familiarity with different models, and a resultant lack of focus on the core elements of CBT: behavioural change and cognitive challenge.

This book aims to confront each of these problems by bringing together the principles of CBT and its evidence base using a fresh approach. It aims to support clinicians to provide the best possible service to adolescents and young adults. Chapter 5 outlines this approach.

References

APA, 2013. *Diagnostic and statistical manual of mental disorders* (5th edn). Washington, DC: Author.

Becker, C.B., Zayfert, C., and Anderson, E., 2004. A survey of psychologists' attitudes towards and utilization of exposure therapy for PTSD. *Behaviour research and therapy*, *42*(3), pp. 277–292.

Bieling, P.J. and Kuyken, W., 2003. Is cognitive case formulation science or science fiction? *Clinical Psychology: Science and Practice*, *10*(1), pp. 52–69.

Brosan, L., Reynolds, S., and Moore, R. G., 2007. Factors associated with competence in cognitive therapists. *Behavioural and Cognitive Psychotherapy*, *35*, pp. 179–190.

Brosan, L., Reynolds, S., and Moore, R. G., 2008. Self-evaluation of cognitive therapy performance: do therapists know how competent they are? *Behavioural and Cognitive Psychotherapy*, *36*, pp. 581–587.

Butler, G, 1998. Clinical formulation. In A.S. Bellack and M. Hersen (eds) *Comprehensive clinical psychology*. Oxford: Pergamon, pp. 1–24.

Chadwick, P., Williams, C., and Mackenzie, J., 2003. Impact of case formulation in cognitive behaviour therapy for psychosis. *Behaviour Research and Therapy*, *41*(6), pp. 671–680.

Corrigan, P.W., Watson, A.C., and Barr, L., 2006. The self-stigma of mental illness: implications for self-esteem and self-efficacy. *Journal of Social and Clinical Psychology*, *25*, pp. 875–883.

Franklin, M.E. and Foa, E.B., 2002. Cognitive behavioral treatments for obsessive compulsive disorder. In P.E. Nathan and J.M. Gorman (eds) *A guide to treatments that work* (2nd edn). London: Oxford University Press, pp. 367–386.

Gil, P. J. M., Carrillo, F. X. M., and Meca, J. S., 2001. Effectiveness of cognitive-behavioural treatment in social phobia: a meta-analytic review. *Psychology in Spain*, *5*(1), pp. 17–25.

Ishikawa, S.I., Okajima, I., Matsuoka, H., and Sakano, Y., 2007. Cognitive behavioural therapy for anxiety disorders in children and adolescents: a meta-analysis. *Child and Adolescent Mental Health*, *12*(4), pp. 164–172.

Jacobson, N. S., Dobson, K. S., Truax, P. A., Addis, M. E., Koerner, K., Gollan, J. K., et al., 1996. A component analysis of cognitive-behavioral treatment for depression. *Journal of Consulting and Clinical Psychology*, *64*, pp. 295–304.

Johnsen, T.J. and Friborg, O., 2015. The effects of cognitive behavioural therapy as an anti-depressive treatment is falling: a meta-analysis. *Psychological Bulletin*, *141*(4), pp. 747–768.

Johnstone, E.C., Frith, C.D., Crow, T.J., Owens, D.G.C., Done, D.J., Baldwin, E.J. and Charlette, A., 1992. The Northwick Park 'functional' psychosis study: diagnosis and outcome. *Psychological Medicine*, *22*(02), pp. 331–346.

Johnstone, L., Whomsley, S., Cole, S., and Oliver, N., 2011. *Good practice guidelines on the use of psychological formulation*. Leicester, UK: British Psychological Society.

Kinderman, P., Read, J., Moncrieff, J., and Bentall, R.P., 2013. Drop the language of disorder. *Evidence Based Mental Health*, *16*(1), pp. 2–3.

Kirk, S. and Kutchines, H, 1994. The myth of the reliability of the DSM. *Journal of Mind and Behaviour*, *15*, pp. 71–86.

Kuyken, W., Fothergill, C.D., Musa, M., and Chadwick, P., 2005. The reliability and quality of cognitive case formulation. *Behaviour Research and Therapy*, *43*(9), pp. 1187–1201.

Link, B.G., Struening, E.L., Neese-Todd, S., Asmussen, S., and Phelan, J.C., 2001. Stigma as a barrier to recovery: the consequences of stigma for the self-esteem of people with mental illnesses. *Psychiatric Services*, *52*(12), pp. 1621–1626.

Lysaker, P.H., Buck, K.D., Taylor, A.C., and Roe, D., 2008. Associations of metacognition and internalized stigma with quantitative assessments of self-experience in narratives of schizophrenia. *Psychiatry Research*, *157*(1), pp. 31–38.

McGorry, P.D., Purcell, R., Hickie, I.B., Yung, A.R., Pantelis, C., and Jackson, H.J., 2007. Clinical staging: a heuristic model for psychiatry and youth mental health. *Medical Journal of Australia*, *187*(7 Suppl), pp. S40–S42.

McManus S., Bebbington P., Jenkins R., and Brugha T. (eds), 2016. Mental health and wellbeing in England: Adult Psychiatric Morbidity Survey 2014. Leeds, UK: NHS Digital.

Matheson, S.L., Shepherd, A.M., Pinchbeck, R.M., Laurens, K.R., and Carr, V.J., 2013. Childhood adversity in schizophrenia: a systematic meta-analysis. *Psychological Medicine*, *43*(2), pp. 225–238.

Matuszak, J. and Piasecki, M., 2012. Inter-rater reliability in psychiatric diagnosis: collateral data improves the reliability of diagnoses. *Psychiatric Times*, *29*(10), pp. 12–13.

Mayo-Wilson, E., Dias, S., Mavranezouli, I., Kew, K., Clark, D.M., Ades, A.E., and Pilling, S., 2014. Psychological and pharmacological interventions for social anxiety disorder in adults: a systematic review and network meta-analysis. *The Lancet Psychiatry*, *1*(5), pp. 368–376.

Nelson, E. and Rice, J., 1997. Stability of diagnosis of obsessive-compulsive disorder in the Epidemiologic Catchment Area study. *American Journal of Psychiatry*, *154*(6), pp. 826–831.

NHS England n.d. Adult Improving Access to Psychological Therapies Programme [online]. Available at www.england.nhs.uk/mental-health/adults/iapt. (Accessed 22nd September 2017).

Nordt, C., Rössler, W., and Lauber, C., 2006. Attitudes of mental health professionals toward people with schizophrenia and major depression. *Schizophrenia Bulletin*, *32*(4), pp. 709–714.

Norton, P.J. and Barrera, T.L., 2012. Transdiagnostic versus diagnosis-specific CBT for anxiety disorders: a preliminary randomized controlled noninferiority trial. *Depression and Anxiety*, *29*(10), pp. 874–882.

Padesky, C.A. and Mooney, K.A., 1990. Clinical tip: presenting the cognitive model to clients. *International Cognitive Therapy Newsletter*, *6*(1), pp. 13–14.

Pain, C.M., Chadwick, P., and Abba, N., 2008. Clients' experience of case formulation in cognitive behaviour therapy for psychosis. *British Journal of Clinical Psychology*, *47*(2), pp. 127–138.

Patel, V., Flisher, A.J., Hetrick, S., and McGorry, P., 2007. Mental health of young people: a global public-health challenge. *The Lancet*, *369*(9569), pp. 1302–1313.

Powers, M. B., Sigmarsson, S. R., and Emmelkamp, P. M. G., 2008. A meta-analytic review of psychological treatments for social anxiety disorder. *International Journal of Cognitive Therapy*, *1*, pp. 94–113.

Rachman, S., 1997. A cognitive theory of obsessions. *Behaviour Research and Therapy*, *35*(9), pp. 793–802.

Read, J., Haslam, N., Sayce, L., and Davies, E. 2006. Prejudice and schizophrenia: a review of the 'mental illness is an illness like any other' approach. *Acta Psychiatrica Scandinavica*, *114*, pp. 303–318.

Redhead, S., Johnstone, L., and Nightingale, J., 2015. Clients' experiences of formulation in cognitive behaviour therapy. *Psychology and Psychotherapy: Theory, Research and Practice*, *88*(4), pp. 453–467.

Rüsch, N., Corrigan, P.W., Todd, A.R., and Bodenhausen, G.V., 2010. Implicit self-stigma in people with mental illness. *The Journal of Nervous and Mental Disease*, *198*(2), pp. 150–153.

Rüsch, N., Hölzer, A., Hermann, C., Schramm, E., Jacob, G.A., Bohus, M., Lieb, K., and Corrigan, P.W., 2006. Self-stigma in women with borderline personality disorder and women with social phobia. *The Journal of Nervous and Mental Disease*, *194*(10), pp. 766–773.

Ruskin, P.E., Reed, S., Kumar, R., Kling, M.A., Siegel, E., Rosen, M., and Hauser, P., 1998. Reliability and acceptability of psychiatric diagnosis via telecommunication and audiovisual technology. *Psychiatric Services*, *49*(8), pp. 1086–1088.

Salkovskis, P.M., 1985. Obsessional-compulsive problems: A cognitive-behavioural analysis. *Behaviour Research and Therapy*, *23*(5), pp. 571–583.

Salkovskis, P.M., Forrester, E., and Richards, C., 1998. Cognitive-behavioural approach to understanding obsessional thinking. *The British Journal of Psychiatry. Supplement*, (35), pp. 53–63.

Saunders, K.E.A., Bilderbeck, A.C., Price, J., and Goodwin, G.M., 2015. Distinguishing bipolar disorder from borderline personality disorder: a study of current clinical practice. *European Psychiatry*, *30*(8), pp. 965–974.

Schomerus, G., Matschinger, H., and Angermeyer, M.C., 2014. Causal beliefs of the public and social acceptance of persons with mental illness: a comparative analysis of schizophrenia, depression and alcohol dependence. *Psychological Medicine*, *44*(2), pp. 303–314.

Shafran, R., Clark, D.M., Fairburn, C.G., Arntz, A., Barlow, D.H., Ehlers, A., Freeston, M., Garety, P.A., Hollon, S.D., Ost, L.G., and Salkovskis, P.M., 2009. Mind the gap: improving the dissemination of CBT. *Behaviour Research and Therapy*, *47*(11), pp. 902–909.

Stobie, B., Taylor, T., Quigley, A., Ewing, S., and Salkovskis, P.M., 2007. "Contents may vary": A pilot study of treatment histories of OCD patients. *Behavioural and Cognitive Psychotherapy*, *35*(03), pp. 273–282.

Thornicroft, G. 2007. *Shunned*. Oxford: Oxford University Press.

van Os, J., Gilvarry, C., Bale, R., Van Horn, E., Tattan, T., and White, I., 1999. A comparison of the utility of dimensional and categorical representations of psychosis. *Psychological Medicine*, *29*(03), pp. 595–606.

Van Os, J., MacKenna, P., Murray, R., and Dean, K., 2003. *Does Schizophrenia Exist?* London: Institute of Psychiatry.

Waller, G., 2009. Evidence-based treatment and therapist drift. *Behaviour Research and Therapy*, *47*(2), pp. 119–127.

Weich, S., Blanchard, M., Prince, M., Burton, E., Erens, B.O.B., and Sproston, K., 2002. Mental health and the built environment: cross-sectional survey of individual and contextual risk factors for depression. *The British Journal of Psychiatry*, *180*(5), pp. 428–433.

Wells, A., 2013. *Cognitive therapy of anxiety disorders: a practice manual and conceptual guide*. Chichester, UK: John Wiley & Sons.

Wright, E.R., Gronfein, W.P., and Owens, T.J., 2000. Deinstitutionalization, social rejection, and the self-esteem of former mental patients. *Journal of Health and Social Behavior*, pp. 68–90.

Chapter 5

A fresh approach

Emotions are a sign that I'm alive, I'm a human being. They're nothing to be afraid of, it's just not getting caught up in them.

(22-year-old male)

It's nice [to understand things in this way] because it means that I'm essentially normal, I am supposed to respond in this way. It makes me feel like less of a crackpot!

(23-year-old female)

In the fresh approach outlined in this book, adolescents and young adults are given the opportunity to understand their difficulties and receive intervention without having to view themselves as 'disordered' or 'ill'. The practice of CBT is separated from the diagnostic model and is grounded instead in emotion science. A scientific understanding of emotions provides a normative framework that is clear, easy to understand, and suggests interventions that are entirely consistent with the evidence upon which CBT is based. Adolescents and young adults learn about their emotions and emotional 'traps', view themselves as fundamentally similar to their peers, and as capable of bringing about change so that they can continue their development into adulthood.

The use of the science of emotion rather than the science of diagnosis also means that the process is simpler (e.g. one fear trap instead of multiple anxiety-disorder models) and it rebalances our practice to better include 'neglected' emotions such as anger.

This chapter briefly outlines the theoretical principles of this approach, before detailing the five pillars of understanding we can use with adolescents, young adults, and their families, to understand their difficulties.

Theoretical approach of this book

The four principles that form the theoretical basis of the approach are:

- the inclusion of a developmental context;
- the grounding of understanding in the normal;

- an emphasis on education and clarity;
- adherence to the evidence base.

Developmental context

There is a great deal of developmental change during the course of adolescence and early adulthood (Chapter 2). Any work offered to adolescents and young adults should be contextualised in an understanding of their developmental trajectory.

Incorporating the developmental context has an impact on our work in a variety of ways. It might affect decisions about with whom we choose to work, when we choose to work, how we proceed with the work, and the ultimate goals of intervention. These ideas are developed later in the chapter.

Grounded in emotion and emotion regulation science

The difficulties facing adolescents and young adults are understood using the science of 'normal' development, such as the models and understandings outlined in Chapter 2. Where there are significant difficulties, these are understood to be an interruption to normal development, rather than an illness or disorder. The difficulties faced by adolescents and young adults are seen as difficulties with regulating emotions, either specific emotions like fear or sadness, or more broad emotion regulation difficulties as outlined in the emotion dysregulation chapter (Chapter 9).

In grounding the approach in the normal human experience of emotion, we have a categorical way of describing the difficulties that individuals face without resorting to diagnostic, illness-based language. For example, we can use phrases such as 'problems with fear, 'fear-based problems', or 'caught in the fear trap'.

Education and clarity

Adolescents and young adults are at a stage of life in which learning is central. In this approach, adolescents and young adults are supported to learn about emotions and their emotional experience by providing new knowledge and perspectives.

Solid learning derives from good teaching and so it is important that the educational components of the model are presented with clarity and confidence, and that they fit together in a coherent fashion to help explain a number of different experiences. This book provides clear, simple ideas and formulations that can be understood by clinicians, young people, and families alike, which lead to the implementation of cognitive-behavioural techniques to facilitate change.

The basis in emotion science rather than diagnostic science means there are fewer models to learn. For example, the fear trap is a trap that works with all fears, regardless of the feared stimulus. This means that, as clinicians, we can become experts at using a few clear, straightforward models and explaining them in a way that others will understand.

Based on best available evidence

Adolescents and young adults deserve high quality intervention that is based on the best available evidence. While this book outlines a fresh approach as an alternative to the diagnostic basis of the majority of clinical trials, it does maintain the value of evidence-based practice. It links to the evidence base in three ways:

- **General CBT**. As outlined in Chapter 3, there is strong support for CBT at the broadest level. Across presentations and across populations, interventions that involve behavioural change and cognitive challenge have a basis in evidence.
- **Specific Interventions**. While the route and explanation for intervention might be different using emotion rather than diagnostic science, in practice, the approach results in using the same kinds of interventions for the same kinds of people. The link between the approach of this book and the available evidence is outlined at the end of each chapter.
- **Implementing CBT in practice**. The quality of CBT as delivered in practice falls worryingly short, compared to CBT in research trials (see Chapter 4). This book provides a few simple cognitive-behavioural models that clinicians can use for a variety of presentations with high levels of familiarity and confidence. This supports the processes of explaining and implementing the interventions with the strongest evidence.

Five pillars of the approach

The theoretical principles lead on to five pillars for adolescents, young adults, and their families to make sense of their experience and the interventions that can help. The five principles covered in this chapter are:

1. What are emotions?
2. What are the functions of emotions?
3. How are emotions regulated?
4. A basic model of development
5. The hand brain.

1. What are emotions?

We begin not with disorders, their symptoms, and their prevalence, but with emotions and an understanding of how they work. The first part of the process is to explore and understand what are emotions.

Emotions are generally agreed to comprise various components. The most obvious component and that usually first named by adolescents and young adults is the feeling; the conscious experience of the emotion. However, there are also other components such as the physiological changes occurring in the body and cognitive components. We refer to five different components of emotions: feeling, physiology, facial expression, cognition, and behaviour. The next section goes through each of these in turn and then looks at how the components fit together.

Feeling: conscious experience

The conscious experience of emotion, the feeling, is the most salient experience of emotion. Each emotion is associated with this awareness of an emotional state. These feeling states are labelled with hundreds of different emotional words and phrases (Plutchik, 2001), ranging from the more basic (e.g. sad, angry) to the more colourful (e.g. 'on cloud nine' or 'bricking it'). The conscious experience of emotion is separate from the other components of emotion.

This distinction can be illustrated using the example of someone who stubs their toe. A gentle tap of the toe produces an awareness of pain in the toe that can be pushed away and the degree of interference in their ability to continue the previous task can be limited. In this case the individual is aware of the physiological state of their toe, but is able to continue regardless. However, if they stub their toe while running and really damage it, they would still be aware of the pain as originating in the toe but the pain might overwhelm their attentional systems and lead to them hopping up and down, shouting in agony, and being unable to concentrate on anything other than the pain. In this way, we can understand the difference between the physiological state of their toe, and the conscious experience of, in this case, pain, relating to this physiological state.

If an adolescent or young adult is told that they are 'depressed' or they have 'depression', they are likely to label the conscious experience as 'depression' with a corresponding expectation that this can and should be got rid of or eradicated. A similar process will follow for 'anxiety'. In this context, a diagnostic label can be seen to actively interfere with the processes of emotional understanding and emotion regulation. As a result, in the approach advocated in this book, this diagnostic language is avoided. We come back to this in the chapters on specific emotions later in the book.

Physiology: body sensations

The nervous system of vertebrates is made up of two main structures: the central nervous system, which consists of the brain and spinal cord, and the peripheral nervous system, which consists of long bundles of nerves that connect the central nervous system to the rest of the body. The peripheral nervous system is separated into three further systems. The sensory nervous system, which communicates sensory information (e.g. touch and taste) to the central nervous system. The somatic nervous system, which is under voluntary control and sends messages from the central nervous system to the muscles, for example, to enable voluntary movement. The autonomic nervous system is a 'self-regulating' system not usually under conscious control, and includes the digestive system and the respiratory system.

The system most linked with our emotional state is the autonomic nervous system. It is always activated but is in either the sympathetic or the parasympathetic state. Different emotions are characterised by different levels of activation of these two states of the autonomic nervous system. These different levels of activation result in the characteristic bodily sensations associated with different emotions.

SYMPATHETIC ACTIVATION: ACCELERATE!

The sympathetic state is like the accelerator pedal: it involves the simultaneous activation of many different parts of the body ('in sympathy'). This state is triggered by the release of epinephrine, also known as adrenalin, as well as cortisol. Epinephrine increases activity; cortisol increases the supply of energy to sustain this increased activity. The combined effects of these two processes are:

- an increase in heart rate;
- an increase in rate of breathing;
- dilation of blood vessels in the muscles;
- liberation of energy sources (e.g. fat and glycogen);
- increasingly dilated pupils;
- increased muscle tension;
- attentional focus on threat;
- constriction of blood flow for other areas of the body;
- suppression of digestive and immune systems.

The body is geared up for quick, physical activity: the muscles are tense and receiving maximum blood flow and energy, the mind is alert and focused on potential threat. This state of physical and psychological preparedness is achieved by the inhibition of other less-acutely necessary tasks, such as digestion, immunity, and attentional demands that are not immediately important. The emotions of fear and anger are characterised by intense activation of the sympathetic nervous system, which is often labelled 'fight or flight' (see Chapters 6 and 8).

PARASYMPATHETIC ACTIVATION: BRAKE!

The parasympathetic state is like the brake pedal and proceeds primarily via acetylcholine, with a number of different outcomes:

- heart rate slows to conserve energy;
- salivary secretion is enhanced to aid swallowing of food;
- gastric muscular activity is stimulated to aid digestion;
- secretion of enzymes is enhanced to break down food and to store nutrients;
- sphincter muscles are relaxed to aid urination and secretion;
- pupils contract and the lens adapts for near-focused vision;
- sexual system is stimulated, at times producing sexual arousal.

The result of these processes is that the body is slowed down to conserve energy and to allow the slow, gradual processes of digestion, absorption, and expulsion. The heart rate is slowed, the muscles relaxed and heavy, the energy of the body directed inward. This characteristic activation of the parasympathetic nervous system has been dubbed 'rest and digest' or 'feed and breed'.

Facial expression

A number of researchers have investigated emotion through facial expression. They began research by investigating the way facial expressions thought to convey emotion were interpreted in different cultures around the world. These studies concluded that, across cultures, each emotion appears to be associated with a distinct facial expression (Elfenbein and Ambady, 2002).

In many ways, the facial expression is related to the physiology of the emotion. The emotions associated with an aroused emotional state – anger and fear – have widened eyes which increases the field of vision and the speed of movement of the eyes, facilitating visual response to threat. The facial expressions associated with disgust involve constricted airways to reduce intake of noxious gases and sticking out the tongue to eject something distasteful.

While there is debate about whether the neurobiology of the facial expression is important in the experience of emotion, it is nevertheless a central aspect of its social transmission (Izard, 2009).

Appraisals/cognitions

One of the most basic ways in which emotions differ between individuals is on the basis of their interpretation of different situations. This is known as an appraisal: a cognitive process that mediates the relationship between a person and the environment. Appraisals might be consciously experienced thoughts or might be less explicitly known and more fused with other aspects of the emotional response (Lazarus, 1991).

A simple way to explain the importance of appraisal or cognition in the experience of emotion is to use an example, for example that outlined in Chapter 3, where somebody messaged a friend and received no reply. There are a number of different ways in which this ambiguous situation could be interpreted:

1. "Their device has run out of battery": leading to a neutral or mildly annoyed state;
2. "They're bored of me": leading to sadness;
3. "I've done something to offend them": leading to fear;
4. "Something terrible has happened to them": also leading to fear.

Each appraisal is associated with a different emotional response highlighting the importance of appraisal or cognition in emotion.

Behaviours

Each emotion is associated with a behavioural urge or action impulse, which might include running away, fighting, shouting, crying, hugging, or laughing. These behaviours can be over-ridden or inhibited, but there is an urge or behavioural tendency associated with each emotion. In many theories, this is thought to be the 'point' of the emotion, or the adaptive function that the emotion serves (see section below).

Fitting the components together

There have been a variety of theories of emotion that have placed different emphasis on the components outlined above (e.g. Cannon, 1927; Schacter and Singer, 1962; Lazarus, 1991). More recent theories of emotion have asserted that emotion feeling is a phase of neurobiological activity (Izard, 2009), and therefore that emotion arises out of the interaction between all these different elements. This model is consistent with the premise of CBT and supports the idea that a change in any one component of emotion will bring about a change in the overall experience. This idea that the components of emotions come together to produce the overall experience is easily shared with adolescents and young adults.

2. What are the functions of emotions?

Charles Darwin followed up his seminal work 'On the Origin of Species' (1859) with another volume specifically about emotion and its expression, in which he applied the theory of evolution by natural selection to the phenomenon of emotion (Darwin, 1872). The central tenet was that emotions and their expression had evolved, like other characteristics and traits of humans and animals, because they had aided the survival of the species. Emotions were thought to serve some purpose or function that enabled the species to survive and develop over time. In Darwin's theory, emotions served to coordinate and synchronise a number of diverse bodily systems to ensure a coherent response when required, which aided longer-term survival.

The majority of the theories of emotion since this time have accepted and embraced this premise. Indeed, in one current theory of emotion, the first of seven principles is that "emotion feeling derives from evolution and neurological development . . . and is more often inherently adaptive than maladaptive" (Izard, 2009: p. 3). Given this focus on the evolutionary adaption of emotions, a variety of functions have been proposed, at both individual and group levels.

At an individual level, the most obvious function of emotion is protection from threat. In the presence of threat, various systems in the body are activated simultaneously (sympathetically) to facilitate the overall energising of the body and behavioural impulses to enable the individual to survive. The emotion felt in this situation may be fear, in which case the main behavioural urge will be to flee, or anger, in which case the main behavioural urge will be to fight. Fear and anger can therefore be seen as different responses to threat.

Of course, any organism in any environment has to do more than just protect itself; cowering in a corner out of range of threat is an insufficient strategy for longer term survival. An organism must seek food, shelter, and a mate. Emotions therefore also provide a motivating force to explore the environment and play or interact with others. Happiness is an emotion associated with a broad attentional focus and a tendency to try out new things or new behaviours (Fredrickson, 2004).

These functions of emotion are most easily understood at the individual level. However, emotions also serve a function in a social context. Shame and guilt are often referred to as the 'social emotions' and these emotions are important in holding groups together. Shame, for example, is an extremely aversive emotion that is felt when an individual does something inconsistent with the norms of the group. The easiest way to avoid shame is to uphold the group norms, which results in fairly coherent and stable groups.

The function of emotions in modern life is nicely illustrated in a quote from the *Stanford Encyclopedia of Philosophy*, "No aspect of our mental life is more important to the quality and meaning of our existence than emotions. They are what make life worth living, or sometimes ending." (de Sousa, 2014: p. 1).

In summary, emotions are considered to be coordinating phenomena that serve important functions at both the individual and the societal level. No emotion is 'positive' or 'negative'; all have value in life, but some tend to be experienced more pleasurably than others. The functions of emotions are different depending on the particular emotion under consideration. Each chapter in this book has a section on the specific function of that emotion.

3. How are emotions regulated?

So far, we have covered what emotions are, and their function. However, emotions do not always function in adaptive and helpful ways otherwise there would be no need for this book! In order to understand what goes wrong with emotions, we need to return to the ideas of emotion regulation outlined in Chapter 2.

Emotion regulation is the ability to consciously adjust and respond to emotional states. It does not involve the control or restraint of emotion, nor its suppression, but can be defined as the ability to attenuate and curtail the intensity and duration of emotions as needed, as well as amplify and extend emotion states when necessary (Thompson, 1994).

In this book, emotional difficulties are seen to arise from problematic emotion regulation strategies. The task is to help adolescents and young adults to understand the emotion regulation strategies that they are using and the reasons that they are proving ineffectual. Each of the chapters outlines a trap that highlights the usual emotion regulation strategies that cause problems. The next step is to help them to modify their approaches in one of the areas of emotional experience: environment, physiology, facial expression, thoughts, and behaviours. All the interventions in this book focus on making change in one or more of these areas in order to bring about a change to the overall emotion experience.

Many difficulties with emotion regulation are particular to specific emotions so there are detailed chapters in the book on fear, sadness, and anger, as well as briefer chapters on guilt, shame, and disgust. Sometimes, difficulties with emotion regulation are more global, hence the chapter on emotion dysregulation. Given the emphasis on emotion regulation, and experiencing the full range of emotions, there is also a chapter on happiness.

4. A model of development

Chapter 2 provides a detailed summary of the process of development through adolescence and on into adulthood. While this is important for us clinicians to understand, we would obviously not call on the entirety of this knowledge during the course of our clinical work. Nevertheless, a continued reference to the developmental stage in ways that are relevant to the individuals with whom we work is important. From a practical point of view, there are a number of ways in which we might refer to development in our work.

Adolescence and early adulthood is a time of change

It is useful to remind ourselves, adolescents, young adults, and their families, that adolescence/early adulthood is a time characterised by rapid change in many areas:

- physical;
- cognitive;
- social cognitive;
- identity;
- sexual;
- changing relationships with families;
- changing relationships with peers.

It is also useful to remember that adolescence is an expanding phase of life, beginning earlier than in previous generations, and ending later; age ranges of 10–25 are now accepted. The science showing a second period of rapid brain development in adolescence and continuing through the twenties is also often powerful information for adolescents, young adults, and families.

As we noted in Chapter 2, the idea that adolescence and early adulthood are inevitably plagued with difficulty is not supported; the majority of individuals make their way fairly smoothly through adolescence, early adulthood, and onwards. Dismissing the difficulties individuals face as 'adolescent angst' or 'a phase of life' is therefore unwarranted and unhelpful. However, we do need to bear in mind the context of high levels of change as a background against which to conceptualise the difficulties with which adolescents and young adults might present.

Theories of adolescent development

Models such as the focal model (Chapter 2) provide a way of thinking about this level and variety of change. The focal model suggests that the majority of individuals manage adolescence and early adulthood by focusing on one issue at a time, before moving on to the next. For example, they might put off thinking about their parents' upcoming divorce in favour of revising for exams, and then deal with the family issues during the summer. There are two potential reasons for difficulty in adolescence: the first is there were difficulties prior to adolescence, and the magnitude of the change becomes overwhelming. The second is that there are too many different changes happening all at once, and so it becomes overwhelming.

This model is quick to explain and can be a powerful clinical tool to help adolescents, young adults, and their families to think about what is going on at an overarching level. It provides a useful framework in which issues can be prioritised and decisions can be made about whether CBT might be helpful at this point, and what might be the goal of any work.

Collaborating or guiding?

CBT has a heavy emphasis on collaboration with the individual seeking help (see Chapter 3). However, when working with adolescents and young adults, this needs to be adapted. Expecting adolescents and young adults to be able to collaborate on an equal footing with a clinician is unrealistic; attempts to achieve this often lead to adolescents and young adults feeling that they have to 'make themselves better' and saying things such as "that's what I'm here for!" or "you're the expert!." Emotion science and the traps outlined in this book can provide us with a tighter framework within which adolescents and young adults can fit their individual experience, and can help us to make educated guesses about their experiences in life.

The process of guessing or trying to empathise with their experience can be particularly important as one of the many issues with which adolescents and young adults present is a lack of somebody in their lives who has been able to stop and think about them as an individual, and consider their needs, wants, and desires (see Chapter 9 on Emotional dysregulation in particular). Sometimes, this is precisely the role that they need us, as clinicians, to take. We can be open about this process, drawing upon our knowledge of adolescent development to enable us to guess or suggest what might be in their best interests, or what they might want, feel, or need. Sometimes this might involve more self-disclosure on our parts, to talk about our experience of the world, or to use ourselves as examples of how things might be for them.

Throughout this process, collaboration is still important and we need to do this tentatively and to keep checking during the course of work, but the balance of suggestion to checking might be different to that of adult work.

Matching therapy to the developmental stage

Another area of development that should remain in the forefront of our minds is the impact that development has on abilities relevant to our work. As outlined in Chapter 2, adolescents and young adults develop rapidly during the course of these years, and the abilities required to work cognitively (e.g. formal operational thought) will simply not be present until a particular stage of development.

As a result, we need to monitor the comprehension of adolescents and young adults as we move through the work, frequently checking and eliciting feedback to ensure we have explained things properly and that we are working together.

It is also sobering to speak to individuals about what they might remember from previous therapeutic input and to note how little they recall. Certainly, as a general rule, simple is best!

Involving families and wider networks

Families and wider networks are extremely important in the lives of adolescents and young adults, so the way in which we involve families and wider networks is crucial in our work. Change for adolescents and young adults can be facilitated by change in these networks and families are often keen to understand what can be done to support the processes of therapy. At other times families and other systems might be involved in maintaining problems, sometimes unwittingly, and so helping others understand what is going on can be of particular importance.

One of the principle concerns is to remember that we should be led, as far as possible, by the adolescent or young adult themselves; they are not children. We need to ensure that we provide an opportunity for them to talk to us without others present, as well as to discuss with them how best others might be involved. Each subsequent chapter refers to the role of families and networks in the different presentations.

Therapeutic aims

Incorporating a developmental model has important implications for the ultimate aims of our work. We can too easily find ourselves expecting adolescents or young adults to reach the position of a fully-functioning adult! The aim, within a developmental context, must be to support adolescents and young adults to continue the process of development between childhood and adulthood. We need to remember that our task is to provide knowledge and care to support them to continue their development.

5. The hand brain

Paul Maclean was a neuroscientist and theorist who brought together the concepts of neuroscience and the study of the brain, together with theories of evolution. His resulting construct, known as the triune brain (e.g. 1990), has been highly influential not only in neuroscience but also in social science.

The theory of the triune brain suggests that the brain is made up of three relatively distinct parts, which correspond to the phases of evolution through which the human brain is thought to have progressed. According to the theory, there have been periods of relative stability in terms of brain development, and the bursts of expansion in evolutionary terms have resulted in distinct developments to the brain, which map on to the increasingly complex neurological systems seen in different species.

Maclean began developing his model in the 1960s and it was published in a fairly complete form in 'The Triune Brain and Evolution' (MacLean, 1990). Since this time, it has been roundly critiqued (Heimer et al., 2007) and there are a variety of issues with the model, most of which relate to its over-simplicity. While the model does simplify a complex science, it nevertheless provides a useful way of thinking and talking about the brain for those of us outside the field of neuroscience. Indeed, many argue that the concept of the Triune Brain is still by far the best concept we have for linking neuroscience with social science (Cory and Gardner, 2002).

Daniel Siegel (2015) has developed this concept and linked it to the hand, calling this the 'hand brain'. In this model, outlined in Figure 5.1, different parts of the hand relate to the three different structural regions of the brain outlined by Maclean. The hand brain is used in this book as a way of helping clinicians, adolescents, and young adults understand some basics of brain function to inform the way in which they approach themselves, their emotions, and their emotional difficulties.

The hand brain is formed of the fist, with the thumb folded inside the fingers. Adolescents, young adults, and families can make this model with their own hands to involve them in the explanation; the physical activity also increases attention and serves as a useful reminder.

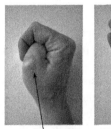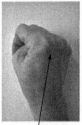

Reptilian Brain   Mammalian Brain   Rational Brain   "Flipped Lid"

Figure 5.1 Demonstrating the hand brain

Reptilian brain

The reptilian brain is represented by the wrist and the base of the thumb. In neurobiological terms it includes the brain stem, the basal ganglia, and the mid-brain. It is the oldest part of the brain in evolutionary terms, around 300 million years old. The reptilian brain is concerned with a range of basic survival behaviours such as defending the self, defending territory, hunting, foraging for food, and mating. This collection of activities is sometimes known as the 'four Fs': fleeing, fighting, feeding, and fornicating.

Mammalian brain

The mammalian brain is represented by the thumb that is tucked into the fist. This mammalian brain is younger than the reptilian brain, but still very old, around 200 million years in evolutionary terms. It consists of the amygdala, hippocampus, hypothalamus, and other smaller parts of the limbic system. The main difference between mammals and reptiles, according to MacLean, is that mammals are social creatures that are born in a helpless state and require maternal care to grow and develop. The mammalian brain can therefore be seen as responsible for the social emotions, playfulness, and maternal instinct.

Rational brain

The final major phase of the evolution of the human brain was the development of what MacLean called the neomammalian brain or the neocortex; what we refer to as the 'rational brain'. This part of the brain is around 80% of the mass of the human brain and is represented by the back of the hand and all the fingers. It developed much more recently in evolutionary terms, homo sapiens first appearing around 200,000 years ago. It is unique to humans and contains functions not commonly seen in other mammal species: language, planning, abstraction, and perception. It is called the 'rational brain', as it contains the functions that enable rational thought, although, as we will see, it is not always particularly rational.

Hand brain together

The three different parts of the hand brain often work well together, harmoniously. However, there are times when there is conflict or when one part of the brain over-rides another.

The clearest example of this is when the fight–flight response is activated. As we saw above, the fight–flight response is stimulated by the autonomic nervous system moving into the sympathetic state, a response produced by epinephrine or adrenalin. The body moves into threat mode and the response is quick. At these times, the reptilian brain can be seen to be in charge and the rational brain is offline; Dan Siegal (2015) calls this 'flipping the lid' (Figure 5.1). This concept is useful for fear and anger. Alternatively, the rational brain can find itself sucked in and restricted, so that its rationality is compromised, as highlighted in the sadness trap (Chapter 7).

Summary

In this chapter, we have outlined the theoretical principles and five pillars of the approach of this book. These pillars stand in place of a medical, diagnostic understanding of the difficulties young people face and fit together to form a coherent, normative approach to CBT with adolescents and young adults.

These principles and the five pillars are central to understanding the remainder of the book and provide a continual reference point when encountering obstacles and help keep us, as clinicians, and the adolescents and young adults with whom we work, focused on the task at hand.

References

Cannon, W.B., 1927. The James-Lange theory of emotions: a critical examination and an alternative theory. *The American Journal of Psychology, 39*, pp. 106–124.

Cory, G.A. and Gardner, R., 2002. *The evolutionary neuroethology of Paul MacLean. Convergences and frontiers.* Westport, CT: Greenwood Publishing Group.

Darwin, C., 1859. *On the origin of species by means of natural selection.* London: John Murray.

Darwin, C. 1872. *The expression of emotions in man and animals.* London: John Murray.

Elfenbein, H.A. and Ambady, N., 2002. On the universality and cultural specificity of emotion recognition: a meta-analysis. *Psychological Bulletin, 128*(2), pp. 203–235.

Fredrickson, B.L., 2004. The broaden-and-build theory of positive emotions. *Philosophical Transactions of the Royal Society B: Biological Sciences, 359*(1449), pp. 1367–1378.

Heimer, L., Van Hoesen, G.W., Trimble, M., and Zahm, D.S., 2007. *Anatomy of neuropsychiatry: the new anatomy of the basal forebrain and its implications for neuropsychiatric illness.* New York: Academic Press.

Izard, C.E., 2009. Emotion theory and research: highlights, unanswered questions, and emerging issues. *Annual Review of Psychology*, *60*, pp. 1–25.

Lazarus, R.S., 1991. Cognition and motivation in emotion. *American Psychologist*, *46*(4), pp. 352–367.

MacLean, P.D., 1990. *The triune brain in evolution: role in paleocerebral functions.* London: Plenum Press.

Plutchik, R., 2001. The nature of emotions. *American Scientist*, *89*(4), pp. 344–350.

Schachter, S. and Singer, J., 1962. Cognitive, social, and physiological determinants of emotional state. *Psychological Review*, *69*, pp. 379–399.

Siegel, D.J., 2015. *The developing mind: how relationships and the brain interact to shape who we are.* London: Guilford Press.

de Sousa, R., 2017. Emotion. In Edward N. Zalta (ed.) *The Stanford encyclopedia of philosophy* (Winter 2017 edition). Available at https://plato.stanford.edu/archives/win2017/entries/emotion/.

Thompson, R.A., 1994. Emotion regulation: a theme in search of definition. *Monographs of the Society for Research in Child Development*, *59*(2–3), pp. 25–52.

Chapter 6

Fear

> You can look at the fear trap and it makes sense. You can see where the feelings are coming from, the results of the feeling, and how it feeds back on itself. Because it's logical, it's easy for me to see how it fits with what's going on in my head.
>
> (21-year-old male)

Fear is an emotion that is relatively infrequently experienced but is extremely unpleasant and aversive; being rated as the most dreaded emotion. Adolescents and young adults, facing a great deal of change, are likely to experience fear fairly regularly and often get into difficulties managing fear. Given the evolutionary response of flight to feared stimuli, many adolescents and young adults attempt to manage fear through avoidance of contact with the object of their fears. This can result in significant disruption to their education, to peer association, to family connection, and to the world in general. As a result, problems with fear can constitute a real threat to the developmental process.

CBT has a relatively strong evidence base in fear presentations, which is based on different models for different feared stimuli. The interventions involved, while conceptually relatively simple, are often extremely challenging for adolescents and young adults to undertake. As a result, helping them to properly understand why they have to do these difficult things and how it will help is of paramount importance. Given the variety of different models of CBT available for fear-based presentations, however, it can be difficult to for clinicians to decide which model to use and then to use it with sufficient clarity to achieve this aim.

This chapter begins with the science of fear, exploring what fear is and its functions. Next, the fear trap is outlined, a simple but powerful cognitive-behavioural formulation for almost all fear-based presentations, which builds on the understanding of fear outlined in the first part of the chapter. The formulation is described in detail, paying particular attention to the links between the elements to ensure high levels of understanding and clarity. The fear trap is then used to outline the process of intervention when working with fear-based presentations. Case examples are used to illustrate this process.

The end of the chapter provides examples of how the fear trap can be used with a variety of different difficulties with fear. The last section highlights the ways in which the evidence base informs the recommendations of the chapter.

What causes fear?

Many different situations produce fear. An analysis of online searches for "fear of . . ." in 2008 found that the top ten were flying, heights, clowns, intimacy, death, rejection, people, snakes, failure, and driving (Tancer, 2008). In 2005, adolescents in America were asked what they feared most and reported terrorist attacks at number one, shortly followed by spiders, death/dying, failure, war, and heights (Lyons, 2005).

At its most basic level, fear is a response to threat. In evolutionary history, the predominant threats were potential predators or attackers. In modern life, with greater access to information about the world, potential threats are more diverse and include politics, money, social success, and the future.

What is fear?

In Chapter 5 we outlined five different elements of the human emotional experience. The next section covers each of these elements in relation to fear. When exploring these different aspects with adolescents and young adults, it can be useful to use the principles of guided discovery (Chapter 3) to build up a sense of what fear is, the idea that there are things going on in different areas of experience, and then to move on to consider what function these different changes might serve.

Feelings

Fear is relatively infrequently experienced, it is energetic and intense but fades rapidly, and is consciously experienced as cold (Scherer and Wallbott, 1994). It is extremely aversive: across seven different cultures it was identified more often than any other emotion in response to the question "Which emotion do you dread the most?" (Izard, 1971).

Fear is often used synonymously with the word 'anxiety', which derives from the Latin 'to choke'. It describes one aspect of the physiology of fear (see next section). However, because of its frequent use in psychiatric diagnosis, it has come to be associated with illness and disorder. This invitation to externalise the experience of fear results in a sense that anxiety is something some adolescents and young adults 'have' that can be 'got rid of', rather than an emotion that is normal, functional, and can be regulated. Consequently, it is best to avoid using the terms 'anxiety' or 'anxious' when referring to the emotional experience of fear.

A quick scale on which the intensity of fear can be rated (e.g. on a 0 to 10) is a helpful way to invite adolescents and young adults to think about fear as an emotion that can be experienced to different degrees, rather than a symptom that is either present or absent. Words can be added to help define different parts of the scale, for example: calm, relaxed, apprehensive, concerned, nervous, worried, fearful, scared, alarmed, panicked, terrified, and 'bricking it'.

Physiology

Fear has a dramatic impact on the body. Of the two systems of the nervous system outlined in Chapter 5, it is the sympathetic system that is activated in fear; the parasympathetic system is supressed.

Activation of the sympathetic system results in increased heart rate, deeper breathing, tension in the muscles, heightened senses, and attentional focus on threat. This can explain experiences such as shaking, things appearing louder, or touch being more sensitive. The attentional focus on threat explains how difficult it can be to concentrate on other tasks when scared.

Suppression of the parasympathetic system results in digestive system suppression, for example a dry mouth or 'butterflies' in the stomach. In extreme cases food might be expelled from the body either through needing the toilet (hence the phrase 'bricking it' which derives from visiting the brick outhouse prior to indoor facilities!) or being sick. Prolonged suppression of the para-sympathetic system can lead to reduced immune function and reduced sexual interest.

Facial expression

Fear is an emotion that can be read quickly on a face. The facial muscles are tense, the senses are alert. This is seen in a widening of the eyes to ensure good vision, an opening of the mouth, which is associated with improved hearing and breathing. For lower intensities of fear, the expression is one of thought and consideration.

The face, in addition to facilitating the senses, also communicates emotion to others. Fear on the face of another can prompt a search for danger (see the function of fear below).

Appraisals/thoughts

Fear is associated not only with physiological activation but also psychological activation. Thoughts are energised and focused on the feared object. They tend to be quick and impulsive rather than slow and methodical and can feel as though they are racing or spiralling. Thoughts are motivating, such as "I need to get out of here!" or "Help!!" Alternatively, thoughts may race to find the best response to the threat.

Attention and thoughts are directed towards the perceived threat and it is difficult to concentrate on anything else. In addition, it is difficult to use a slow, rational, decision-making process. With intense fear, it can become almost impossible to think clearly at all.

Behaviours

The behavioural urges associated with fear are quick dramatic physical responses, such as running; getting away from the feared object as quickly as possible. This is often followed by subsequent avoidance of the feared object. Another common response is to freeze: to stop and remain completely still, often remaining this way until the threat has passed.

What is the function of fear?

As we covered in Chapter 5, emotions serve important functions in human life. Fear links clearly to self-protection, being one possible emotional response to threat in the environment (the other being anger). This links to the fight–flight response as described by Walter Bradford Cannon (1929). The flight response is linked with fear; the fight response with anger.

The different elements of fear all link directly to its function. Where there is an environmental threat, a physical response is likely to be required. The effects as outlined above prepare the individual both physiologically and psychologically, by gearing up the body for physical action, ensuring an attentional focus on threat, and increasing the acuity of the senses. This occurs alongside the inhibition of non-essential tasks (both from a physiological and psychological point of view). All of this is experienced consciously as aversive, which motivates escape behaviour. Often this behaviour will involve fleeing to a safer place, which clearly is an adaptive response. Examples of these would be jumping out of the way of oncoming traffic, or running away from an attacker. Sometimes the behaviour might be to freeze, which can be adaptive as it reduces the likelihood of detection – many animal species detect potential prey by movement.

A simple example we can use with adolescents and young adults is the idea of a tiger being close by, perhaps in the street, or in the corridor outside the room. We can use guided discovery to build up a sense that the best course of action would be to run away, making sure that we are aware of where the tiger is, where our best route of escape might be, and making sure that we run as fast as we can (not necessarily as fast as the tiger, just faster than somebody else also running away!). This explains the increase in breathing to get more oxygen, which is then pumped around the body through increased heart rate, to the muscles which use this for energy and tense up ready. The facial expression is wide to enable high levels of sensory input, the attention is focused on the threat (the tiger and escape-route, not the nice car nearby). Digesting the lunch is stopped and lunch might even be 'dumped'. In this way, we can show how all of the different changes that occur with the experience of fear function to support this action.

That fear is a necessary emotion is illustrated by the unusual case of an individual known as SM, who sustained damage to a part of the brain associated with the fear system with the result that she experienced almost no fear. This is despite a life in which she has been held up at knife- and gun-point, been almost killed in a domestic violence incident and has received many death threats. These experiences are attributed partly to the neighbourhood in which she lives, but also to her tendency to approach rather than avoid potentially dangerous situations as a result of her inability to feel fear (Tranel et al., 2006).

Fear is also an emotion that can be experienced as enjoyable: the experience of intense emotion in an environment known to be the safe, for example riding a roller-coaster or watching a horror film. There is also an intense feeling that derives from having survived and overcome something that was feared and this can be an important part of the enjoyment of the experience (Izard, 1991).

Finally, the experience of fear or stress in a group often enhances the bonds between group members. This is highlighted by the tend-and-befriend pattern described by Taylor et al. (2000), which operates at a group level, bringing organisms together to support and protect each other. In humans, the shared experience of fear can therefore lead to deepened bonds and enhanced emotional closeness.

Fear and the hand brain

At this point we can return briefly to the idea of the hand brain, outlined in Chapter 5. In the model of the brain, there are three sections, the reptilian brain, the mammalian brain, and the rational brain. The fear response is located in the oldest part of the brain; the reptilian brain. The feelings of fear and fright are located within the reptilian brain – it is the reptilian brain that is scared. The reptilian brain is worried about different situations and the reptilian brain is the one running away and feeling better as a result. This is an important idea to explore in therapy as the reptilian brain is known not to be capable of rational thought. This allows adolescents and young adults to have irrational fears, to be scared of things they know, rationally, are not scary. It is also an important concept when we come to intervention.

Adolescent development and fear

As outlined in Chapter 2, adolescence is an important time of change; individuals are moving from a position within a wider family to a position of greater independence. In moving away from the family and forming their own identities, they are pushing themselves into the unknown, facing new environments and new experiences, and taking greater risks. Alongside this they are taking on increasing levels of responsibility and there are greater expectations of them as individuals. All of this means that adolescence is a time when fear is likely to be a fairly commonly experienced emotion.

Fear trap

Having covered what fear is and what it is for, we know that fear is usually a useful emotion; it functions to protect from threat. There are times, however, when fear becomes unhelpful, when it becomes the dominant emotion in the lives of adolescents and young adults, and where it represents a significant barrier to their development.

In these cases, fear has taken over and the adolescent or young adult is struggling to regulate its intensity. As a result, our starting point in any work with fear is not to get rid of fear, but to support its better regulation. This is an important departure from the diagnostic approach, where the aim is often assumed to be an eradication of anxiety (see Chapter 4).

In our work with adolescents and young adults, it is important that we validate the difficulties that they experience, help them to understand these difficulties, and develop a treatment plan together. This is all possible using the fear trap.

The fear trap is a diagrammatic cognitive behavioural formulation, which takes the essence of disorder-specific models and distils them into a simple maintenance cycle that can be used for almost all fear-based difficulties regardless of the object of the fear. The fear trap highlights the ways in which the elements of the model are causally linked to each other, using the psychological understanding of fear as outlined above. The model of the hand brain further serves to highlight the mechanisms in operation.

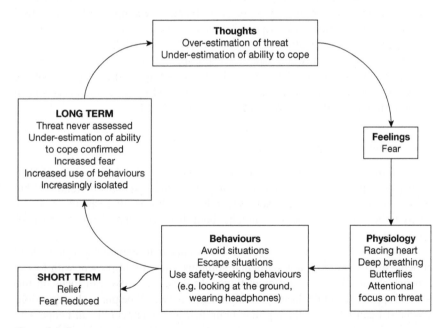

Figure 6.1 Fear trap

The fear trap is illustrated in Figure 6.1. Each element of the trap is described in detail next, to highlight the principles and theory behind the trap. Afterwards, there is an example of how the fear trap can be drawn with an adolescent or young adult.

Appraisals/thoughts

While there is no need to start at any particular point in the fear trap, the thoughts often provide a sensible starting place. In the fear trap, there are two types of thought.

Over-estimations of threat

These thoughts are predictions or fears about what might happen in a given situation. Given that they sustain the fear trap and the high levels of associated fear, they are usually extreme, often catastrophic. They are also usually irrational and known to be irrational by the adolescents and young adults experiencing them. As a result, they can be seen to be the fears of the reptilian brain; the irrational, primitive part of the brain, which can exist even when the rational brain is aware that they are unlikely or over-estimated. As a result, they are usually simple statements about the world, rather than questions or more complex ideas. Examples include "I'm going to die," "I will be sick," or "I'll be attacked." Sometimes there will be many different kinds of thoughts, but where this is the case, they usually cluster around a deeper, more basic sense of threat; for example: "I'll be rejected" or "Something terrible will happen." Imagery around the feared outcome or catastrophic predictions often highlights the over-estimated threat.

It is really important, when using the fear trap, that the exact nature of the fear is clarified. While the model outlined by the fear trap works regardless of the object of the fear, the interventions that follow need to target the exact fear in order to maximise efficacy. We will return to this idea later.

Under-estimations of ability to cope

These thoughts are predictions and fears about the individual's sense of their ability to cope. These are predictions not about the external environment, but about what the individual themselves will do, how they might respond. These are likely to be extreme and so we can talk about these as feared thoughts or worst-case scenario predictions.

Sometimes, adolescents and young adults appear to experience fear without it being associated with any particular stimulus; they might present with lots of worries about all sorts of different things. In these cases, we can focus on this second appraisal. While these types of thoughts may well be phrased as questions "What if I can't cope?," the reptilian brain fear is a statement "I can't cope with anything" or "I'm extremely vulnerable." There might also be appraisals around the experiences associated with fear, for example "I can't cope with worrying thoughts" or "I can't possibly manage all this stress," which are consistent with meta-cognitive appraisals (Wells, 1995).

Feelings

In the fear trap, as in all of the other traps in this book, feelings are central. The feelings are the motivating force behind the trap and are also the location of the distress. In the fear trap, it is essential that fear (or a synonym of fear) is elicited, as this is what drives the formulation.

Physiology

The physiology associated with fear can be included at this point, if it would be of benefit. This is not always necessary, but for people who have specific worries around their bodies it can be really helpful. This is often the case for those who are afraid of panicking or being sick, or where there is a fear that others will perceive physiological changes (see specific sections at the end of the chapter).

It is important that the causal links between the emotion and the physiological responses are made to ensure that adolescents and young adults understand that the physiological changes are associated with the emotion and that there are reasons why this is the case. We need to ensure a good level of understanding of fear more generally in order for this to make sense. Where we, as clinicians, think it would be helpful to include physiology, the most important physiological changes can be included; it is often important to highlight the attentional focus on threat.

Behaviours

As outlined above, the function of fear is to coordinate disparate bodily systems to collective action. It is the emotional experience of fear that provides the motivation for action, and so, in the traps in this book, the behaviours are driven by the emotional experience. The hand brain model helps us to understand that this motivational force arises from primitive and basic parts of the brain; the reptilian brain. This means that behaviours tend not to be logical, reasoned actions undertaken to reduce the actual risks of specific situations. Using the hand brain in this way helps us to include all behavioural responses to threat, no matter how apparently illogical they may seem.

Behavioural responses to fear fall into three groups:

Avoidance

Simply not going anywhere near the feared situation is the most common behavioural response to fear. Avoiding situations entirely avoids the associated experience of emotion.

Escape

Leaving the situation at the first sign of discomfort is similar to avoidance, in that the feared situation is avoided, as is the associated emotion.

Safety behaviours

Safety behaviours are used in the feared situation to increase the sense of safety and reduce the experience of fear. They can include a variety of different behaviours, some of which are deliberate, others of which become habitual over time and are almost automatic and not noticed.

It is important to understand that safety behaviours are not strategies arising from the rational brain to increase safety in reality, but are behaviours driven by the reptilian brain that increase the feeling of safety and decrease the feeling of fear. This means that the majority of safety behaviours are illogical and may be missed as a result.

Examples of safety behaviours include:

- clutching the seat when travelling in a car;
- looking at the ground when in a crowd;
- checking a door is locked multiple times;
- checking the body for physiological changes;
- seeking reassurance from others;
- self-reassurance;
- distraction.

In these examples, we can highlight how the behaviours serve to make the reptilian brain feel safer, while not increasing the real levels of safety as perceived by the rational brain. Safety behaviours that are often missed include tensing muscles, gripping things, distraction, closing eyes at crucial moments, or looking away. Despite the fact that these have no impact on actual levels of safety, they are often important factors in maintaining the fear trap.

It is important to remember that sometimes other people will be drawn into doing some of these behaviours. This is particularly the case for adolescents and young adults. Reassurance seeking is a common safety behaviour for adolescents and young adults, and one that families will often engage in to try to help. For example, families will often repeatedly tell adolescents and young adults that they need not worry, or that everything is going to be OK. Other behaviours include colluding with avoidance, for example making certain meals, or making other exceptions to support the adolescent or young adult to better manage. Finally, they may engage in other safety behaviours to support adolescents and young adults, for example checking that windows are locked, or ensuring that clothes remain off the floor. Generally speaking, families engage in these behaviours from a point of care and concern and are unaware of the extent of the impact that these can have in maintaining the difficulties.

Short term consequences

It is important to acknowledge the power of the behaviours elicited in the previous section. This is because the behaviours adolescents and young adults adopt to manage their fear actually work. In the short term, they feel much calmer, more relaxed and much better as a result of avoiding, escaping, and safety behaviours. This is an important part of the model, as it validates the experiences of adolescents and young adults by illustrating that they are reasonable; they are not engaging in behaviours that are ridiculous or stupid. The behaviours they use do exactly what they are supposed to do: they provide comfort and relief.

Long term consequences

While the behaviours work in the short term, they cause problems in the long term.

There are clear reinforcing cycles between the behaviours and the two groups of thoughts: over-estimation of threat and under-estimation of ability to cope. If adolescents and young adults avoid putting themselves in the feared situation, they are never in a position to test the level of threat and they never find out what would have happened. This means that the next time they face the situation they still over-estimate the threat and still experience high levels of fear. Also, if adolescents and young adults repeatedly avoid the things of which they are afraid, they confirm to themselves that they can't cope. This makes it likely that they will continue to under-estimate their ability to cope.

Escape behaviours have the same impact as avoidance behaviours as adolescents and young adults do not remain long enough in the situation to test out these thoughts.

Safety behaviours block learning experience via one of two routes: either adolescents and young adults are not focusing their attention on the situation and so do not witness that the reality of the world differs from their feared predictions, or the non-event of the feared prediction is attributed to the presence of the safety behaviour. Highlighting the illogicality of the reptilian brain is important here. For example, in their rational brains, adolescents and young adults know that gripping the passenger seat of the car does not make them any less likely to be involved in an accident, however, their reptilian brain is responding to this as if this is the case. More will be said about this in the section on graded exposure.

It is also important to note that all these behaviours reinforce the initial appraisals, which leads, in the longer term, to escalations in the feelings, in the level of fear, as well as to increased likelihood of using the behaviours: avoidance, escape, and safety behaviours. This can result in increased isolation and a significant negative impact on social and educational life.

Fear trap and families

We know that the environmental context is really important for adolescents and young adults and the family is a major part of the context. Fear is a powerful emotion and when adolescents and young adults have difficulties with fear, their families and peers have no choice but to become involved.

Given this, it is often useful to share the fear trap and the ideas behind it with families. In some cases, the family will attend the sessions and can be involved throughout. In other cases, we can invite the adolescent or young adult to take a copy of the fear trap away and to explain it to their family themselves. Having such a clear and easy to understand formulation can be really powerful for families as well as adolescents and young adults themselves and can give them the clarity and courage to do what they thought was probably the right thing anyway; many families will already have ideas about 'facing fears' or 'pushing through'. The implementation of these ideas can be supported by the circles, outlined later in the chapter.

Families may also have to alter their own behaviour to support movement out of the fear trap, and it is helpful to ensure that they understand the reasons why this is the case. As outlined earlier, families may do all sorts of things to try to improve the situation, some of which are helpful and others that serve to maintain the problem. Helping families to understand the fear trap enables them to help in the best ways possible.

Summary of the fear trap

The fear trap is a cognitive behavioural formulation, incorporating thoughts, feelings, and behaviours. It incorporates a negative reinforcing loop, in which behaviour that brings about the removal or reduction of an aversive stimulus (i.e. an aversive emotional experience) is reinforced and hence repeated. The fear trap, however, differs from other cognitive behavioural formulations in terms of its clear focus on a few important elements and the causal relationship between them, as well as the emphasis placed on feelings as the root of the trap.

Given its simplicity, the fear trap is not specific to particular presentations and the model remains the same regardless of the object of the fear. This same model fits for fears of going out, fears of specific stimuli, fear of social situations and so on. That being said, it is extremely important to spend time ensuring that the exact nature of the fear has been clarified as it is this precision that leads to focused interventions. There are minor adjustments that can be considered for some specific presentations (see later sections in this chapter) but they are not fundamental or structural variations, just ways to ensure that the exact fear is targeted in the processes of intervention.

It is important to remember that, where people are experiencing difficulties with fear, **all of the elements of the trap will always be present**. Adolescents and young adults will not experience difficulties with fear unless they have appraisals that over-estimate threat and under-estimate their abilities to cope, and these appraisals cannot be maintained unless they are doing something, behaviourally, to maintain these appraisals. Sometimes, the appraisals or the be- haviours might be subtle, at other times the behaviours might be cognitive in nature (e.g. counting or thought suppression), but they will always be present. This principle is useful to remember where presentations might, at first glance, not fit the norm.

Drawing the fear trap

It is most helpful to draw the fear trap from scratch, on a blank piece of paper, so that the model gradually builds up during the conversation. This ensures we use the important principles of collaboration and guided discovery, rather than adolescents and young adults feeling that we are fitting them into a box. Nevertheless, the fear trap is a model that works for almost all fear-based presentations and so it should not look structurally different for each case, although it will be tailored to each individual.

As with any maintenance cycle, it usually helps to use a recent example in which there has been a particular difficulty. This helps to ensure that there is a meaning behind the cycle and that the different elements fit together. Therefore, it is best to begin by asking the adolescent or young adult to think of a recent event that made them scared or worried and that perhaps they have a tendency to avoid. Often, asking them to imagine themselves in the situation just prior to the event can elicit fear in session and help elicit thoughts, feelings, and physiological states.

Take, for example, the case where an adolescent or young adult is worried about attending college (Figure 6.2). We could ask: "so take yourself back to last

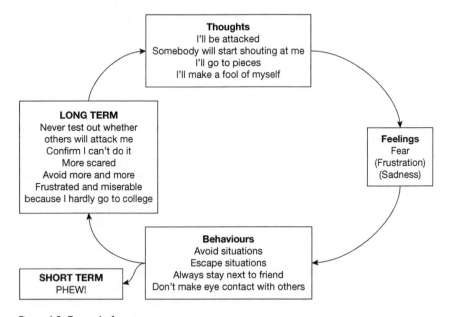

Figure 6.2 Example fear trap

Tuesday morning, you're outside college, you're just about to go in, what are you thinking?" The thoughts that come up can be written down. In our example, these might be thoughts such as "I will be attacked," or "Somebody will start shouting at me," both of which are over-estimates of threat. Where thoughts of only one type are volunteered, it is useful to prompt for the others so that both groups are included in the trap: "Do you have thoughts about how you might respond if this did happen?" Once thoughts that illustrate these two groups have been elicited, it can be helpful to show that the thoughts/appraisals fall into two categories.

It is important to get these thoughts right, and to clarify at a later stage if necessary. Interventions to move out of the fear trap will be designed to specifically target particular appraisals, and the clearer the identification of the thoughts, the more focused will be the intervention. Methods of clarification include using imagery to highlight the worst possible situation, asking about what the reptilian brain fears, or increasing the levels of fear in session using the techniques outlined later in this chapter (Physiological intervention: regulating fear in the moment) and asking about the appraisals when the adolescent or young adult is more connected with the fear.

Once we have identified the appraisals, we can ask something like "How do these thoughts make you feel?" This makes it clear that feelings are causally related to the thoughts, reinforcing that each element of the trap is clearly causally linked to the others. We can write down the feelings, as they are expressed, regardless of what they are. However, it is important to include somewhere in this list a word that relates to fear, which is the key emotion that sustains the fear trap.

It is helpful to highlight the emotion of fear at this point, by circling or putting other emotions in brackets, so we can see that fear sustains the trap rather than anger or sadness. We can come back to these other feelings later on in drawing the trap, as they fit with the long-term consequences of being stuck in the trap. In our example (Figure 6.2), the adolescent or young adult has said they feel scared of going into college and frustrated with themselves for finding it so difficult. We have highlighted fear by putting brackets around the other emotions to return to it later.

To make the link between the experiences so far outlined and the resulting behaviours it can be helpful to summarise: "Let's look at what we have drawn out so far. You have lots of thoughts about bad things happening, which make you feel really scared and frightened and causes you to have a fast heart rate and to feel sick, do you like feeling like this?," "No, OK, so what do you do to try not to feel like this?" or "So what do you do about these feelings, if you don't want to feel this way?" In this way, we are working to ensure that through each step of the trap the causal link between the elements is explicit and properly understood.

There are three types of behavioural response: avoidance, escape, and safety behaviours. Most adolescents and young adults are aware that they avoid situations. On occasion, however, they can miss this as a strategy, particularly if they avoid things almost completely, but asking something like: "So when was the last time you walked down the main corridor at college?" generally helps them to see that they tend to manage their fears by avoiding things entirely. We can use similar prompts to elicit escape and safety behaviours, such as "Do you do anything to make yourself feel better in these situations?" It is important to keep an eye out for more subtle safety behaviours, particularly when it appears that adolescents or young adults are not using avoidance or escape.

The next task is to elicit the impact of these behaviours, in both the short and the long term. Avoidance is often the easiest example to illustrate the power of these behaviours. Adolescents and young adults can be asked to imagine themselves just prior to doing the thing they are scared of: "OK, so you're just about to go into college, and then you turn around and walk home instead, how do you feel?" Phew! It's a powerful feeling.

It can be helpful, at this point, to summarise the model so far.

> So, you're thinking about going to college, you're having lots of negative thoughts about what might happen and how you might cope. You're feeling really scared and you can feel this in your body, and you're just about to do it, when you turn around and go the other way and you feel a massive sense of relief. What happens the next time you are faced with this situation? What happens if every time you face this situation you turn around and go the other way?

Here we might include some of the emotional consequences that might have come up earlier when asking about feelings; in our example, the frustration is an emotional consequence of becoming increasingly isolated, falling behind at college, or losing touch with friends. These are often the most easily elicited of the long-term consequences.

The most important of the long-term consequences are those that relate directly back to the trap. It is important to get these links right so that adolescents and young adults can see how the trap has causal links all the way around and constitutes a tight cycle. To achieve this, we can use guided discovery for each aspect of the fear:

Clinician:	"Just before you went into college, what did you imagine would happen, what was your reptilian brain's fear?"
Young person:	"I thought everybody would start shouting at me, or maybe attacking me without reason."
Clinician:	"OK, so what happened to that fear, given that you never actually went into college?"
Young person:	"I never found out that they probably weren't going to attack me."

To help understand the often-illogical nature of the process, as a result of the heavy involvement of the reptilian brain, we can also talk about eye contact:

Clinician:	"Great, what happens if you never make eye contact?"
Young person:	"I don't see what people are doing."
Clinician:	"So what does your reptilian brain make of that?"
Young person:	"It probably thinks they are really threatening."
Clinician:	"Exactly, it's as if your reptilian brain thinks 'It's a good job I didn't make eye contact with anybody, otherwise something awful would have happened.'"

The next part is to elicit what happened to the under-estimation of ability to cope:

Clinician:	"What happened to your fear that you wouldn't be able to cope?"
Young person:	"Well, I didn't cope, I ran away."
Clinician:	"OK, so you confirmed to yourself that you couldn't cope."

Finally, it is important to get the sense that, over time, the fears have grown and have got worse. Sometimes we can predict that this is what has happened; that over time, they have gone around and around the cycle and it has got increasingly difficult.

One of the important benefits of using models or having common ways of talking about things is that it can help adolescents and young adults feel less alone. We can achieve this by naming the diagram we have drawn as the fear trap, which is something that we draw out regularly with all sorts of different people. This helps them to see that this is a common problem that many individuals, at some point in life, will face.

It is important to go over the trap to ensure that adolescents, young adults, and their families understand it. It can also be helpful to use colours to draw it out so that it looks nice and they will want to look at it, rather than it being drawn in messy black biro on a scrap of paper! Where there is more than one specific fear, it can be helpful to show the adolescent or young adult how other fears might fit in the same pattern. The same can be true where a parent or carer is present, as they too might have fears that could fit into the fear trap.

Breaking the fear trap: intervention

The fear trap, with just a few, very important elements, is an ideal place from which to consider what needs to happen to break the cycle; to break out of the fear trap. Once we have drawn out the fear trap and checked it is understood, we can simply say "With any vicious cycle, the cycle can be broken at any point and it will fall apart, so where do you think we could start?" Most people will say either the thoughts or the behaviours or both and we can ask for further options until we have these two. If we have family members in the room, they too can be asked to contribute.

Behavioural change

This book has a focus on providing clear, understandable formulations that follow clear lines of intervention. The fear trap has the clearest intervention: **the only way out of the fear trap is to change behaviour; to do something different**. This is consistent with evidence for exposure in fear-based presentations (Ale et al., 2015; Norton and Price, 2007).

Indeed, if we return to the hand brain, we can explain this focus on the behavioural level of intervention. Thoughts are a function of the rational brain; the fear response is held by the reptilian brain which is not rational. We can explain that trying to think your way out of the fear trap is like trying to explain to a reptile that it does not need to be scared. While the rational brain might be able to rationally understand that the feared object is not as scary as it thinks it is, it is not until the reptilian brain is **shown**, through experiencing the situation, that the fear trap can be broken and the fear can be reduced. The conclusion is that the only way out of the fear trap is to change the maintaining behaviours: avoidance, escape, and safety behaviours.

Circles

The explanation so far has provided a clear rationale for behavioural change. The question usually asked next by adolescents, young adults and their families, is how?

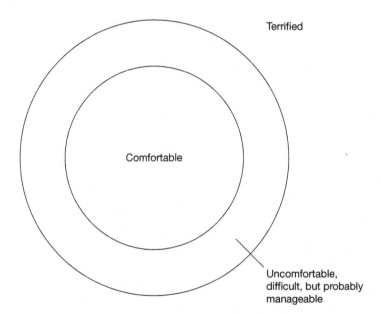

Figure 6.3 Circles

The processes of intervention flowing from the fear trap are distilled using a very simple model based on drawing two circles on a blank piece of paper (Figure 6.3).

The first circle encompasses everything that the adolescent or young adult finds comfortable and not concerning; they are asked to come up with some ideas about things in this zone. Where they find this difficult, we can make suggestions of things that they do that fall in this zone, for example staying at home watching TV. The second circle is drawn around the first circle; everything outside this circle is considered terrifying. If the adolescent or young adult cannot come up with anything here, we can suggest things such as going shopping in the city on a Saturday afternoon, or doing a bungee jump. We can then draw their attention to the gap between the two circles; the gap between things that are comfortable and things that are terrifying. We can describe things in this zone as difficult, uncomfortable, but probably manageable. Activities in this area are those that are tricky, but they think they could probably manage.

The idea behind these three circles is that humans, like most species, are creatures of habit; they like to do the same things over and over again. Regular activities become comfortable and fall into the comfortable zone; rare activities fall into the terrified zone. Activities in the uncomfortable, difficult, but probably manageable zone that are repeated, will, over time, move into the comfortable zone. Adolescents and young adults quickly understand that, over time, the comfortable zone will expand to include these things and eventually, things that were in the terrified zone will move into the uncomfortable, difficult, but probably manageable zone.

The hand brain further supports the understanding behind the circles. In the comfortable zone, nothing new is being tackled so the reptilian brain is offline and cannot learn anything new. In the terrified zone, the reptilian brain dominates and is in a state of over-arousal that is not conducive to learning. This can be illustrated by the 'flipped lid' (Chapter 5). In the uncomfortable, difficult, but probably manageable zone, the rational brain is online, the reptilian brain is also active and scared, the two can operate together to remain in and learn from new experiences. This can be illustrated with the hand brain by hovering fingers over the thumb to illustrate a balanced struggle between the reptilian and rational brains.

So far, the fear trap has enabled us to explain to adolescents and young adults that the short-term processes of avoidance, escape, or safety behaviours all work in the short term, but all lead to negative long-term consequences. The fear trap combined with the hand brain has helped to understand that it is these behaviours that adolescents and young adults need to work with to begin the process of breaking the fear trap. The circles have helped us to think about which behaviours adolescents and young adults need to start with when they are going to do something different.

There are two options in terms of the way in which this can be achieved. The first is graded exposure which is an intervention operating at the behavioural level.

The second is behavioural experimentation which operates at the behavioural level but is catalysed by the incorporation of a cognitive process of prediction and belief-testing. Each is outlined in turn.

Graded exposure

Graded exposure is a behavioural technique developed by Wolpe and Lazarus (1966) in the 1950s. The model in based on the principle of desensitisation, in which organisms cease to respond to an environmental cue that is repeatedly presented in the absence of meaningful association. In the fear trap, desensitisation is the process through which the reptilian brain is repeatedly presented with the environmental situation it believes to be threatening, in the absence of actual danger; hence the fear decreases over time. Graded exposure relies on exposing individuals to the feared stimulus so that they habituate to it, at gradually increasingly levels of intensity.

The first task is to ensure that the fear trap has been drawn with sufficient clarity to identify the main fear. The advantage of the fear trap is that a single model can be used irrespective of the nature of the fear. However, this does mean that the specification and the clarification of the fear is really important. Exposure, as an intervention, needs to target the exact fear, otherwise it will not work. A common example of this is with panic attacks. In panic attacks the primary fear is usually "I'm going to die," which is fuelled by the physiological changes associated with fear and the resulting behaviours. Doing graded exposure to leaving the house or to going out can bring about slight improvements, but misses the primary fear, which is "when my body feels like this, it means I'm going to die." Effective intervention needs to involve exposure to the physiological experience that is appraised as an over-estimated threat (for more on this see later section on specific presentations).

Once the exact nature of the fear has been identified, we can build our intervention around the four common principles of graded exposure, namely 'graded', 'prolonged', 'repeated', and 'without distraction' (Öst, 1989), which are detailed next.

Graded

Using the circles, we can explain that the process of learning only continues while adolescents and young adults push themselves into the uncomfortable, difficult, but probably manageable zone. Once something has become easier and is moving towards the comfortable zone, the intensity needs to be increased. The circles make it clear that emotion drives the process – if adolescents and young adults are feeling scared, then they are doing the right things. Given that this is the case, the adolescent or young adult themselves is in the best position to determine what is the best next step in terms of exposure: they will feel it.

Prolonged

Adolescents and young adults need to stay in the situation long enough for their reptilian brain to learn that the things it fears are not as scary as it thinks they are. If they do not remain there long enough then the reptilian brain does not have the opportunity to learn and is left with the belief that the feared event would have happened had they remained there longer.

Repeated

Adolescents and young adults need to repeat the behavioural changes so that, over time, the things that are in the uncomfortable, difficult, but probably manageable zone will gradually move into the comfortable zone. This is true of any learning; practice is key. As clinicians, we can suggest a task every day would be most effective.

Without distraction

Distraction refers to safety behaviours. Research varies according to the degree to which it recommends allowing or forbidding safety behaviours during exposure (e.g. Salkovskis et al., 1999). In this model, the issue is quickly dealt with using the circles; as long as the behavioural change involves adolescents and young adults pushing themselves into the uncomfortable, difficult, but probably manageable zone, then something new is being learned. If the safety behaviours serve to make the behaviour feel entirely comfortable then they need to be reduced or altered. If they serve to move the behavioural change from the terrified zone into the uncomfortable, difficult, but probably manageable then they are OK to use for a short period, as part of the grading of the exposure levels, but the longer-term aim should be to drop them altogether.

Graded exposure and the fear trap

Graded exposure in the context of the fear trap is not fundamentally different to graded exposure as a stand-alone intervention. There are two important factors the fear trap adds to the process.

The first is the grounding of the technique in the clear, straightforward understanding outlined in this chapter. We can encourage adolescents and young adults to engage in the process of graded exposure not just because we know that it works and the evidence supports this assertion, but because they understand **why** it should work. Many people will probably have told adolescents and young adults that they should face their fears, but the process of listening, understanding the difficulties they face, and helping them to understand where and why they are stuck and how they can get out of the fear trap is powerful. Working through the information in this chapter in one or two sessions is often enough to help adolescents and young adults to make dramatic shifts in their behaviour after months or years of gradual decline into the fear trap and increasing avoidance. In addition, the circles provide a clear understanding of where facing the fear has not worked. Adolescents and young adults or their families will often say that they have tried to face their fears, but that it did not work. Usually, what has gone wrong in these cases is that they have pushed too hard and have gone from the comfortable zone into the terrified zone and then straight back again, so avoiding the uncomfortable, difficult, but probably manageable zone and avoiding the possibility of any learning taking place. Alternatively, they might have done tasks too infrequently, or tried too many different tasks all at once.

The second benefit of the fear trap is that adolescents, young adults, and their families understand how everything fits together and so are in a good position to hang on to the responsibility for setting tasks themselves. The responsibility for deciding which tasks are appropriate and which might be too easy or too difficult sits best with the adolescent or young adult; only they will feel the level of fear faced in each task. Given that we want them to do as much practice and repetition as possible, it makes sense that responsibility for deciding exactly what the tasks will be and when they will be done does not sit with the clinician, who will often only have weekly appointments, but with the adolescent or young adult and/or their families. This is an important distinction to be made with graded exposure based on a traditional hierarchy where the clinician often finds themselves holding responsibility for picking the next stage and judging the pace.

Example

In the example fear trap outlined (Figure 6.2), graded exposure needs to target the specific fears associated with going to college. Some of the fears are about being attacked and so graded exposure will need to include attending college (not avoiding), remaining in college even when feeling scared (not escaping), spending time in college away from the friend, and starting to look up a little and make eye contact with others (not using safety behaviours). The principles outlined earlier (graded, prolonged, repeated, and without distraction) need to be included, so the adolescent or young adult needs to ensure that they stay in college for long enough, ideally until the fear levels reduce, and that they do it regularly, perhaps once or twice per week initially, but quickly building up to every day. The circles can be used to support conversations about how much they can manage. It is important to remember that the harder they can push themselves, the more difficult it will be but the faster they will get to their goal. From a clinician's point of view, it also makes sense to err on the side of too much rather than too little; to encourage a sense of self-belief in the adolescent or young adult and a sense of confidence in the approach.

While exposure work continues, it is important to keep revisiting the fears to ensure that exposure is targeting the specific appraisals that are driving the fear. In our example, we might need to consider targeting the appraisals around making a fool of themselves or going to pieces, by setting particular tasks for example around asking questions in class, or getting things wrong. We would also check that new behaviours do not develop to interfere with exposure, for example taking the same routes through college, or avoiding lunchtimes.

Behavioural experiments

The alternative way of breaking out of the fear trap is via behavioural experiments.

Behavioural experiments still involve behavioural change, but are understood as tests of cognition rather than behavioural desensitisation to feared stimuli. In the language of the fear trap they act simultaneously on the thoughts and the behaviours, compared to graded exposure which acts primarily on the behaviours alone.

There are a variety of methods for setting up behavioural experiments. We will use the simplest (Bennet-Levy et al., 2004). The model has been laid out as a flow diagram for ease of use with adolescents and young adults (Figure 6.4).

To begin a behavioural experiment, we begin with a thought or appraisal. The thought is usually a prediction about what might happen in a particular situation. In the fear trap, the prediction will be either be an over-estimation of danger or an under-estimation of ability to cope, or perhaps both.

As with graded exposure, identification of the fear is important. We need to ensure that we are testing the appraisal or thought that is associated with the highest level of fear.

There are two further considerations to remember when eliciting these predictions. The first is to ensure that they are sufficiently extreme; the second is to make sure that they are sufficiently broad.

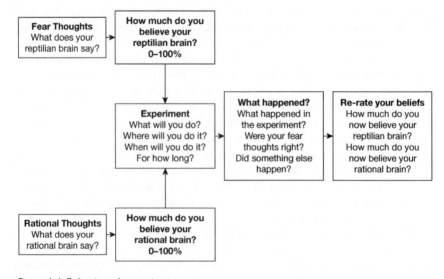

Figure 6.4 Behavioural experiments

Extreme

Extreme emotions are associated with extreme predictions. Often, adolescents and young adults will express a thought that is an amalgam of the feared thought and the rational thought e.g. "I'll be worried in this situation," so it will appear to be a feared thought, but the associated emotion would be a low level of fear such as trepidation or apprehension. However, the emotions we usually see are terror or extreme fear, which indicates that the feared thought is likely to be more extreme.

To help connect to the feared prediction, we can use the hand brain and elicit the 'reptilian brain's thought': "What is it that your reptilian brain expects in this situation?" or "Your reptilian brain is really scared in this situation, what does it expect in the worst possible scenario?" Alternatively, there might be a feared image which can help elicit the feared prediction. Often, adolescents or young adults feel embarrassed or silly about their predictions and tone them down as a result. Encouragement to the extreme, often using humour, and making it clear that the rational brain knows that this is unlikely, but it is the reptilian brain making this prediction, can help adolescents and young adults to feel more comfortable about revealing the true and extreme feared predictions. The example in this case might be "I'll be so terrified I'll die," rather than "I'll be worried in this situation."

Broad

The most powerful behavioural experiments are those that are based on predictions that are broad, generalised statements about the world (i.e. core or conditional beliefs, Padesky, 1994). If we can test a broad statement about the world then even small shifts in the conviction with which this belief is held will lead to significant change. There are common techniques used in CBT to guide adolescents and young adults to this point, such as the downward arrow technique, "What would be so bad about that?" which would be a repeated question (using rephrasing) until we have got to a core belief (Burns, 1999).

An example (see Figure 6.5) is an adolescent who is testing a belief about what might happen when entering a lesson at school. The initial prediction might be "Some of my classmates will look at me" and this prediction would be sufficient to conduct a behavioural experiment. However, if we can help them to think about what this would mean, why they might look, what would be so bad about that, we could conduct the same behavioural experiment with the feared prediction "Everybody will laugh at me" or perhaps "I am a laughing stock." A behavioural experiment to test this latter belief, with the associated prediction of what would happen in this case if it were true is more likely than the initial prediction to be the catalyst for significant change.

Having a sense of the prediction to be tested, we then ask adolescents and young adults to identify the alternative prediction or belief. It is best if this is also a broad statement about themselves or the world so "I'm similar to everyone else" would be more powerful than "Nobody will laugh at me."

At this point we ask adolescents and young adults to rate their degree of conviction of each of these predictions on a percentage scale from 0% (don't believe it at all) to 100% (completely convinced it's true). Obviously, given that these are ratings of different beliefs they don't have to add up to 100.

The next step is designing the experiment. This should be specific in detail and cover what the adolescent or young adult will do, with whom they will do it, when, and for how long. The detail is important to ensure that the adolescent or young adult undertakes the experiment in a way that will most likely test their two predictions and will be able to measure the outcome.

The adolescent or young adult then carries out the experiment, evaluates the outcome, and re-rates the beliefs.

This process covers behavioural change as outlined in the previous section, but, in testing beliefs also covers a cognitive element that can assist with generalisation and the pace of change.

Motivation

Whether we use graded exposure or behavioural experiments, these interventions are difficult. We are asking adolescents and young adults to face things they are

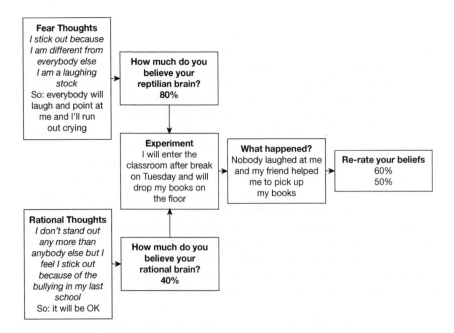

Figure 6.5 Example behavioural experiment

terrified of and have avoided, often for significant periods of time. Two factors can help us enhance motivation.

Confidence is the first. As outlined in Chapter 5, adolescents and young adults benefit from clear, confident explanations about their experiences. Using the fear trap, we can be really confident that the best way out of the trap is via the behaviours. Adolescents and young adults really want to know that things work and confidence on the part of clinicians in this approach is important. We can enhance motivation by being confident that if people reduce their avoidance, reduce their escape, and reduce their use of safety behaviours, and do it properly, then they **will**, over time, feel less scared. This is more likely to help them to challenge themselves than a vague sense that this kind of activity sometimes works. The ability to use the model to explain why previous attempts might not have worked (e.g. pushed too hard, or not done sufficiently regularly or for long enough) can further enhance confidence.

Reward is the second. The most powerful form of reinforcement is reward; a behaviour that receives a reward is more likely to be repeated. Traditional behavioural manuals of graded exposure recommend using a linear hierarchy of feared events to build up gradually towards a particular goal. This results in a list of all of the scariest things that an adolescent or young adult faces, which is not often an appealing prospect! To counterbalance this, we can ensure that the graded exposure programme or the behavioural experiments contain tasks that are scary, but also contain an inherent reward. The most powerful reward is a clear tie to the adolescent or young adult's main goal. Reward can also be built into the activities in a more casual manner, for example leaving the house might involve going to the shop to buy a treat, or to visit a friend. Sustaining motivation in the face of difficult tasks is a really important and often neglected part of the work of both graded exposure and behavioural experiments.

Physiological intervention: regulating fear in the moment

So far, we have drawn the fear trap and moved through to graded exposure and behavioural experimentation. This is usually enough for the majority of adolescents and young adults and they can use these ideas to make changes and get back onto their developmental trajectory. Sometimes, however, there are issues with the regulation of fear when doing graded exposure or behavioural experiments. Adolescents and young adults are sometimes extremely reluctant to engage in this kind of work and will say things like "What if I start to panic?," or "What happens if I can't stop shaking?." Alternatively, the fears might relate to a perception within the body, for example in panic or fears of being sick, and so we might need to do experiments, in session, exploring these phenomena.

The easiest way to tackle these issues is to do things, in session, to regulate levels of fear. This will involve both up-regulating (intensifying) and down-regulating (reducing) the experience of fear in session. Through this process we have the opportunity to demonstrate the impact of physiological intervention, and also to test out appraisals that might link to the experience of fear itself.

As outlined earlier in the chapter, fear has a dramatic physiological impact. This impact derives from sympathetic activity in the autonomic nervous system, so-called because the majority of its functions lie outside conscious control. However, there are three areas of the system that can be brought under conscious control: breathing, the direction of attention, and muscle tension. It is these aspects that we can target to regulate the experience of fear.

Breathing. During activation of the sympathetic nervous system the breathing alters to increase the volume of oxygen available to the body. If this process is enhanced, the experience of fear will intensify. For individuals concerned about breathing when they get scared, moving their attention to their breath and increasing the depth of breath can induce feelings of panic. Alternatively, consciously over-riding and counteracting this process by gently slowing the breathing down, influences other aspects of the autonomic nervous system such as the heart rate, blood pressure, and muscle tension. Bringing the awareness to the breath and using this to calm has long been a practice in many eastern parts of the world, and is central to meditation and yoga, for instance.

Muscle tension. The sympathetic nervous system functions to energise the body for intense physical activity and muscles become tense. Consciously targeting the muscles, increasing their tension and the attentional focus on their tension will intensify feelings of fear; relaxing the muscles will lessen fear. Relatedly, posture is an important part of emotion regulation: sitting in a calm versus a fearful manner has an impact on the experience of fear.

Focus of attention. With the activation of the sympathetic nervous system comes an attentional focus on threat. In the case of fear this will be the source or the cause of the fear. Focusing attention on the threat will intensify the experience of fear, moving the attention away will lessen it.

Before engaging in this kind of work, we need to check first for any physical conditions that might interfere with this process, for example heart problems or asthma. The work involves starts with a fear scale, a 0–10 scale upon which we can add some descriptive terms. We can explore predictions about what happens at different intensities of fear, what happens to make it go up, to go down, what the characteristics of different levels are, and so on. Next, we spend some time directing attention, muscle tension, and breathing, to increase and then decrease the levels of fear. An example is provided next.

Example

In the earlier example (Figure 6.2), where the adolescent is fearful of going to college, they may need some ideas about what they can do when they go in to college, to keep their levels of fear in the uncomfortable, difficult, but probably manageable zone, and prevent its tipping into terror. We can use the 0–10 fear scale with some of their own words on it, for example, calm (0), worried (2), scared (6), and terrified (10). We can then talk about where would be manageable on this scale, "OK, up to an 8 is just about alright." The task then is to increase the intensity of fear in the session. We never do this by making ourselves the object of fear, as this will interfere with the therapeutic relationship, but we can use imagination to bring a feared stimulus into the room. This is relatively easy to begin, all we need to do is to ask about a time when they were scared, or, even better, something that they are worried about in the future. Once they have come up with something, we can use these three areas to increase the intensity of fear:

Clinician:	"What worries you about this situation?" *[moving attentional focus towards threat]*
Young person:	"There will be loads of people there."
Clinician:	"OK, focus your attention on all the people, visualise all of the people there, crowds of them." *[sharpening attentional focus to the specifically feared aspect]*
Young person:	"OK."
Clinician:	"What do you notice in your body as you do this?" *[bringing awareness to physiological changes]*
Young person:	"I can feel my heart rate increasing."
Clinician:	"OK, focus on that increase in heart rate, feel it pumping in your chest, where are you on the fear scale now?" *[check in with level of fear]*
Young person:	"I'm at a 5."
Clinician:	"Can you go a bit higher?" *[ensure young person is on board with process, encourage discomfort but don't force it]*
Young person:	"Yes."
Clinician:	"OK, notice the sounds, hear all the noise in the corridor, focus on your heart beating in your chest, feel your muscles tensing up." *[using tone of voice, tensing own muscles to mirror an increase in fear and ensure that own calm stance does not lessen intensity of emotion]*
Young person:	"OK."
Clinician:	"OK, good, what do you notice now, what thoughts are you having?" *[bring attention to thoughts and fears]*
Young person:	"I'm worried I'm going to lose control, I'm going to panic."
Clinician:	"OK, where are you on the fear scale now?" *[check in]*
Young person:	"An 8, I'm really scared now, I feel I'm going to lose control."
Clinician:	"OK, so the fear now is that you're going to lose control, that's good to know. Can you stay there longer?" *[naming this new cognition that we were not previously aware of]*
Young person:	"No, it's too much."
Clinician:	"OK, OK, good, we'll come back down now. So, take a deep slow breath in, focus on the out breath, notice the breath coming out, and at the same time allow those muscles to

loosen, the shoulders to drop. Then sit back in your chair, sit in a really comfortable position, the position you're in when you're really calm." [PAUSE] "Good, now focus your attention on the sound of the traffic outside, really focus your attention on that, notice the noise of those cars going past on the wet road." [PAUSE] "Good, now bring your attention to the music in the waiting room, hear the faint noise there." [PAUSE] "Great, where are you now on the fear scale?"

Young person: "Down to a 4."

Clinician: "OK, great, we'll just keep going with the breathing, slowing it down, loosening those muscles. Pick something in the room to look at, focus your attention on that, notice the different colours, the light and shade, the shadows from the light."

Throughout this kind of process, it is important that we model the effect we're hoping to produce. When intensifying the emotion, we need to model this ourselves, raising our voices, tensing our own muscles, adjusting our own breathing, otherwise we will be too much of a calming influence. We might even want to invite the adolescent or young adult to get up, and to get up ourselves to increase the intensity of the feeling. Likewise, on the way down, we want to join in the breathing, the focusing of attention, the sitting back in our chairs, which allows the adolescent or young adult to join us without feeling silly, and also further regulates the emotion; if we remain tense it will be hard to support them to relax!

This exercise is something that can be really powerful for a variety of different reasons. Firstly, it can challenge beliefs about what happens at the higher levels of fear. This is particularly important for presentations where there are threat-based appraisals associated with the experience of fear (e.g. "I'll have a heart attack," "I won't be able to cope," "If I get really scared I'll never calm down and it will ruin the rest of my day"). Secondly, it demonstrates the efficacy of physiological strategies in reducing levels of fear and can motivate people to try things that otherwise might sound too basic. Thirdly, it can enable access to information that was otherwise hidden, for example particular fears that become evident only when the individual is really scared. Finally, it allows us to demonstrate that we, as clinicians, are not scared of fear; that fear is an emotion that we can understand, regulate, and that does not need to dominate life.

In our example, the adolescent or young adult becomes scared that they're going to lose control. It will be necessary to do the task again in future, so that the reptilian brain can learn that the experience of fear at this level of intensity is not associated with losing control. This might well involve increasing the fear to an 8 and keeping it there, but this needs to be separately set up and agreed with the adolescent or young adult.

There are a variety of ways in which adolescents and young adults can enhance their abilities to regulate fear and to calm the reptilian brain. Yoga, mindfulness, attention training and relaxation all involve, to varying degrees, processes of manipulating breathing, attentional focus, and muscle tension. There is evidence in support of all of these strategies and they have been linked to a variety of improved health outcomes (see evidence section). Which of these strategies is chosen and which is most likely to help is down to the individual adolescent or young adult and also the clinician. While these techniques will often have been mentioned or recommended to adolescents and young adults previously, the use of the hand brain model, neuropsychological explanations, associated evidence, and the experience in session can provide more of an impetus to try them.

Regulating fear versus safety seeking

There is a risk, in using fear regulatory strategies, that these behaviours will become safety-seeking behaviours and sustain the fear trap. The hand brain distinguishes between helpful strategies that regulate fear, and short-term strategies that maintain it in the longer term. The key distinction is between:

Rational brain strategies arising from a calm position aiming to regulate fear

versus

Reptilian brain strategies arising from a panicked position aiming to reduce threat.

For example, in panic attacks, many adolescents and young adults (and indeed older adults) have been taught relaxation or breathing techniques. If these techniques are used by the reptilian brain "because otherwise something terrible will happen" they will fuel and exacerbate the difficulties. If these techniques are used by the rational brain "To cope with high levels of unwarranted fear, when I know I'm OK," then they will be helpful in both the short and long term. Adolescents and young adults understand the difference between these types of strategies, when explained in this way.

Summary of breaking the fear trap

Intervention in the fear trap is focused around behavioural change. There are two intervention options: graded exposure and behavioural experimentation. Both require commitment to behavioural change, motivation for which can be gained through helping adolescents and young adults to develop the understanding outlined in this chapter. Physiological regulation in the moment can be used, where necessary, to supplement the other interventions.

Specific presentations

The fear trap is a powerful tool that can be used for any fear-based difficulty. This section outlines how the trap can be used for different types of fear, and how it can be used to target specific types of fear. Physiological fears, social fears, and obsessive-compulsive presentations are covered below.

Physiological fears: panic attacks, health fears, fears of being sick

Panic attacks, health fears, and fears of being sick all involve appraisals of physiological changes in the body that contribute to heightened levels of fear. In these cases, it is essential to include the physiological changes associated with fear and this follows with intervention.

Firstly, we need to capture the extremity of the over-estimation of threat. In panic, this is often "I'm going to die," or "I'll faint." Other health fears tend to have similarly extreme appraisals, but are longer-term "I'll get cancer/a brain tumour and die." Fears of sickness are usually, unsurprisingly "I'm going to be sick." It is important that these appraisals of over-estimated threat are extreme and are written as statements. The hand brain model reminds adolescents and young adults that these are reptilian brain thoughts, which can co-exist with rational thoughts like "I know it's not really going to happen."

Fear is the driving force behind the trap. Physiological changes must be included for panic attacks, health fears, and fears of being sick. The most important physiological aspects will relate directly to the appraisals, for example an increase in heart rate where the fear is a heart attack, an increased sense of dizziness where the fear is fainting, or digestive changes for fears of being sick. In addition, we must include the attentional shift towards threat as attention shifts to the internal workings of the body, magnifies the changes experienced, and feeds the over-estimation of threat.

Behaviours in the case of panic, health fears, and fears of being sick include avoidance, escape, and safety behaviours. Avoidance is often obvious, but could be subtle, for example avoiding certain foods, or times of eating, or avoiding physical exertion. Safety behaviours are likely to include a number of physiological behaviours. These might include attempts to control breathing, sitting or lying down, or tensing or loosening particular muscles. They might also include attempts at attentional control, for example distraction or thought suppression. All of these behaviours provide short term relief but, in the longer term, serve to maintain the over-estimation of threat and under-estimation of ability to cope.

Interventions for all fears are primarily behavioural, involving graded exposure or behavioural experiments. For all of these presentations, interventions need to include exposure to the physiological sensations with which the over-estimation of threat is associated. In panic, this will need to involve exposure to a faster heart rate, deeper breathing, or feeling dizzy. In fears of being sick this will need to involve exposure to digestive discomfort and in other health fears will need to relate to whatever physiological change is appraised as an over-estimated threat. The section on physiological intervention earlier highlights ways in which we can use attentional focus, breathing, and muscle tension to increasing the intensity of fear in session and work on exposure to these feared stimuli.

With physiological fears, it is particularly important to use the hand brain to distinguish between rational brain strategies that aim to regulate emotion, and reptilian brain strategies that aim to reduce threat. Controlling breathing, for example, is a common safety behaviour in panic, driven by the reptilian brain to avoid a heart attack, but a calmer breathing pattern, driven by the rational brain to reduce the intensity of fear is often recommended as a good way to regulate emotion.

Panic example

A young adult is off sick because they experienced a panic attack at work and are worried about it happening again. Initially, the threat is difficult to identify, something about not wanting to lose control, but asking the young adult to imagine themselves back at the time helps connect them to the fear in that moment, which was "I'm going to lose control," underneath which was "I'm going to die," which is a common appraisal in panic attacks. The under-estimate of ability to cope is "I can't manage." While this presentation is linked with work, the main threat-based appraisal relates to the internal physiological experience, particularly the heart rate, rather than the external environment.

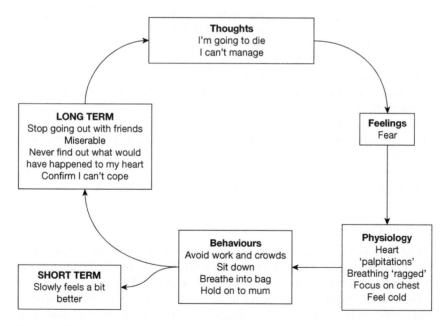

Figure 6.6 Example fear trap for panic

Behaviours in this example of the fear trap include avoidance of work and crowds, but most are physiological safety behaviours: controlling breathing, sitting down, and holding on to mum. These are all reptilian brain attempts to avoid the over-estimation of threat ("I'm going to die") associated with the physiological experience. There is some short-term relief provided by these behaviours, which is elicited by asking the young adult how they would feel if they did not do these behaviours ("Even worse!"). In the longer term the behaviours maintain the difficulties through preventing re-appraisal of the over-estimated threat, as shown in Figure 6.6. The fear trap, used in this way, is almost identical to Clark's model of panic (Clark, 1996).

Exposure in this case needs to focus on the physiological experience and the associated over-estimation of threat ("I'm going to die"), which may well include the perception of increased heart rate, dizziness, shortness of breath, or chest pain.

The task is to experimentally manipulate the physiological experience of the young adult, to test out what actually happens and then to allow re-appraisal of the over-estimated threat. There are a number of different ways in which this can be done, depending on the nature of the appraisal.

It is usually best to do these experiments in the way outlined earlier in this chapter (Physiological intervention: regulating fear in the moment). This ensures a gentle increase in levels of fear and we can bring up the level of intensity over time, primarily by manipulating attentional focus. In this case, focusing attention on the heart rate might be sufficient to bring about an increase in fear. We could further increase intensity by using hyperventilation, in which the breathing is artificially increased in depth and rate. This tends to increase heart rate, dizziness, jelly legs, and can easily induce the fear response outlined in the fear trap (Figure 6.6). Full-lung breathing involves breathing normally but with the lungs already full, which can induce feelings of chest pain. Visual disturbances can be created with particular visual stimuli (see Clark, 1996 for more information on these techniques).

In this way, we increase exposure to the feared stimulus (physiological change) while preventing the usual behavioural response, to begin the process of re-appraisal. Given that this is an unpleasant process, we might set it up as a behavioural experiment using the template in Figure 6.4 to gather predictions from the reptilian and rational brains before carrying out the task.

Fears of sickness example

An adolescent has developed fears of being sick in their senior school years. They fear being physically sick and this is exacerbated, as it often is, by the fact that they had occasionally been sick primarily as a result of these fears. The over-estimation of threat is "I'm going to be sick," which, while not completely inaccurate, is agreed to be over-estimated. In addition, the level of fear about being sick is over-estimated relative to the likely consequences of this outcome.

The associated under-estimation of threat is "I'm useless." The emotion is fear, and we explore the physiological response to make the link between the digestive system and fear.

Behaviours include avoiding social situations (particularly eating out), deliberately making themselves sick to avoid needing to be sick in social situations, and managing their portions. More subtle behaviours include monitoring their body for signs of sickness (a physiological/attentional behaviour), an almost-automatic tightening of the chest, and adjustment of breathing to prevent sickness.

In line with the fear trap, the task is to work behaviourally to reduce the behaviours so that the threats can be re-appraised. Exposure work involves a reduction in avoidance of social situations and a reduction in avoidance of food-related safety behaviours. The work also involves adjustment of physiological monitoring and control and uses the ideas of the rational brain regulating emotion rather than the reptilian brain monitoring risk of sickness.

Social fears

Fears about social situations cover a range of different appraisals. These might include fears of negative evaluation by others, of letting others down, of offending others, or even of attack by others. The first priority is to accurately identify the appraisals; we need to pinpoint the fear. Asking adolescents and young adults to imagine the worst-case scenario or the reptilian brain's worst fear can help here. Imagery is often powerful in social fears and the image of the worst-case scenario provides details of the over-estimations of threat and under-estimations of ability to cope. There is often an overlap between shame and social fears, as evident in experiences such as reddening or suddenly feeling at a loss as to what to do (see Chapter 11).

Most social fears involve an appraisal that the individual will be viewed in a negative light by others. Appraisals include "I'll make a fool of myself" or "Everybody will think I'm useless." These kinds of appraisals result in the experience of fear, and the associated physiological responses. Importantly, the attentional focus moves towards the threat: the way that the individual is perceived by others. This results in an attentional focus in the imagined (or feared!) perception of the individual by others. This is often labelled the 'processing of the self as a social object' (Clark and Wells, 1995).

This attentional focus combined with the physiological response to fear, is often appraised as consistent with the feared outcome; "Everyone will notice that I'm shaking (and think I'm incompetent)," "I'll go bright red (and everyone will laugh at me)," or "My mind will go blank (and I'll look stupid)." Behaviours fall into the same three categories: avoidance, escape, and safety-behaviours, and are attempts to escape the threat and relieve the fear. Safety-behaviours in these situations are often attempts to manage the manifestations of fear, such as looking down, avoiding eye contact, gripping the chair or lectern, rehearsing responses, or wearing lots of clothes or makeup.

Behavioural experiments are often extremely powerful in social fears. Where there are appraisals about shaking, reddening, looking in particular ways, these appraisals can be tested using behavioural experiments. The therapy situation can be used as an experimental situation and adolescents and young adults can practise meeting somebody in therapy, or can practise giving a talk to their therapist. Alterations can be made to the situation, to where they focus their attention, and to how much they use their safety behaviours, to test predictions about how helpful or otherwise these behaviours are. Video feedback can be used to explicitly test appraisals about how the individual appears from an observer perspective. These tasks can be extremely challenging, so it is important to tailor them closely to the appraisals, to derive maximum benefit.

Example

A young adult has just started a new job. Early in the role, a manager suddenly asked them a question, their mind went blank, and they could not answer. They are now scared about meeting senior people and appearing incompetent. The over-estimated threat is "Everyone will think I'm incompetent." This is a reptilian brain appraisal as in their rational brain they know that their immediate colleagues are pleased with their work. The under-estimate of ability to cope is "I can't manage at work."

The emotion is fear, which drives an attentional focus on threat, specifically on the way in which they are seen by others, and they have an image of themselves as standing looking stupid not knowing what to say. The risk is that this consumes their attentional resource meaning that there is none left to consider what to say. Behaviours include avoiding managers and meetings at work, trying not to talk and not to be noticed. Safety behaviours include planning/rehearsing conversations, sticking to 'safe' topics, and running comments through the mind before saying them. All these behaviours prevent the reptilian brain re-appraising the situation as less threatening and prevent development of confidence-building appraisals.

Intervention needs to target the behaviours: to involve reduced avoidance and reduced safety behaviours. It also needs to focus on shifting of attention away from threat-focused imagery and towards the situation at hand, which will reduce the likelihood of the mind going blank (as a result of being focused internally rather than externally). Clark and Wells (1995) recommend beginning with a behavioural experiment to explore the impact of attentional focus on threat and safety behaviours. In this situation, the young adult can role play talking to a manager while accentuating the attentional focus on threat and their usual behavioural strategies (of rehearsing, sticking to 'safe topics' and running potential comments through the mind). They can then perform the same role play, but push their attention outwards to the other person and the conversation between them, as well as trying not to use the usual behavioural strategies. Video feedback and feedback from the other participant in the role play (which might be the clinician or perhaps an assistant) can be used to provide additional information.

Predictions from the reptilian and rational brains can be made prior to the experiment (as in Figure 6.5), and these can be evaluated after the experiment. Areas of interest would be the level of fear experienced, the degree to which the conversation flowed, and how noticeable was the fear from the other person's point of view.

Behavioural experiments can then move into real world situations and the young adult can think of situations that they could build up to, using the circles as a guide to how hard to push themselves. Examples might include practicing saying hello in the lift, or asking a question in a meeting. It is likely that physiological intervention will need to be included, so that the young adult has some ideas about what to do if their mind does go blank (which can happen when their attention is so focused on threat). This might involve some breathing, taking a moment, or directing the attention away from threat and back to the present moment. These things can be practised in session, first increasing the levels of fear by imagining a difficult social situation, perhaps inviting the threat focused thoughts about the mind going blank, and then using the techniques of breathing and relaxation of muscles, and focusing the attention away from these thoughts to bring the rational brain back on line and continue with the conversation. The hand brain can distinguish between reptilian brain safety behaviours and rational brain fear regulatory strategies.

Obsessive compulsive presentations

Many adolescents and young adults present with fears of situations they know to be unlikely, but which drive behaviour nonetheless. These kinds of thoughts often fit a pattern of 'if I don't do x then y will happen'; for example, 'If I don't wash my hands six times, then I'll get ill' or 'If I don't step in this particular way, then my mum will have an accident', or 'if I have this thought I'll go to hell'. These difficulties are often described as obsessive-compulsive, where the **obsession is the thought** and the **compulsion is the behaviour**. Obsessions are repeating patterns of thought; compulsions are repeating patterns of behaviour.

Obsessive compulsive presentations can be formulated using the fear trap, the circles, and the hand brain in the same way as the other fears outlined in this chapter. All presentations with obsessive or compulsive elements will have each element of the fear trap – it is not possible to have compulsions without a threat-based appraisal and it is not possible to have obsessions without behaviours to maintain them. There may be occasions where different elements are more subtle than usual, but all elements will always be present.

The important part to get right is the thoughts and appraisals; specifically, the over-estimation of threat and the under-estimation of ability to cope. Intrusive thoughts might relate directly to threat, for example thoughts about a partner cheating, or thoughts about harm coming to a loved one. Sometimes, thoughts might not relate to threat at all, and might be violent or sexual in nature. Importantly, it is the meaning or the appraisal of these thoughts that constitutes the over-estimate of threat (Wells, 2013). For example, an adolescent or young adult who has thoughts about harm coming to somebody else might appraise these thoughts "Having these thoughts makes them more likely to happen." An adolescent or young adult with intrusive sexual thoughts might appraise these thoughts "Having these thoughts makes me an awful person." Another way to explain it, is that the reptilian brain is reacting to these intrusive thoughts as if these thoughts are a direct threat to survival in the same way as is a predator or attacker. It is this appraisal of these intrusive thoughts that leads to fear.

The behaviours following on from fear fall into the same three categories outlined above: avoidance, escape, and safety behaviours. For obsessive compulsive presentations, safety behaviours include compulsions and/or reassurance seeking. Compulsions can include all sorts of behaviours, including checking, hand-washing, or repeating actions (e.g. closing doors or entering rooms). It is important to look out for subtle behaviours as compulsions might be cognitive in nature, for example thought suppression (trying not to have the thoughts or push the thoughts away), repeating/replacing thoughts, or internal counting. Reassurance seeking can include asking others "Have I locked the door?" or "Is it OK?," or self-reassurance, which can be more subtle and difficult to spot.

All behaviours are seen to be driven by fear and all bring relief in the short term. In the long-term, the level of threat is not tested and the under-estimation of ability to cope is confirmed.

Intervention is exposure with response prevention (i.e. graded exposure without the use of safety behaviours), which is delivered in the same way as previously outlined. The fear trap is a good model for this presentation given its focus on the behavioural route out of the trap; evidence supports behavioural intervention for obsessive compulsive patterns (Wells 2013). Any and all behaviours associated with the fear trap need to be reduced, gradually, over time, using the circles to support the process. This will allow exposure to the feared stimulus and a re-evaluation of the two appraisals. It is important to be clear about the exact fear so that the intervention can be clearly targeted. For example, if an adolescent or young adult is worried that their violent thoughts will lead to their causing violence, we need to support them to expose themselves to violent thoughts while not engaging in the usual behaviours (e.g. thought suppression, or self-reassurance) and experience the fear of this exposure for long enough for it to reduce. This can often be an in-session task. As long as these behaviours are reduced the appraisals will reduce and things will improve. This idea is really helpful in cases where behavioural experiments are not possible (e.g. with obsessions about going to hell).

Example one: illness and hand-washing

A young adult fears becoming seriously ill and washes their hands frequently to relieve the fear of this prospect. In this case the over-estimation of threat is

"I'm going to die," which is triggered by an obsessive thought (e.g. "That's dirty" or "I'll get ill"), which causes fear. The behaviours are avoidance (for example of various surfaces and situations) and the compulsion of handwashing. Avoidance and handwashing provide short-term relief, but prevent assessment of the true level of threat.

Exposure in this case focuses primarily on reducing hand-washing, perhaps reducing the number of pumps of soap, or number of times hands are washed on each occasion, or time spent washing hands. Over time this can build up to touching certain things and not washing hands, to eating foods without washing hands and so on. The way to determine the best rate of change is to use the circles and to do as much as possible, without moving into the terrified zone. Ideally, tasks are completed every day within a structure that the young adult can follow during the week to sustain the challenge. We need to ensure that subtle behaviours do not develop to interfere with the progress, for example reducing eating except at meals, or avoiding hand-held foods such as crisps. All of this will enable exposure to the feared situation without the behaviours (exposure with response prevention) which will allow the reptilian brain to learn that it is over-estimating the threat.

Behaviours in this case could be combined with cognitions in a behavioural experiment, and the adolescent or young adult could be asked to predict what might happen if they were to eat a packet of crisps without first washing their hands and to specify what they will do, when they will do it, and when they might experience the results. The behavioural task is the same, but the inclusion of a cognitive component can support the process and increase the rate of change.

Example two: intrusive sexual thoughts and thought suppression

Another example, outlined in Figure 6.7, is an adolescent who has intrusive sexual thoughts (obsessions) that they fear make them more likely to behave that way and make them an awful person. Importantly, in this example guilt is also present and needs to be included in the intervention (see Chapter 11). They manage these thoughts by avoiding particular people and by trying to replace thoughts with 'good' thoughts, as well as trying to persuade themselves that they are not going to do something bad. The obsessions are the intrusive sexual thoughts, the over-estimation of threat is the appraisal of these obsessions "Having these thoughts makes me a bad person," there is avoidance and reassurance-seeking (self-persuasion) and the compulsions are having 'good' thoughts.

We can explain that the reptilian brain is responding to the intrusive thought as if it were a threat in-and-of itself. By exposing the individual to the intrusive thought without the associated behaviour, we can help the reptilian brain to learn that the thought is just a thought and does not represent a threat. Intervention of this kind can begin in-session, with exposure to a sexual thought or image that will be uncomfortable, difficult, but probably manageable to tolerate, and repeated

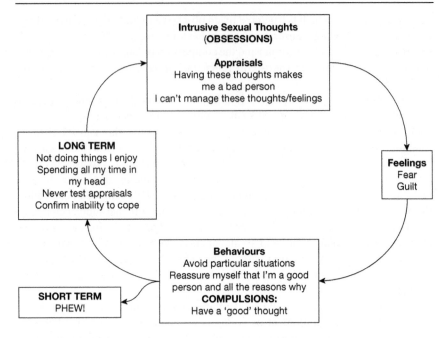

Figure 6.7 Example fear trap with obsessions and compulsions

drawing refocusing of attention on the thought or image to prevent pushing the thought away, replacing it, or the self-reassurance processes. During in-session tasks, we increase the intensity of these thoughts or images up to the most feared. In between sessions, adolescents and young adults can practise staying with the thoughts rather than pushing them away or replacing them.

The ultimate aim is to get to the point at which the thoughts do not prompt any particular behaviour at all; they are responded to as any other thought, and so this can be something to practise in the longer term. In this case, where there is arguably a greater disconnect between the rational and reptilian brains, a behavioural experiment is perhaps less likely to add much to the intervention.

Summary of specific presentations

In this section, we have highlighted some specific types of fears for which we can use the fear trap. It is important to note that these are illustrations of how the fear trap can be used, and there is no expectation that adolescents and young adults will fit neatly into these kinds of examples. While some will, it is more likely that the majority will experience a combination of different types of fears, or will have fears that result in a combination of different kinds of behaviours or attentional focus.

The beauty of the fear trap is that, regardless of the type of fear, we can use the same model to understand it, which will lead to focused and targeted intervention. The important things to remember are to ensure that we take time to accurately identify the appraisals associated with the fear, and accurately identify the behaviours that maintain the fear trap. As long as our interventions are designed to reduce the behaviours and expose the individual to their fears, then the interventions will work.

Evidence base

Meta-analytic reviews support the use of CBT for those diagnosed with anxiety disorders, whether adults (e.g. Hoffman et al., 2012) or children and adolescents (James et al., 2015).

For children and adolescents, the evidence is unequivocal for comparisons of CBT against non-active controls (e.g. wait list), but less strong in relation to comparison with active controls, medication, or treatment as usual (James et al., 2015). It does also appear that the effects of CBT are maintained at follow-up of over one year (Davis et al., 2014).

Despite the variety of models available, there is little evidence to support the use of one model of CBT over another; a recent meta-analytic review found no evidence that disorder-specific CBT was more effective than generic CBT for children and adolescents (Oldham-Cooper and Loades, 2017). In adults, there is evidence to support the use of the Clark and Wells (1995) model of social anxiety over more generic models, but there are caveats that all trials were conducted by the developer, and there is no such evidence in children or adolescents (Mayo-Wilson et al., 2014).

This chapter outlines a generic CBT formulation for fear-based difficulties that leads to interventions that are consistent with the evidence base: a focus on behavioural intervention and behavioural experimentation that is designed to target the specific fears of adolescents and young adults. The resulting interventions are consistent with disorder-specific interventions, as outlined in the section on specific presentations.

References

Ale, C.M., McCarthy, D.M., Rothschild, L.M., and Whiteside, S.P., 2015. Components of cognitive behavioral therapy related to outcome in childhood anxiety disorders. *Clinical Child and Family Psychology Review, 18*(3), pp. 240–251.

Bennett-Levy, J. E., Butler, G. E., Fennell, M. E., Hackman, A. E., Mueller, M. E., and Westbrook, D. E., 2004. *Oxford guide to behavioural experiments in cognitive therapy.* Oxford: Oxford University Press.

Burns, D., M.D., 1999. *The feeling good handbook* (Revised edition). New York: Penguin.

Cannon, W.B. 1929. *Bodily changes in pain, hunger, fear, and rage.* New York: Appleton-Century-Crofts.

Clark, D. M. 1996. Panic disorder: from theory to therapy. In P.M. Salkovskis (ed.) *Frontiers of cognitive therapy.* New York: Guilford Press, pp. 318–344.

Clark, D.M. and Wells, A., 1995. A cognitive model of social phobia. In R.G. Heimberg, M. Liebowitz, D. Hope, and F.R. Schneier (eds) *Social phobia: diagnosis, assessment, and treatment.* New York: Guilford Press, pp. 69–93.

Davis, R., Souza, M.A.M.D., Rigatti, R. and Heldt, E.P.D.S., 2014. Cognitive-behavioral therapy for anxiety disorders in children and adolescents: a systematic review of follow-up studies a systematic review of follow-up studies. *Jornal Brasileiro de Psiquiatria. Rio de Janeiro, 63*(4), pp. 373–378.

Hofmann, S. G., Asnaani, A., Vonk, I. J. J., Sawyer, A. T., and Fang, A., 2012. The efficacy of cognitive behavioral therapy: a review of meta-analyses. *Cognitive Therapy and Research, 36*(5), pp. 427–440.

Izard, C.E., 1971. *The face of emotion.* New York: Appleton-Century-Crofts.

Izard, C.E., 1991. *The psychology of emotions.* New York: Plenum Press.

James, A.C., James, G., Cowdrey, F.A., Soler, A., and Choke, A., 2015. Cognitive behavioural therapy for anxiety disorders in children and adolescents. *Cochrane Database of Systematic Reviews,* Issue 2. Art. No.: CD004690. DOI: 10.1002/14651858.CD004690.pub4.

Lyons, L., 2005. What frightens America's youth? *Gallup.com,* March 29.

Mayo-Wilson, E., Dias, S., Mavranezouli, I., Kew, K., Clark, D.M., Ades, A.E., and Pilling, S., 2014. Psychological and pharmacological interventions for social anxiety disorder in adults: a systematic review and network meta-analysis. *The Lancet Psychiatry, 1*(5), pp. 368–376.

Norton, P. J., and Price, E. C., 2007. A meta-analytic review of adult cognitive-behavioral treatment outcome across the anxiety disorders. *The Journal of Nervous and Mental Disease, 195*(6), 521–531.

Oldham-Cooper, R. and Loades, M., 2017. Disorder-specific versus generic cognitive-behavioral treatment of anxiety disorders in children and young people: a systematic narrative review of evidence for the effectiveness of disorder-specific CBT compared with the disorder-generic treatment, Coping Cat. *Journal of Child and Adolescent Psychiatric Nursing, 30*(1), pp. 6–17.

Öst, L.G., 1989. One-session treatment for specific phobias. *Behaviour Research and Therapy, 27*(1), pp. 1–7.

Padesky, C. A., 1994. Schema change processes in cognitive therapy. *Clinical Psychology & Psychotherapy, 1*(5), pp. 267–278.

Salkovskis, P. M., Clark, D. M., Hackmann, A., Wells, A., and Gelder, M. G., 1999. An experimental investigation of the role of safety behaviours in the maintenance of panic disorder with agoraphobia. *Behaviour Research and Therapy, 37*(6), pp. 559–574.

Scherer, K. R. and Wallbott, H. G. 1994. Evidence for universality and cultural variation of differential emotion response patterning. *Journal of Personality and Social Psychology, 66*(2), pp. 310–328.

Tancer, B., 2008. *Click: what millions of people are doing online and why it matters.* Paris, France: Hachette Books.

Taylor, S.E., Klein, L.C., Lewis, B.P., Gruenewald, T.L., Gurung, R.A.R., and Updegraff, J.A., 2000. Biobehavioral responses to stress in females: tend-and-befriend, not fight-or-flight. *Psychological Review, 107*(3), pp. 411–429.

Tranel, D., Gullickson, G., Koch, M., and Adolphs, R., 2006. Altered experience of emotion following bilateral amygdala damage. *Cognitive Neuropsychiatry*, *1*(3), pp. 219–32.

Wells, A. 1995. Meta-cognition and worry: a cognitive model of generalized anxiety disorder. *Behavioural and Cognitive Psychotherapy*, *23*(3), pp. 301–320.

Wells, A. 2013. *Cognitive therapy of anxiety disorders: a practice manual and conceptual guide*. London: John Wiley & Sons.

Wolpe, J. and Lazarus, A.A., 1966. *Behavior therapy techniques: a guide to the treatment of neuroses*. New York: Pergamon Press.

Chapter 7

Sadness

Even sadness is a good thing, without it there'd be no compassion in the world.

(22-year-old male)

When you're sad, you just think about being sad, you don't see it with the thoughts and behaviours and see how it all goes together. The trap is really useful.

(15-year-old female)

Sadness is a fairly infrequent emotion associated with loss and limitation. It is consciously experienced as intense and aversive and tends to be more enduring than other emotions, often lasting for days or weeks. Sadness is associated with a turning inward and withdrawal from the world, as well as a slowing down of the body. It is this physiological response which gives rise to the diagnostic term 'depression' for problems with sadness.

In adolescence and early adulthood, there are a great many environmental changes and challenges, many of which are likely to bring about feelings of sadness. Given that the predominant behavioural response to sadness is withdrawal, difficulties with sadness can represent significant barriers to ongoing development for adolescents and young adults. Difficulties with sadness in adolescents and young adults may be more subtle than many expect, as older children and adolescents are able to completely inhibit the expression of sadness and mask it with another emotion (Izard, 1991).

In this chapter, we explore sadness from an evolutionary point of view, and look at the impact it has on thoughts, the physiology of the body, the face, and behaviour. We then explore the functions of sadness, which are often fairly new ideas for adolescents and young adults and their families. This under-standing is used to build the sadness trap, a cognitive-behavioural model of what happens when adolescents and young adults get stuck in sadness, with a particular emphasis on the way in which the elements of the trap pull together to form a tight knot.

This trap is used to outline the main ways in which we can support adolescents and young adults with difficulties with sadness, and also the importance of involving families and peers in this process.

What causes sadness?

Like all emotions, sadness is a response to the environment. Specifically, it is a response to the loss of something in the environment, something that was either possessed or desired. Importantly, sadness is only felt when this loss is accepted. Anger, being a motivating and approach emotion, is more likely where the individual is working to regain what has been lost, or trying to get what is desired. Sadness is associated with the loss of something possessed or desired, **combined** with an acceptance of an inability to get it back (Stein and Levine, 1990). It is therefore an emotion associated both with loss and with limitation.

This means that sadness can be associated with the sense of loss of the desired environmental object, but it can also be associated with the loss of power to influence the environment in the desired fashion. An environmental loss that, for one person might be relatively insignificant, for another can have a much more dramatic impact as it affects the way in which the individual views themselves and their level of influence over their environment and their lives. Extreme sadness can therefore lead to feelings of powerlessness and hopelessness.

What is sadness?

In Chapter 4 we outlined the five different elements of the emotional experience. We now consider each of these elements in relation to sadness. It is important to allow sufficient time to explore these ideas, as thinking of sadness as an emotion, and particularly a potentially useful one, is often a new idea to adolescents, young adults, and their families.

Feelings

Sadness is a fairly infrequent emotion, but when experienced tends to endure, often lasting for a period of days or more. Indeed, sadness appears to be the longest lasting of the common emotions (Scherer and Wallbott, 1994). Sadness is experienced as cold. It is also experienced as intense and aversive.

The word "depression" derives from the Latin meaning to press down, depress. It has been adopted by the medical profession where it is used to describe the lowering of function, both in terms of activity and physiology, often seen in cases of extreme and prolonged sadness. Depression is a word that is used interchangeably between medical and emotional contexts and is sometimes given extra weight by adding the word 'clinical' such as 'clinically depressed'. In this book, the word 'depression' is avoided as a result of its tendency to invite an understanding of emotional experience in medical terms (see Chapter 4 and Horwitz and Wakefield, 2007). This book will stick to the term sadness to ensure reference to an emotional experience. We will also avoid using the term 'mood' which is variously defined, but usually unhelpful in being associated with diagnosis or a value judgement about emotion.

Like other emotions, sadness can be experienced to different degrees. It is helpful to encourage this perception of the different intensities of emotion, rather than just their presence or absence. A 0–10 sadness scale might include words such as: blue, disappointed, gloomy, miserable, despondent, forlorn, dejected, bleak, heart-broken, hopeless, and wretched. Where young people use the term 'depressed' or 'depression', it can help to add other synonyms such as 'miserable' or 'really sad' to encourage this perception of an emotional experience rather than a medical illness.

As outlined above, sadness is an emotion that is associated not just with the loss of something in the environment, but an experience of limitation and lack of power. As the level of sadness intensifies, the experience of this sense of limitation and reduced power to influence the environment also intensifies, with the result that extreme sadness is usually associated with feelings of powerlessness and hopelessness. This combination of loss, powerlessness, and hopelessness often also leads to a sense of pointlessness and purposelessness.

Physiology

Sadness has a similarly dramatic impact on the body as does fear. However, the impact is almost opposite. In Chapter 5, we outlined the two systems of the nervous system: the sympathetic and the parasympathetic systems. In sadness, the parasympathetic system is activated, the brake system. This system tends to activate each organ discretely and gradually in comparison to the mass whole-system activation of the sympathetic system associated with fear.

The result of parasympathetic activation is that the body is slowed down to conserve energy and to allow the slow, gradual processes of digestion, absorption, and expulsion. The heart rate is slowed, the muscles relaxed and heavy, the pupils of the eyes contract and the lens is near-focused, the energy of the body is directed inward. This characteristic activation of the parasympathetic nervous system has been dubbed 'rest and digest'. Sadness is the only emotion dominated by this physiological state.

Facial expression

Sadness is often not expressed vocally and yet it is often expressed intensely through non-vocal mannerisms. One of the primary expressions of sadness is through facial expression.

The facial expressions associated with sadness are, like its physiology, characterised by withdrawal; a lowering and drawing down of the face, facial features are reduced in form and no particular aspect is highlighted.

The face displays this withdrawal of the senses, but also communicates sadness to others. A sad face tends to elicit an approach response in others (Seidel et al., 2010). This tendency for others to approach somebody that appears sad is important when we consider the purpose of sadness later in the chapter.

Interestingly, sad facial expressions are also associated with increased perceived age by strangers (Hass, Western, and Lim, 2016).

One of the most characteristic facial traits associated with sadness is crying. The tears associated with sadness appear unique to humans and are a powerful signal of the emotion (Bard, 2000).

Appraisals/thoughts

Sadness is an emotion that is characterised by a turning inward and a search for meaning. The mind is engaged and introverted in a manner quite different from other emotions such as fear, anger, or happiness. The slow burning intensity combined with the withdrawal from others tends to invite long periods of thought.

Appraisals in sadness tend to centre, as we have outlined, around loss and limitation. Thoughts around loss include "I wanted that" or "I didn't want them to leave." Appraisals focusing on limitation might include "I can't do it" or "I'm not as good as I thought I was." Further thoughts might move through the reasons for the loss, perhaps through thoughts about whether the loss was deserved or not, whether anything might have been done to prevent it, or whether things might be done to prevent it in the future.

As well as thoughts and appraisals with this kind of content, research suggests that particular thinking styles are more prominent in sadness. For example, memory is biased in favour of negative emotional experiences, the ability to read others' emotional expressions is reduced, and processing tends toward detail and minutiae rather than the overall and the bigger picture (e.g. Isbell, Lair, and Rovenpor, 2013). Predictions about future self-efficacy are also much more negative when sad compared to when happy (Kavanagh and Bower, 1985).

At higher levels of intensity, and as a result of these thinking styles, sadness and the associated powerlessness and hopelessness can lead to more extreme appraisals, such as "I'm useless," "Nothing will ever turn out right," or "Everything will always be terrible." This thinking style can lead to a focus on whether it is worth continuing if things will not change, and then towards thoughts of ending life altogether. There is logic in this convergence of thoughts on one of the few choices over which the individual feels they still have an influence, and this process of considering mortality is particularly understandable where the loss is a death. Furthermore, for adolescents and young adults for whom a major developmental process is deciding how they want to live their lives, the counter-option of not living life is never too far from consciousness. It is important to remember that thoughts about not living or being dead are very different from behaviours carried out to this end.

Sadness is therefore associated with an appraisal of loss and limitation, followed by a great deal of cognitive processes, often directed towards discovering the source and meaning of the sadness.

Behaviours

The main behavioural impulse associated with sadness is withdrawal. We have seen that sadness is the only emotion characterised by the predominant activation of the parasympathetic nervous system. The body is focused inward, the energy levels kept low, the heart rate slowed, the focus internal. The face too is directed inward, as is the focus of attention and the thought processes. Behavioural urges are similarly directed inward and sadness is characterised by a behavioural urge to withdraw; to move away from stimulation, people, and to seek out quiet and often aloneness.

A powerful example of this withdrawal can be seen in football. At the end of an important match, the winning side come together as a team and join together in their happiness. The losing side sit down on the pitch, looking downward at the grass and turning in, alone.

When sadness becomes intense and powerlessness and hopelessness really take hold, thoughts of ending life might lead towards suicidal behaviour. It is important to remember that completed suicide is an extremely rare event and that, despite media and popular perceptions that it is most common in adolescence and early adulthood, it remains most likely in middle age (Scowcroft, 2016). Suicidal activity and behaviour, however, do occur where there is extreme sadness, hopelessness, and powerlessness.

What is the function of sadness?

Sadness is an emotional response to the loss of something in the environment; something either possessed or desired. It is associated both with this environmental loss and also with an acceptance of personal limitation to remedy this loss. The body is slowed to conserve energy; the face is turned inward along with attention and thought processes. The main behavioural response is withdrawal and the seeking out of quiet, and sometimes aloneness. In higher levels of intensity thoughts can turn to suicide and suicidal behaviours can occur.

As we covered in Chapter 5, emotions serve important functions. Sadness is an emotion that adolescents and young adults often find difficult to understand in terms of function, but there are a variety of situations in which sadness exerts a powerful force.

Most obviously, sadness is an emotion that communicates to the individual themselves and to others that all is not well. As a result of this communication, sadness is likely to elicit feelings of empathy in others and therefore the provision of care from others. The withdrawal associated with sadness is often withdrawal back to a place of safety where this comfort and care is most likely to arise. This is particularly the case in infants and children where sadness brings adults fairly quickly to the rescue (Izard, 1991). One of the most obvious human facial characteristics of intense sadness is crying. While Darwin (1965) concluded that tears in humans were incidental, Vingerhoets (2013) argues that tears signal help-lessness, especially during childhood, which is the most vulnerable time of life. He suggests that tears constitute a focused, close-range signal of emotional distress, which is a safer signal of emotional distress than an auditory scream emitted in all directions. Certainly, the tears of children can elicit quick and powerful responses from adults.

Sadness involves a slowing down and turning inward and is characterised by a search for meaning and long periods of thought. This process of withdrawing from life, reducing usual activity in order to take stock and re-evaluate can lead to important changes in an individual's approach to life. Indeed, it is often a period of sadness that leads to important decisions and an adjustment of the relative value placed on different activities. Decisions to change school, to change job, to move house, to begin or end relationships are all often preceded by a period of sadness. As a result of these changes, connections are usually strengthened; connections with the self in terms of doing things more consistent with an individual's own values and beliefs, or connections with others and increased investment in relationships with friends, family, or partners (Izard, 1991). In this sense, the experience of sadness, with its tendency to withdrawal and introspection is extremely important, and attempts made to alleviate the feeling, to dampen or lessen it might prevent or delay important decision-making processes. Furthermore, sharing experiences of sadness with others is often what brings people together. This is particularly evident in the prevalence of books, films, and music that elicit sad feelings and hence feelings of connection and empathy.

Sadness is also an important emotion in a social context; the joy and the happiness of connection with others (see Chapter 12) has its counterpart in the sadness felt when these connections are severed. Given that humans are social beings and are dependent to varying degrees on others for care and nurture, the threat of sadness with the loss of connection is important in holding communities together. Even where separation cannot be avoided – the most obvious example being when a loved one dies – sadness that is shared within a community brings people together in a shared sense of grief. This is illustrated across the world, with most communities coming together for some kind of commemoration (e.g. funeral) of the individual who has died. Sadness, in these contexts, can reunite a family and strengthen social bonds (Izard, 1991).

Extreme sadness can lead to extreme behaviours, for example suicidal communications or behaviours, and these can be seen in the context of attempts to communicate to others that all is not well. Of course, this is more usually the case where other attempts to communicate such information have been unsuc-cessful and the individual is resorting to less functional means of communicating. Where suicidal behaviour is an attempt to end life and to eliminate the ongoing distress, this tends to be the result of entanglement in the sadness trap (see next section).

Overall, sadness is an emotion that is particularly important in human life. It is a powerful emotion that signals that all is not well, often being the main driver of important life changes. It brings people together, deepens connections between them, and encourages empathy and supportive behaviour. The threat of the experience of such an aversive emotion also keeps people and communities together. Clearly, for a species that has evolved to live in complicated communities, sadness has provided an evolutionary advantage.

Adolescent development and sadness

Adolescence and early adulthood is fundamentally a time of development and change (Chapter 2). Any change involves loss, for example the loss of close bonds with family, or the loss of friends at previous schools. This means that environmentally, there are a great many events that might contribute to feelings of sadness.

Adolescents and young adults, as part of this process of change, are also experimenting with their identities and capabilities (Chapter 2). This means that they are potentially more likely at this life stage than at others, to come up against their own flaws and limitations (consider the number of exams and assessments during this phase of life relative to others!). Processes of growing but not-yet established independence are also likely to result in experiences of limitation and sadness.

Given that older children and young adolescents are able to completely inhibit the expression of sadness and even mask it with another emotion (Izard, 1991), sadness in adolescence and early adulthood may be less obvious than we expect, and many individuals will experience high levels of sadness and isolation without others' awareness. This is likely to perpetuate the problems (see the sadness trap, below).

All of this means that sadness is likely to be a fairly common experience during this phase of life and adolescents and young adults do indeed report high levels of sadness (Bertha and Balázs, 2013).

Sadness trap

We have looked at what sadness is and what it is for; we know that it is a useful emotion directed towards survival, the seeking of help, the holding together of relationships, and taking stock and re-evaluation. As a result, our aim should not be to get rid of sadness in the way that a diagnostic model of depression might encourage but to understand and to work with sadness.

Like in fear, however, there are times when humans can find themselves stuck in intense circular experiences of sadness. In these cases, sadness is no longer a helpful response to the environment but an internal state that persists regardless of it. It is at times such as these when individuals might find themselves with a diagnosis such as depression.

In adolescents and young adults, it is arguably unhelpful to provide this kind of diagnostic label (see Chapter 4) but it is important to validate the difficulties that they face, to help them to understand these difficulties, and develop a treatment plan. All of this can be achieved using the sadness trap.

The sadness trap, like the other traps in this book, is a diagrammatic cognitive behavioural formulation. It highlights the ways in which the elements of the model are causally linked to each other, using the psychological understanding of sadness as outlined above. The hand brain is used to highlight the mechanisms in operation.

The sadness trap is illustrated in Figure 7.1. It is different to the fear trap in that it is not a vicious cycle, but a tight knot of thoughts, feelings, physiology, behaviours, and environment, each of which links with, and is consistent with the other elements. It is similar in nature to Padesky and Mooney's (1990) five-part model. We outline the principles and theory behind the trap before providing an example of how the sadness trap can be drawn with an adolescent or young adult.

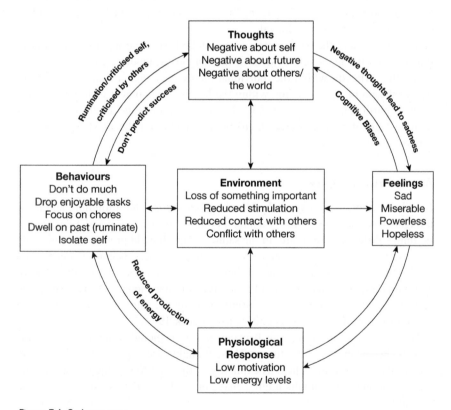

Figure 7.1 Sadness trap

Environment

As we have outlined so far in this chapter, sadness is an emotional response to environmental loss and personal limitation. In the sadness trap, the environment is important and interacts with the other elements of the trap. The environment can include the physical environment, but is more likely to include the social environment and the relationships and interactions between the adolescent or young adult and those around them. For adolescents and young adults, the social environment will include a mix of family and friends.

Difficulties in the environment can include life events characterised by loss (e.g. death of a family member or friend), or can include environmental limitations, such as lack of friends, bullying, conflict within the family, or a lack of stimulation. Genograms or timelines can highlight less obvious environmental factors, such as a lack of closeness in the family or a sense that the adolescent or young adult has not felt accepted in a peer group.

Environmental factors interact with all the other elements of the trap, feeding negative thought processes, leading directly to experiences of sadness, powerlessness and hopelessness, impacting on the physiology of the body, and leading to behaviours such as withdrawal.

The inclusion of the environment as an integral and central part of the sadness trap reduces the tendency, evident in the diagnostic model (see Chapter 4), to locate the difficulty within the individual themselves, and encourages a perception of the problem as existing within the life and the context of the individual. This is particularly important for adolescents and young adults, given their relative lack of influence over their environments and the need for others to support change.

Appraisals/thoughts

In sadness, there is a great deal of thinking about loss and limitation, and these thoughts often move towards reaching a point of re-evaluation and a decision to do things differently in future. In the sadness trap, thought processes do not tend to be so productive and assume a more repetitive process, becoming deeper and more generalised. The **processes** of thought in the sadness trap are often known as rumination, a particular kind of repetitive, circular thought (Nolen-Hoeksma, Roberts, and Gotlib, 1998). The **content** of thoughts common in the sadness trap was outlined by Beck in his cognitive triad (Beck 1979).

Beck proposed a strong link between negative thoughts about the self, the world/other people, and the future. These thoughts are expressed explicitly, but appraisals are not always held as explicitly as they are highlighted here. Instead, adolescent and young adults might behave or think 'as if' these statements were the case.

Negative thoughts about the self

There are often many negative thoughts about the self. Often, these thoughts are specific to different situations, but underlying these thoughts tend to be core beliefs in the areas of self-defectiveness, responsibility, and control. The kinds of thoughts seen in the sadness trap are outlined in Table 7.1 and illustrated in the example outlined next.

All of these types of negative thoughts and beliefs are often seen where people are stuck in the sadness trap. Beliefs about a lack of control or ability to influence, however, are particularly important, as they are particularly likely to lead to inactivity and hence to getting stuck in the sadness trap. They are also likely to lead to negative thoughts about the future, below.

Other negative thoughts about the self, include present focused thoughts such as "I haven't done anything useful," which might relate to the core belief "I'm useless," or "I should have done more," which might relate to the core belief "I'm to blame." In extreme cases, present-focused thoughts might include "I would be better off dead," which could be linked to core beliefs in the domain of self-defectiveness.

Negative thoughts about the future

Thoughts and predictions about the future tend to be extremely negative, often representing hopelessness about the possibility of change. Examples include

Table 7.1 Negative thoughts about the self common in the sadness trap

Area	Example thoughts
Self-defectiveness	I am dull
	Nobody likes me (I'm unlikable/unloveable)
	I'm worthless
	I'm not good enough
	I'm ugly
	I'm insignificant
	I'm unimportant
	I'm undeserving
Responsibility	It's all my fault
	I'm to blame
	I'm a bad person
	I'm evil
Control	I'm useless
	I'm hopeless
	I'm helpless
	I'm powerless
	I'm a failure
	I can't cope

"I will always be like this," "Nothing will ever get better," and "There is no hope for me." These kinds of negative thoughts about the future are likely to be linked to negative thoughts about control, and likewise to inactivity as a result of a lack of belief that activity will bring about change. Thoughts in the sadness trap can follow the path of powerlessness and hopelessness, with the result that thoughts can become focused on the belief that things will not change, that change is not within the individual's influence to achieve, and that things will never improve. This pattern of thought is often known as rumination, which is characterised by a focus on distress and its causes and consequences, with little focus on solutions, which are believed to be outside of the individual's control (Noelen-Hoeksma, 1998).

Negative thoughts about the world/others

Thoughts about the world and other people include "Nobody loves me," "The world is unpredictable," "The world is dangerous," "The world is unfair," "Other people are horrible." Negative thoughts relating to the predictability of the world are likely to be linked to beliefs about having control (without predictability it is impossible to have control and influence).

Feelings

Negative thoughts about the self, about the future, and the world/other people all lead to feelings of sadness. The degree and intensity of these thoughts has an impact on the intensity of these feelings of sadness, and lots of negative beliefs about the self, particularly relating to control, the future, and the unfairness or unpredictability of the world are likely to lead to intense feelings of sadness, hopelessness, and powerlessness.

It is the emotion that is central to the sadness trap; it is this intense feeling that is so intolerable. It is also the feeling that makes sense of the biological and behavioural responses associated with the emotion, as outlined in the section above. In the sadness trap, it is essential to elicit an emotion consistent with sadness (not 'depression' which is a diagnosis). Where they exist, it is also important to elicit hopelessness and powerlessness. It is the emotion that drives the formulation.

Negative thoughts are therefore clearly linked to a resulting feeling of sadness. There is also a strong link between the feelings of sadness and the negative thinking styles and thoughts outlined above. We saw in the earlier part of the chapter how sadness is associated with memory recollection and particular thinking styles. This means that feeling sad is likely to lead to thought processes that are consistent with this emotion; for example, a focus on the event that precipitated the sadness, a focus on the personal limitation that it highlighted, or a tendency to recall similarly difficult life events.

Physiology

Unlike in the fear trap, where physiology is an optional extra to the trap, in the sadness trap the physiological response is essential. The physiological response to sadness is intense and drives the downward trend of motivation and energy levels seen at these times. It is important that the causal links between the emotion and the physiological responses are made, ensuring that young people understand that the physiology is associated with the emotion, and that there are reasons why this should be the case.

We saw, earlier in the chapter, that sadness is the only emotion characterised by a dominant activation of the parasympathetic nervous system. This results in a shift of activity in the body towards internal functions such as digestion and immunity rather than the external muscular activity seen in fear. Feeling sad is associated with an intense physiological response which gears down the body, reduces energy levels and motivation, and turns the body inward.

Behaviours

Reduced motivation and energy levels are very likely to lead to reduced activity, so the primary behaviour seen in the sadness trap is **withdrawal**. This withdrawal can be obvious, in which it occurs from everything and everybody resulting in a state of intense isolation. In its lesser forms, it might be a withdrawal from activities that were previously enjoyed or from social contact with others. It is common for adolescents and young adults to withdraw in more subtle ways, to withdraw from many activities but continue studying, or to continue to see friends, but to become quieter for example. This withdrawal can be associated with repetitive processes of thought, often labelled rumination, which can, in some cases, be included as behaviours in the sadness trap.

Behaviours in the sadness trap, unlike in the fear trap, are not seen as a way to avoid the emotion, but are entirely consistent with it. The act of withdrawing is consistent with the feeling of sadness and does not reduce the feeling of sadness. There is no real relief to be gained by withdrawing but it is effortful to do anything else.

This withdrawal has an impact on all of the other elements of the trap.

Physiology. Reduced activity leads to reduced production of energy; the less the body does, the less energy it produces. There is tight knot between these two elements of the trap.

Environment. Withdrawal and turning inward moves the individual away from the external world and away from environmental connections. Reduced involvement with activities, be they pleasurable, or focused on achievement and progression leads to further impact on thoughts, feelings, and physiology. Reduced involvement with others leads either to isolation and loneliness, or to conflict, both of which often result in further withdrawal.

Thoughts. Reduced activity is likely to lead to confirmation of negative thoughts about the self. This can occur via self-criticism: "I haven't done anything all day," "I'm a waste of space," and via others criticising "You're useless," "Why can't you do something?" A relative lack of activity also leaves long periods of time for rumination and repetitive thought.

Sadness trap and the hand brain

In sadness, the brain is not seen to be operating at cross-purposes as is the case in fear, but rather in almost too-close unity. In sadness, the brain can be seen to be almost shut-down, sucked together, tightened together like the knot of the sadness trap. It is not that the rational brain is disconnected from the other parts of the brain, but rather that the other parts of the brain are having a heavy influence on the ability of the rational brain to function rationally, and hence the ability to stand back and see the bigger picture is reduced and there are invitations to circular processes of thought (e.g. rumination). As a result, the rational brain is subject to a great many processing biases in sadness.

Summary

The sadness trap is a cognitive behavioural formulation, incorporating thoughts, feelings, behaviours, the physiology of the body, and the environment. It is a very different cycle from the fear trap, which is more of a dance between fear and relief; the sadness trap is a tight knot of consistent behaviours that merge together to lead to a descent into increasing misery and hopelessness. The sadness trap is similar to other cognitive behavioural formulations but is clearer in the ways in which each element is causally linked to the others and underpinned by an understanding of sadness and of the brain.

Drawing the sadness trap

It is best to draw the sadness trap from scratch so that the different elements and the ways in which they fit together can be explored and understood in turn. It also ensures that young people feel involved in the process and are more likely to own the resulting diagram. The basic principles and structure of the sadness trap are common to all sadness-based difficulties so it should not differ significantly for each individual. The fact that we have a structure and a way of drawing the trap also supports us, as clinicians, with the increased presence and guidance that we often need to bring to our work with adolescents and young adults.

Given that the sadness trap is a knot of interacting elements rather than a swing between different states, as seen in the fear trap, it is not necessary to take a specific example. However, we do need to ensure that young people are connected to the feelings and state of sadness so that the elements can be properly elicited. To achieve this, it can be helpful to help them to recall a time when they felt particularly sad or unhappy and to imagine themselves back at this point.

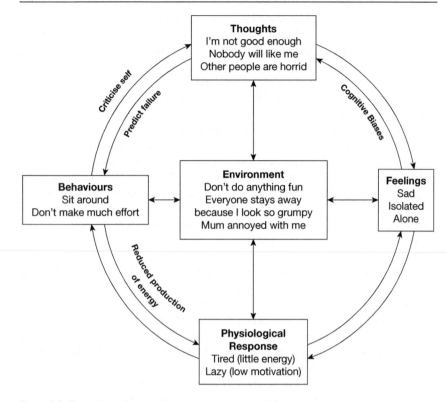

Figure 7.2 Example sadness trap

In this example, a 17-year-old remembers feeling particularly sad after returning home from a bad day at school and finding nobody home.

Often in the sadness trap, adolescents and young adults will verbalise their negative thoughts. Where this is the case, we can start with the thoughts and write some of the most powerful ones down. We can then explore these thoughts to distil them to core beliefs about themselves, the world, and others. We can do this by asking about how they must see themselves, if these are the kinds of thoughts they have about themselves, or what does this group of thoughts mean about them? Where more prompting is required, we can make suggestions, again, picking some, for example "It sounds as though you have a really negative view of yourself, that you see yourself as worthless, or bad, or a failure?" Remember that core beliefs, particularly ones powerful enough to get people stuck in traps, are extreme and powerful, and so we need to elicit and name them in this way. For example, "I'm not very good" is not likely to be as accurate as "I'm worthless" or "I'm no good at all." This is also important from an intervention point of view, as more extreme statements give rise to more successful interventions. In our example we have identified three core beliefs about the self, the world, and others.

Given that sadness is an emotion associated with a great deal of cognitive processing, thoughts are often not too difficult to identify. However, the process of naming the underlying core beliefs can be powerful and can elicit strong emotion. The next step is to name this emotion, which is particularly important where emotion is evident in the room, and naming that a certain statement brought tears or seemed difficult to hear, validates the emotional experience and ensures that, even though we are exploring difficult areas, we are sensitive, compassionate, and attuned. When naming the emotion, we need to ensure that sadness or a synonym is identified. This can take some time, as there are often lots of other emotions around, and sadness, as an emotion is often confused with depression as an illness, but we must make sure that we include sadness, or the trap does not make sense! Once we have identified the emotion, we can consider the interaction between thoughts and feelings, and talk about the evidence that sadness is associated with a tendency to remember sad times in the past, to predict poor outcomes in the future, and to focus on the detail rather than the bigger picture.

Sadness, as outlined above, has a powerful impact on the body. It is the only emotional state dominated by the parasympathetic nervous system and we can talk about this impact as a normal emotional response. We need to ensure that we include both energy and motivation. Neither of these are usually difficult to identify, but it is important to help adolescents and young adults to understand that the physiological response is associated with the emotion of sadness. In our example, the young person has identified these as somewhat self-critical concepts (tired and lazy) and so we have included their language, but qualified it with other statements when we have explored why their body is tired and lazy.

The next link is relatively easy to make, between having little energy and motivation, and doing very little. It is important that we identify all types of withdrawal, not just physical withdrawal, but social and emotional withdrawal too. Many adolescents and young adults will 'soldier on' with an apparent continuation of functioning, while underneath they feel disconnected and isolated. In these cases, we need to identify other forms of withdrawal, for example the lack of connection with others or the focus on the things that have to be done and the dropping of more enjoyable tasks.

The next task is to make some more links around the trap. The easiest is the impact on energy and motivation. We can ask about the impact of not doing much on energy levels and motivation, and most adolescents and young adults have a sense of a vicious cycle here: lower energy leads to lowered activity, which leads back to lower energy.

The next link is to the environment. We can ask about how other people respond when they do very little, or when they stop going out, we can ask when was the last time they did something they enjoyed, we can also make links back to losses in the environment, people they miss, or limitations that might be related to the experience of sadness. From here, we can make links to other parts of the trap. In our example, other people respond negatively to the young person and this clearly feeds the thoughts, feelings, and behaviours already identified. The other link to make is from the behaviours back up to the thoughts, asking about what kind of thoughts they might have about themselves after a day of doing very little for example.

Once the trap is complete, with all five elements and each arrow included, with a clear understanding of the link that each arrow represents, we can ask what it is like to see it illustrated on paper. We can name it as the sadness trap, and note that it is all tied together like a tight knot. This is important in validating the experience of adolescents and young adults, and noting that there are reasons why they are stuck, to reduce criticism and blame.

Breaking the sadness trap: intervention

With a clear understanding of how the different elements of the sadness trap come together, the next step is to consider where best to intervene to break the trap. There are two options. The first is the behaviours, the second is the thoughts.

Increasing levels of activity and problem-solving interactions with the environment are the basis of behavioural activation (Jacobson et al., 2001). Challenging negative thoughts is the basis of cognitive intervention, such as Beck's Cognitive Therapy for Depression (Beck, 1979) and Mind over Mood (Greenberger and Padesky, 1995).

It is usually best to do some work around both thoughts and behaviours in the context of the sadness trap (see evidence section later in the chapter).

Behavioural intervention: behavioural activation

We can see from the sadness trap that the behaviours are clearly tied up with each of the other elements. Not doing much reduces energy levels, encourages a ruminative quality of thought and negative thought content. It also reduces positively reinforcing interactions with the environment and is linked with environmental and interpersonal difficulties. It therefore follows that by targeting behaviours and adjusting interactions with the environment, we can loosen some of the tightness in the knot that is the sadness trap.

This behavioural strategy is often the best place to start. For those individuals doing very little with their time, doing more is clearly going to have to be a part of any intervention strategy and so it makes sense to begin here, given its relative simplicity. For individuals who are already doing something, some fairly small changes in their behaviour can lead to quite dramatic changes in the overall picture.

For adolescents and young adults, who have less control over their environments than do adults, beginning behaviourally invites an immediate focus on the interaction between the individual and their environment. Intervening here requires change in both areas, and can often lead to fruitful involvement of others (the social environment) fairly early in the process. This can lead to intervention at the system level, where adolescents/young adults and their family (and friends) are all working together to bring about change, which makes change more likely and more sustainable. Given this, it is helpful, where possible, to involve the family and wider social network as early and as much as possible in the process. How best to do this can be worked through with the individual early in the process of therapy (see Chapter 5).

Behavioural change is ordinarily delivered through a process known as behavioural activation. Behavioural activation, as its name suggests, is a behaviourally-based intervention based on determining the behaviours that have a positive impact on feelings and functioning, and activating these behaviours (Jacobson, Martell, and Dimidjian, 2001). Behavioural activation is a highly structured intervention that proceeds via a number of stages. The stages outlined below are consistent with those of most manuals (e.g. Jacobson, Martell, and Dimidjian, 2001) but use more basic language and are tailored to the adolescent and young adult population.

Understanding the model and setting goals

When beginning behavioural activation, we need to ensure that the adolescent or young adult has a good understanding of the rationale for intervention. This means focusing on the behavioural aspect of the sadness trap and looking at how the behaviours are tied closely together with all the other aspects of the trap, the thoughts, feelings, physiology, and environment. The aim is to progress with a focus on behaviour and **setting behavioural change as the ultimate goal of intervention**. When stuck in the sadness trap, many adolescents or young adults will only do things if they are 'well enough' or have some energy, but the aim of behavioural activation is to put behavioural change ahead of these concerns and go through with the behaviours in spite of difficult feelings, physiology, or negative thoughts. An analogy that can be helpful in these situations is that of a train. They can guide the front of the train, namely the behaviours, to take a particular route, and the other parts of the train, the thoughts, environment, and importantly feelings, will follow along behind. This idea that they can change behaviours and there may well be a delay in improvements in other areas can be important in sustaining motivation.

Behavioural activation does not involve providing adolescents and young adults with lists of pleasurable activities and sending them off to do them. It is an individualised and tailored approach designed to increase specific activities that are likely to bring positive reinforcement to that individual. For many adolescents and young adults this does not mean a return to previous activities that were pleasurable and meaningful, but is part of the process of development and self-discovery: finding out what they enjoy and what is important in their lives. As a result, like in much of our CBT practice, we need to foster a sense of openness to try things out, to experiment with different activities. Activities that are helpful can be built upon; activities that are not can be adjusted or abandoned in favour of others.

As outlined above, behavioural change involves environmental change and so behavioural activation will also involve problem-solving environmental difficulties. Therefore, not only does the adolescent or young adult need to be open to change, but family members and friends need to support them doing things differently and perhaps interacting or connecting with them in different ways. As a result, it can be helpful to involve the wider network, including family and close friends, in the process of explaining the rationale for behavioural activation.

Activity monitoring

In practice, behavioural activation begins with a detailed exploration of current activities and evaluation of these different activities. Sometimes, adolescents and young adults are able to report fairly accurately what they have done and how they have felt. This might be sufficient information from which to start thinking about the balance of activity and the things that they might want to change. However, the sadness trap highlights the impact that sadness has on cognitive processes, specifically inviting a negative recall bias. Therefore, asking a young person to report what they did last week might result in an under-estimate of their levels of activity and/or over-generalised negative responses such as "I didn't do anything" or "I felt terrible all the time." Where this is the case, we can do a more in-depth exploration in real time, using a diary.

There are different ways of collecting the data, and the variation is mostly based on the different time periods involved. Diaries can be divided up by hour, or by two-hour period, others will split the day into three larger chunks. It is often easiest to allow people to choose their own ways of collecting the data, but where individuals are doing very little, it can be best to use broader time periods so that adolescents and young adults are not encouraged into self-punishment by having to write 'nothing' in hundreds of boxes. While we may have paper-based diaries to allow young people to provide this information, there are many apps on smartphones that may well be more likely to be used by adolescents and young adults than pieces of paper.

Initially, the basic monitoring of activity might be all the young person can manage. However, there are lots of other useful pieces of information that can be added to this to further inform the process. The first of these is a sense of the associated emotion. Adolescents and young adults can be asked to label the feeling they had at the time they were doing each task and rate the intensity of this feeling on a 0–10 scale, 0 being neutral and 10 being the most intense feeling imaginable. Using a specific emotion tends to encourage emotional understanding as opposed to a rating of 'mood' which encourages a more linear (and therefore diagnostic) mode of understanding. Another aspect of this process that can be incorporated is to add ratings of Achievement, Connection, and Enjoyment (ACE for short). These are the characteristics of activities that are important in this context and these can support both the understanding of the sadness trap, and the process of finding a way out of it.

This first phase of activity monitoring highlights the way in which adolescents and young adults interact with their environments, and the impact that this has on how they feel, their energy levels, and the other aspects of the sadness trap. Families and wider systems can be encouraged to support the process, which can start to shift the interactions adolescents and young adults have with those around them.

Problem solving (functional analysis)

With an understanding of how adolescents and young adults spend their time, the next task is to consider the main issues with this pattern of behaviour. Some theory about what is necessary to sustain a fulfilling life is helpful here and reinforces the structure of the intervention to adolescents, young adults, and families. Positive psychology provides three helpful principles (Frude, 2014):

Right amount of activity

Doing too little is a common issue for adolescents and young adults, particularly where there are difficulties engaging in education, for example. Too little activity leads to lowering of energy levels, self-critical thoughts, and limited positive interactions with others and the environment more generally. Too much activity can also lead to difficulties, primarily as a result of feeling overwhelmed and powerless. If there is no time to stop and think, no opportunity to plan and make decisions, then interactions with the environment are not likely to be enjoyable, energy levels are likely to be depleted and the sadness trap will result.

Balance of different activities

The second principle for a fulfilling life is a balance of different types of activities. Some activities bring a sense of Achievement, others are Enjoyable for their own sake, and others involve Connecting with others. These three groups of activities (ACE) are generally sufficient to use with adolescents and young adults. Imbalances in these different activities are likely to lead towards the sadness trap.

Routine

The third principle is routine. Routine is an important part of human life; humans are creatures of habit and like to do the same things over and over again. This repetition is important as it creates a sense of predictability, which allows influence, power, and control. In a world of chaos where anything can happen at any time, there is no ability to influence anything. In a predictable world where the same kinds of things happen repeatedly, it is possible to alter behaviour and predict what might be the result. This link between predictability and control, influence, and power, is important in the context of the sadness trap. As we outlined at the beginning of the chapter, sadness is associated with limitation as well as loss, and so powerlessness and hopelessness are features of the sadness trap. Routine and predictability are therefore important ways out of the trap.

Using these three broad principles to identify the main problem areas helps to plan changes to activities. We might focus on increasing the overall level of activity, or on altering the balance of time spent studying (Achievement) with time with others (Connection), for example.

Activity monitoring and the associated conversations around it may well highlight other more specific patterns of interaction between individuals and their environments. While in general, spending time with others reduces sadness and increases feelings of happiness and contentment, we might find that for some individuals the reverse is the case. This might relate to the quality of the interaction adolescents and young adults have with different people in their environment: they may have a critical parent, or a friend who tends to take advantage, conversely a teacher who is particularly supportive. Exploring the quality of interactions between adolescents and young adults and those around them is an important part of this process and will help to inform the ways in which intervention might proceed.

One of the advantages of work with adolescents and young adults is that family members are often available to join sessions and some of the problem solving we might be able to do in session; facilitating more openness within the family, for example, or suggesting family-based activities. In this way we can work not only with the young person, but also directly with parts of their environment, to bring about change to the whole system. Intervening in this way is also consistent with the processes of Interpersonal Psychotherapy (IPT) that has a strong evidence base for this presentation (see evidence section at the end of this chapter).

Activity scheduling (graded task assignment)

Having gained a sense of the behavioural-environmental interactions in the lives of the adolescent or young adult, and spent some time exploring this in detail, the next step is to consider the changes they might need to make to move them out of the sadness trap.

It is important to **aim small**. Keeping the negative thought biases of the sadness trap in mind, it is best to aim small and to be more likely to succeed, rather than to aim to high and feed self-criticism with failure. If we can agree tasks that are likely to be achieved, we can harness the positive reinforcing qualities of success to increase the progress of change.

It is also important to **be specific**. When adolescents and young adults are caught in the sadness trap their default is to make no change, or to carry on as they are. To give the best chance of success we need to be really specific and break down the process into small parts so that adolescents and young adults are most likely to go ahead and implement the change. It is the **behavioural** response that will make the difference.

It is also important to **work with the system**. Adolescents and young adults have less influence over their environments that do adults and so wherever possible it is best to involve the wider family and system in making change. As clinicians, we might also be able to support adolescents and young adults to access different environments. It is always worthwhile having some ideas or making connections with organisations that offer options for young people, particularly in the social arena. Working with the system means that change is more likely to happen, and also supports the process of understanding emotions as an understandable response to the environment rather than a defect of the individual.

The aim is to support adolescents and young adults to adjust the way in which they spend their time and adjust the interactions they have with their environments. Sometimes this can be a fairly quick dramatic change, for example ending a relationship or changing jobs. However, more commonly, it is a gradual process, which requires regular review and adjustment, using the processes of activity monitoring and recording along the way.

Managing rumination

In behavioural activation, cognitive processes can be treated as behaviours. Rumination, which is a particular process of circular thought, can again be understood as a process of turning inward and withdrawing from the aversive experience of the external world. Even in company, an individual can withdraw from others by directing their attention away from the external and inwards. In behavioural activation, individuals can be encouraged to notice the behaviour of rumination and direct their attention outwards so that they are activating themselves mentally, and engaging in the external environment. Ideas about how to work with the content of thoughts is covered in the next section.

Summary

Sadness, like other emotions, is a response to the environment. Using behavioural activation to explore the interactions adolescents and young adults have with their environments and the impact on the way that they feel is an important intervention and supported by evidence (see evidence section). In our work with adolescents and young adults we have opportunities to support them to manage these interactions by involving the wider systems and helping them access different environments.

Example

A 22-year-old man had a job and worked full time while his partner looked after their child. He worked hard all day, came home very tired and felt as though he had to start work all over again at home, helping to tidy up, organise dinner etc. He was also extremely concerned about money as he knew that they were barely able to manage on their current income and there was little available for unforeseen circumstances. He was fed up, exhausted, and could see no way out.

His activity monitoring diary showed that he was very busy, perhaps too busy, and that his days were dominated by tasks and chores; he spent very little time doing things he might enjoy. When drawing the sadness trap he identified particular negative thoughts about being solely responsible and to blame, and he highlighted feeling powerless and overwhelmed.

The behavioural task was fairly clear: to help him alter the balance of how he spent his time. Activity scheduling focused around making choices and decisions about how he spent his time, both at home and at work and supporting him to problem solve in these areas. While he came to sessions alone, he was encouraged to change the way in which he interacted with those around him and he began asking for help and connecting with people and organisations that might support him. The result was that he began to take more decisions in his life, to receive help and support so that his financial situation improved, to spend more time with friends, and more fulfilling time with his partner and child. Over time this resulted in his having more positive thoughts about himself, having more energy and enthusiasm, and feeling more in control and less overwhelmed.

Cognitive intervention: thought challenging

The second class of interventions that follow from the sadness trap are cognitive interventions. In the sadness trap, there are a great many negative thoughts and negative beliefs about the self that are continually fuelling the feelings, physiological responses, behaviours, and interactions with the environment. Thoughts in the sadness trap are also seen to be subject to negative biases, such that the thoughts are more negative than, rationally, they should be. The central tenet of cognitive interventions in the sadness trap, is that highlighting these negative thoughts, highlighting the thought biases, and then testing the thoughts and developing more rational more adaptive thoughts and thinking patterns, should help adolescents and young adults out of the sadness trap.

Working with thoughts is a central part of CBT and consists of four different stages. First, bringing awareness to the thoughts, second, 'decentring' from the thoughts, third, assessing the degree of accuracy of the thoughts, and fourth adjusting the thought in light of this evidential assessment. The next section looks at each of these stages in turn and an example is outlined afterward.

Identifying thoughts

As we have seen in Chapters 5 and 6, a central part of the experience of emotion is the cognitive appraisal, the thoughts. Many of the thoughts experienced on a daily basis are conscious thoughts. Appraisals are cognitive constructs, ways of making sense of the world, that do not always reach the threshold of awareness. This means that the first step in any cognitive intervention is to bring a conscious focus to the cognitive elements of the emotional experience. In CBT, this is often known as 'identifying thoughts' or 'eliciting cognitions'.

The most common way to elicit cognitions/identify thoughts is to use a thought record. Thought records are traditionally paper-based tables comprising a number of different columns. Typically, these contain a column to describe the situation, a column to describe the emotion and also to rate its intensity, and then a column to describe the thoughts. This is often known as a three-column thought record. Some adolescents and young adults may not particularly like the idea of taking these away to fill in, and may also struggle with the concepts they are designed to highlight. As a result, it is best to complete the first few in session, using examples that occurred recently. If adolescents or young adults can begin to complete one or two as homework tasks then so much the better.

The purpose of the three-column thought record is to support the adolescent or young adult to focus in on the thoughts of the sadness trap and to understand the particular role that thoughts and appraisals play in their emotional experience.

When using a thought record to challenge thoughts, it is important to ensure that the thought that we choose fits in the sadness trap; checking that the thought is associated with a feeling of sadness, rather than fear, for example. Exploring the evidence for and against thoughts that fit in the fear trap (threat focused thoughts) tends not to be particularly fruitful and would be better tackled using a behavioural experiment (see Chapter 6).

Decentring

The next step is to help adolescents and young adults to adopt a decentred position in relation to their thoughts. A decentred position is one in which the individual understands that thoughts, appraisals, and feelings are temporary events of the mind as opposed to reflections of the self that are necessarily true (Safran and Segal, 1990). Adolescents and young adults can be encouraged to take a decentred position by returning to the hand brain. While we label the third section of the brain the rational brain, it is not always as rational as its name suggests. The rational brain tends to have different thoughts and different interpretations of events depending on what is going on in the other parts of the brain. For example, thoughts and thought processes are very different in happiness compared to sadness. In addition, different people often view and interpret situations in different ways.

The concept of thought biases follows nicely from this sense that the rational brain is influenced by other factors and not always as rational as it might be. David Burns has identified ten types of cognitive bias, or thinking errors that commonly arise. These are outlined in Table 7.2.

Table 7.2 Ten types of cognitive bias (adapted from Burns, 1999)

Thought bias	Description	Example
All or nothing thinking	Everything is seen in terms of two extremes (all or nothing!). All or nothing thinking can often be expressed as "Either/or."	Either something is perfect, or it is rubbish. You either like me or you hate me.
Over generalisation	A single event is taken to represent a repeating pattern.	"I always get low grades" (after being given a single low grade). "Nobody will ever want to be with me" (after a rejection from a potential partner).
Mental filter	A small aspect of something receives a large proportion of the attention and the perception is filtered as a result.	"This prom dress is awful" (after nine people express a like for the prom dress, but one questions the shape of the back, and this comment receives all of the attention).
Discounting the positive	Positive experiences are discounted through being attributed to chance, to the nicety of the person who might have made a positive comment, or through moving the goal posts.	"I was just lucky the right questions came up." "They're just saying that because they like me." "It wasn't that difficult really."
Jumping to conclusions	Thoughts are interpreted as facts in the absence of any evidence to support the conclusion. Subcategories include mind-reading and fortune-telling.	"They're thinking that I'm ugly." "They're obviously laughing at me." "Something is bound to go wrong today."
Magnification	The importance of problems is magnified and the importance of the things that are going well is minimised leading to a disproportionate interpretation.	"I'll never get over this difficulty." "Everything is absolutely terrible."
Emotional reasoning	Emotions are used to make decisions about the world.	"I'm terrified of him – he must be really dangerous." "I feel miserable, everything in my life must be awful."
Shoulds, musts, and oughts	Statements including the words should, must, or ought tend to indicate a refusal to accept things as they are. They indicate a lecturing style of thought process in which criticism is never far away.	"I should be better at maths." "I mustn't go out tonight." "He shouldn't be chewing so loud." "This computer ought to work better."

continued . . .

Table 7.2 Continued

Thought bias	Description	Example
Labelling	Rather than describing the event or behaviour, it is the character trait of the person ho engaged w in the behaviour that is described.	"I'm such a loser" rather than "That was a bad mistake." "He's horrible" rather than "That was mean." "The world is unfair" rather than "That's not right!"
Personalisation and blame	A tendency to personalise and blame rather than consider the different factors in a situation. Like many of these thinking errors, personalisation and blame can be directed towards the self or towards others.	"I'm such a bad player, that's why we lost the match." "He's so unreasonable, that's why we had that argument."

All these thinking styles can be present in the sadness trap, and, while adolescents and young adults might engage in eight or nine of these different styles, it is unhelpful to go through this many. A maximum of three of four usually serves to help them begin the process of thinking about their thinking and questioning the validity of their thoughts. Some of the easiest for this purpose are 'should, musts, and oughts'', because there are characteristic words that they can practise noticing, and 'labelling', as there may be particular words that they use to label themselves.

This process of highlighting that thoughts and feelings are not facts but are subject to interpretation and bias is central to using the cognitive methods outlined here. This ability to decentre is essentially a meta-cognitive ability, the ability to think about thinking, and this ability develops during the course of adolescence (see formal operational thought, Chapter 2). Without the ability to stand back and to take the position that thoughts are thoughts and not facts, cognitive work as outlined here, will not be possible. When working with adolescents and young adults it is important to assess the degree to which they have this ability and also to spend some time supporting their learning in this area.

Where the individual finds it difficult to think about their thinking, simpler methods of cognitive intervention are available, such as positive self-talk (see later in this chapter).

Testing the thought: finding evidence

The three-column thought record has helped adolescents and young adults identify particular problematic situations, and the thoughts associated with these situations. These thoughts, however, might not be entirely correct, and given that they are associated with powerful emotions, it might be worth spending some time evaluating these thoughts in a more rational way.

This is quite a time-consuming process and also often fairly emotional. As a result, we need to ensure that the thought chosen for this process is important and emotionally salient. Padesky uses the concept of a 'hot thought' to help with this, the 'hot thought' being that associated with the highest level of emotion, in this case sadness (Greenberger and Padesky, 1995). It is also worth making sure that the thought is expressed properly and that, given its association with high levels of emotion, is expressed strongly enough. As we covered in the fear chapter, thoughts and appraisals that are emotionally salient tend to be simply expressed and extreme. Identifying extreme thoughts at this point also makes the rest of the process easier and more likely to be successful. In the example outlined above, the individual might identify a thought on his thought record of "I'm not very important." This thought is more palatable to write than "I'm worthless" but it may well be something along these latter lines that drives the emotion, and so this is the thought to test. A simple line of questioning such as "Is that strong enough?" or even suggesting more extreme versions of the thought, can help adolescents and young adults identify the best thought to test.

The five-column thought record is designed to help with the process of finding evidence. The two additional columns are the evidence in support of the thought, and the evidence against the thought. The idea is to try to be as impartial as possible, and to stand back from the thought in much the same way as a scientist might, to evaluate its accuracy. Again, this requires a certain level of meta-cognition and without it the task simply does not work.

Given that the thought has been identified and given the thought biases outlined above and in the context of the sadness trap, it is far easier to complete the fourth column (evidence in support of the thought) than the fifth (evidence against the thought). The clinician's task, is to support the latter process and have some ideas ready and in store for the unwelcome situation in which the adolescent or young adult cannot come up with anything to put in the fifth column. Of course, where there are supportive family members or friends about, they can be asked to support this process of finding evidence against the thought (but not for it!).

The whole point of the thought record is to challenge the appraisal that the adolescent or young adult has of the situation that they have identified. As a result, we should only embark on this process if we are fairly sure that their perception is biased and that we are able to articulate why, with examples. Given that our task is then to adjust a bias and increase the level of attentional focus on the evidence against the thought, we can use some simple supplementary techniques to support this process. Firstly, for the evidence in support of the thought we can just write down what we are told and even slow and stem the flow if there is too much. For the evidence against, we can ask for lots of detail, including clarification, imagery, examples, and others' responses. Secondly, the thought record, at least in paper form, is a visual object, and so visual techniques can also support the process. If we can balance the amount of visual content in both columns, or perhaps even make the column containing evidence against longer, this can produce a powerful visual effect. This is fairly easy to do by adjusting the level of detail provided for each item in the column (more detail for the evidence against) or using different colours to make the evidence against stand out.

Re-appraising

The fourth and final process is to identify a more balanced thought or an alternative thought that takes account of both columns of evidence. This classic CBT intervention is not about 'changing positives into negatives' or 'positive thinking' as many lay descriptions of CBT have it, but about correcting negative thought biases and rebalancing irrational processes of thought. In the sadness trap, there are clear thought biases that can be corrected through this process. In the problem-saturated negative world of an adolescent or young adult stuck in the sadness trap, these alternative thoughts are very important, representing something more balanced, more positive, and more hopeful. As a result, we can again push to make these as positive or hopeful as possible. These alternative thoughts can then represent building blocks and pillars of something more positive and hopeful that can be developed over time. This is the sixth column.

If we can foster an attentional focus on the evidence against the thought and on the more balanced thought this can often impact on the other elements in the sadness trap and produce a change in overall emotional experience. It is good to recognise this by re-rating the emotion in the seventh and final column of the thought record. If the initial emotion was sadness, it is important to re-rate this, but also to ask whether there is perhaps any other emotion present, relief, happiness, or contentment perhaps. As we note in the continuum section (see next section), the presence of an emotion that is positively experienced, is more powerful than a reduction in a negatively experienced emotion. This final column demonstrates to the adolescent or young adult the power of the cognitive appraisal or thought in the experience of emotion.

This process can be built up over time, and adolescents and young adults can be encouraged to practise this so that they can complete the entire 7 column thought record (example in Table 7.3) by themselves, to support the process of catching thoughts, challenging them, and adjusting them. Given the work required of the clinician, in supporting with reducing the biases and holding the alternative view, it is worth noting that many adolescents and young adults will not be able to go off with a thought record and complete it alone until they have made a fair degree of progress in therapy. Families and the wider network may be able to support this process.

Example

An example of a full seven-column thought record is outlined in Table 7.3. In this example, an adolescent is asked to recall a time when they felt worthless. The example they chose was when a friend was really nasty to them at school. Firstly, we identified the situation, then the feelings. In this case there are a variety of feelings, but, given that the main issue is that they are stuck in the sadness trap, we are looking to focus on the sadness about this situation. In this case too, anger and shock might be associated with less problematic outcomes. We outline the thoughts next. Again, we pay particular attention to thoughts that are consistent with the sadness. We can ask for thoughts that are related to sadness, we can also remind them that this was a situation in which they said that they felt worthless. This part of the thought record is fairly quick. The next part is to identify the 'hot thought', the thought that is most closely linked to sadness, which, in this case, is "I'm worthless." The hot thought is likely, as in this case, to be generalised and extreme. Once identified, we ask them to rate their degree of conviction in the thought, on a 0–100% scale.

Next, we are looking for evidence that supports this hot thought. Given the biases present this is fairly easy to identify and we look for highlights and to move through this column quickly. Next, we move to the evidence against. This is trickier and we need to have kept our attention out for examples that we can use to prompt here. In this case, which is focused on the behaviour of one individual, it is fairly easy to move to others, and ask questions such as "Did anybody else react in a different way?," "Does anybody treat you as if this wasn't the case?." Here, we can move through other people at school and then also consider family and perhaps friends outside school.

Having completed the first five columns, it is time for a summary and to go through what we have found so far, ensuring that we give most weight to the evidence against. Then we can ask for an alternative thought. It is important to push for as positive a thought as possible. Our example might go something like this:

Young person:	"Maybe I'm not worthless."
Clinician:	"What are you if you're not worthless?" *[powerful question to invite a movement into the positive]*
Young person:	"I don't know."
Clinician:	"OK, so are you worthwhile, valuable, important, good?" *[provide lots of examples, all positive value judgements of the self]*
Young person:	"I'm important to others."
Clinician:	"Great, let's write that down."

Then we want to rate their belief in this alternative thought, then re-rate the initial thought, and then re-rate the feelings.

Table 7.3 Example seven-column thought record

Situation	Feelings	Thoughts	Evidence for	Evidence against	Alternative thought	Re-rate feelings
Friend at school was really nasty to me	Angry **Sad** Shocked	It's not fair! Why did he do that? What did I do? I must have done something wrong **I'm worthless – 70%**	He said I was worthless He treated me badly I didn't have any other friends	A lot of people wanted to help People didn't like to see me upset Other people said that they wanted to be my friend	**I'm important to others – 80%** (I'm worthless – 10%)	Happy

There is a power in writing all of this down and it can be important to invite adolescents and young adults to capture it and hang on to it somehow. They might want a copy of the whole thought record, on other occasions they might take a photo on their phone. Sometimes, it can be best to simply have them write down their alternative thought and take that away.

Briefer thought records

Sometimes, a seven-column thought record can seem too much like a school homework task to be likely to help, and so it can make sense to shorten the process. A good option here is a three-step, or three-column process, beginning with noticing the thought most associated with the emotion, then labelling the cognitive bias, and then coming up with a less biased and more rational thought (Burns, 1999). This process often works better with younger adolescents and also where the adolescent or young adult relates particularly well to the idea that they have biases in their thinking.

Positive self-talk

As noted above, the process of thought challenging can be complex and requires a level of abstraction in terms of thinking ability. For some adolescents and young adults this ability may not yet be present or may need some work to develop. The important part of the process, however, is the arrival at a new appraisal at the end and sometimes it is possible to skip the middle process entirely and simply ask what the adolescent or young adult might like to hear or to say to themselves instead of the negative thoughts inherent in the sadness trap. If they can come up with statements that are both positive and that they think they will believe, then this can be a powerful intervention in itself. It is important that these statements are simple and therefore accessible at times of emotional arousal.

Cognitive intervention: continuum work

Continuums are designed to facilitate work with core beliefs about the self, the world and other people, as opposed to thought records, which tend to be used more in here-and-now situations.

Core beliefs, as outlined in Chapter 3, are relatively brief simple statements about the self, the world/others, and the future. They are informed by and derived from the early experience of the individual and inform the ways in which individuals interact and function in the world. Many core beliefs are helpful and functional, but some tend to cause difficulties and problems. It is these latter ones that we might choose to investigate, explore, and challenge. The theory (see Chapter 3) is that core beliefs have developed in a context and for a reason, but that they might no longer fit with the current environment or situation and so it might be worth questioning them.

The approach as outlined by Padesky (1994) fits very nicely with the ethos of this book. She argues that increasing the degree of conviction in a positive belief about the self is more likely to produce a shift than a decrease in the degree of conviction in a negative belief. For example, holding the belief "I am valuable" with 20% rather than 5% conviction, is likely to have a greater impact than holding the belief "I am worthless" 60% instead of 80%. The secondary impact of focusing on the positive or adaptive belief is that the whole focus of the work moves towards the adaptive and more positive. The method is outlined by Padesky in her 1994 paper, but essentially the process is as follows:

Identifying core beliefs

Core beliefs, as outlined in Chapter 3 represent beliefs about the self, the world/ other people, and the future. They tend to be fairly simple global statements and it often takes work to move through from a statement about a specific situation towards a core belief that is generalised and global. The technique most commonly used is down as the downward or vertical arrow technique (Burns, 1999) and essentially consists of asking repeated questions to take the conversation to a deeper level. It is often characterised by the question "What would be so bad about that?" until a statement of core belief is reached. In reality, most adolescents and young adults find the same question repeated over and over frustrating and insulting! However, using rephrasing, summarising, and reflecting we can ask different questions that are designed to get beneath each different scenario.

The core belief to be evaluated needs to be the one with most emotional salience; it should be stated as an absolute and as extreme as possible. The conviction in terms of rating with regards this belief is then evaluated, usually on a percentage scale (Figure 7.3).

Identifying an alternative belief

At this point, the work shifts away from the negative and towards a more aspirational, hopeful position in which a preferred belief becomes the focus of the work.

The first task is to support adolescents and young adults to identify an alternative or preferred belief. The simplest way to do this is to ask, "If you weren't . . ., how would you like to be?," or "If others weren't . . . how would you like them to be?" The alternative belief needs to be stated as an absolute and in simple terms. Often, adolescents and young adults will come up with a double negative, for example "Not worthless," and we need to keep questioning until we have something more positive: "What would you be if you were not worthless? The core belief and its alternative need not be opposites, but they do need to be incompatible. For example: "I'm valuable" is incompatible with "I'm worthless', but "I'm helpful," while positive, need not necessarily be. Having identified the alternative belief, the next step is to rate the degree of belief in this alternative on a 0–100% scale. A zero rating of conviction might indicate that the bar has been set too high and a shift might be difficult, so we can alter the belief a little to get some belief: "I'm confident" might become "I can be confident."

Using continuums

The work is then to investigate and explore this alternative belief and to increase their rating in terms of this belief through the use of the continuum method.

Continuums are lines upon which single constructs can be rated. It is important that each line only represents a single construct, as clinicians often use bipolar continuums with, for example, worthless at one end, and worthwhile at the other. The point at which an individual ceases to become one and becomes the other is therefore ambiguous, and there is a negative focus throughout. It is much better to work with a continuum of worthwhile 0% to worthwhile 100% (Padesky, 1994).

The first continuum is the alternative belief. This is rated on a 0–100% scale at the top of the page. The individual is invited to rate themselves on this scale at the beginning of the process. In Figure 7.3, the alternative belief is "I'm valuable," which is placed at the top of the page, with the initial rating.

The next step is to explore the components of the quality defined by the alternative belief. For example, "What are the different components of value?," "How would we know that somebody was valued or valuable?," "What kinds of qualities would a valuable person have?," or "What properties would make the world a predictable or understandable place?" Once we have a number of different components of the overall belief, these can be drawn as continuums underneath the main one at the top. In our example in Figure 7.3, we have five sub-dimensions.

The task is now to work with the adolescent to rate various different people on the continuums below and then to amalgamate these ratings into an overall score at the top. It is important to make sure that we use the whole of the continuum and so picking extreme examples is important and often a good place to start: "Who can you think of who is the most worthwhile?," "Who can you think of who is the least worthwhile?" Examples such as Dali Lama and Hitler often come up to illustrate the extremities of the continuum. We can continue this process using family members, friends, and others.

Finally, we ask the individual to rate themselves on each of the sub-categories and then on the top category. If we have done it properly, we should see that the individual will have to shift their belief rating upwards as a result of the markers that we have placed through this exercise. This is what has happened in the example in Figure 7.3.

Like with thought records, it is then important to return to the initial belief and to the emotional ratings to establish that thinking differently has a direct impact

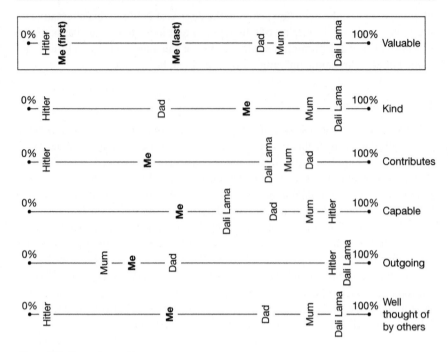

Figure 7.3 Example continuum

on emotion. Reminding the adolescent or young adult to connect with the positive alternative belief, and asking them to write it down, or put it on their phone, can be an important task in between sessions.

Moving into behavioural intervention

Continuums are not just cognitive interventions. The work can move straight into behavioural processes with the alternative ways that the adolescent or young adult would prefer to see themselves, others, or the world. The processes of behavioural activation can be used to support and problem-solve activities that are likely to lead to an increase in the conviction in this belief. In our example, the initial core belief was "I'm worthless" and the alternative was "I'm valuable." Behaviours and interactions with the environment can be targeted towards increasing the degree to which they perceive themselves as valuable by looking at the dimensions on continuums that they would like to develop. In our example (Figure 7.3), this might involve contributing more, building capability, and increasing confidence around others. In this way, behavioural work can arise out of the continuums, and it already has a foundation in a positive view of the self, others, or the world.

Summary of breaking the sadness trap

We have covered two types of intervention: behavioural and cognitive work. As we outlined in Chapter 4, all interventions in CBT are driven by either cognitive challenge or behaviour change and interventions recommended for the sadness trap are no different. Of course, it is difficult to truly separate the two interventions and they do tend to converge as they are tied together so tightly in the trap. If we begin with behavioural activation we end up challenging thoughts and beliefs through behavioural change, if we begin with cognitive challenge the next step is to behaviourally try out the ideas otherwise they will never be properly accepted.

Evidence base

The evidence base for CBT for adults meeting criteria for depression demonstrates efficacy for a variety of different interventions, including CBT, with little evidence of differential efficacy of these interventions (Barth et al., 2013). Thus, CBT appears as effective as Behavioural Activation and Interpersonal Psychotherapy (IPT) with adults, although there are differences in the robustness of these findings as a result of the quantity of evidence upon which the conclusions are based; CBT and IPT having more evidence. A recent trial directly comparing Behavioural Activation and CBT found no difference in outcomes between the groups (Richards et al., 2017).

The evidence for CBT interventions for young people meeting criteria for depression is less strong than for adults; indeed, one meta-analyses found that CBT was more effective than placebo interventions at the end of treatment, but not at follow-up (Weisz, McCarthy, and Valeri, 2006). With larger sample sizes (as a result of studies completed after 2006), later meta-analysis found evidence in support of CBT and IPT, the latter the only efficacious treatment when compared to control conditions at long-term follow-up (Zhou et al., 2015). The majority of CBT studies included in this meta-analysis included both cognitive and behavioural interventions.

Given indications that IPT is as effective, perhaps more effective than CBT for both adolescents and adults, it is worth briefly explaining the model. IPT begins with the premise that depression is a treatable medical condition, it then goes on to state that:

- social support protects against psychopathology;
- whatever the cause of the issue, it occurs within an interpersonal context and usually involves a disruption to the relationships around the individual;
- that interpersonal life events such as death, conflict, life disruptions, and isolation are also significant risk factors for depression;
- it is useful to work on change in social functioning in the 'here and now' to improve functioning. (Markowitz and Weissman, 2012).

As a result, IPT focuses on helping individuals to link their emotions to the circumstances of their lives, to name their feelings, understand them as social cues, and learning to express them in order to improve their interpersonal relationships.

It is this evidence that informs the treatment recommendations in this chapter. There is a focus on using both cognitive and behavioural interventions in the context of the sadness trap, consistent with the evidence outlined above. There is also a focus on the environment of the young person, and supporting the process of bringing about change to the interpersonal context as a part of the process of behavioural activation, which links to the evidence in support of IPT.

References

Bard, K., 2000. Crying in infant primates: insights into the development of crying in chimpanzees. In R.G. Barr, B. Hopkins, and J.A. Green (eds) *Crying as a sign, a symptom and a signal: developmental and clinical aspects of early crying behavior.* London: MacKeith Press, pp. 157–175.

Barth, J., Munder, T., Gerger, H., Nüesch, E., Trelle, S., Znoj, H., Jüni, P., and Cuijpers, P., 2013. Comparative efficacy of seven psychotherapeutic interventions for patients with depression: a network meta-analysis. *PLoS Med, 10*(5), p.e1001454.

Beck, A. T. (ed.), 1979. *Cognitive therapy of depression.* Chichester, UK: Guilford Press.

Bertha, E.A. and Balázs, J., 2013. Subthreshold depression in adolescence: a systematic review. *European Child & Adolescent Psychiatry, 22*(10), pp. 589–603.

Burns, D., M.D., 1999. *The feeling good handbook* (Revised edition). New York: Penguin.

Darwin, C., 1965. *The expression of the emotions in man and animals* (Vol. 526). Chicago, IL: University of Chicago Press.

Frude, N., 2014. Positive therapy. In R. Nelson-Jones (ed.) *Theory and practice of counselling and therapy.* London: Sage, pp. 69–93.

Greenberger, D. and Padesky, C. A., 1995. *Mind over mood.* New York: Guilford.

Hass N.C., Weston T.D., and Lim S-L., 2016. Be happy not sad for your youth: the effect of emotional expression on age perception. *PLoS ONE 11*(3): e0152093.

Horwitz, A.V. and Wakefield, J.C., 2007. *The loss of sadness.* New York: Oxford.

Isbell, L.M., Lair, E.C., and Rovenpor, D.R., 2013. Affect-as-information about processing styles: a cognitive malleability approach. *Social and Personality Psychology Compass, 7*(2), pp. 93–114.

Izard, C.E., 1991. *The psychology of emotions.* New York: Plenum Press.

Jacobson, N.S., Martell, C.R., and Dimidjian, S., 2001. Behavioral activation treatment for depression: returning to contextual roots. *Clinical Psychology: Science and Practice, 8*(3), pp. 255–270.

Kavanagh, D.J. and Bower, G.H., 1985. Mood and self-efficacy: impact of joy and sadness on perceived capabilities. *Cognitive Therapy and Research, 9*(5), pp. 507–525.

Markowitz, J.C. and Weissman, M.M., 2012. Interpersonal psychotherapy: past, present and future. *Clinical Psychology & Psychotherapy, 19*(2), pp. 99–105.

Nolen-Hoeksema, S. S.A., Roberts, J.E., and Gotlib, I.H., 1998. Neuroticism and ruminative response style as predictors of change in depressive symptomatology. *Cognitive Therapy and Research*, 22, pp. 445–455.

Padesky, C.A., 1994. Schema change processes in cognitive therapy. *Clinical Psychology & Psychotherapy*, 1(5), pp. 267–278.

Padesky, C.A. and Mooney, K.A., 1990. Clinical tip: presenting the cognitive model to clients. *International Cognitive Therapy Newsletter*, 6(1), pp. 13–14.

Richards, D.A., Rhodes, S., Ekers, D., McMillan, D., Taylor, R.S., Byford, S., Barrett, B., Finning, K., Ganguli, P., Warren, F., and Farrand, P., 2017. Cost and Outcome of Behavioural Activation (COBRA): a randomised controlled trial of behavioural activation versus cognitive-behavioural therapy for depression. *Health Technology Assessment*, 21(46), pp. 1–366.

Safran, J.D. and Segal, Z.V., 1990. *Cognitive therapy: an interpersonal process perspective*. New York: Basic.

Scherer, K. R. and Wallbott, H. G., 1994. Evidence for universality and cultural variation of differential emotion response patterning. *Journal of Personality and Social Psychology*, 66(2), pp. 310–328.

Scowcroft, E., 2016. *Suicide Statistics Report 2016: including data for 2012–2014*. UK: Samaritans.

Seidel, E.-M., Habel, U., Kirschner, M., Gur, R. C., and Derntl, B., 2010. The impact of facial emotional expressions on behavioral tendencies in females and males. *Journal of Experimental Psychology. Human Perception and Performance*, 36(2), pp. 500–507.

Stein, N.L. and Levine, L.J., 1990. Making sense out of emotion: the representation and use of goal-structured knowledge. *Psychological and Biological Approaches to Emotion*, pp. 45–73.

Vingerhoets, A., 2013. *Why only humans weep: unravelling the mysteries of tears*. Oxford: Oxford University Press.

Weisz, J.R., McCarty, C.A., and Valeri, S.M., 2006. Effects of psychotherapy for depression in children and adolescents: a meta-analysis. *Psychological Bulletin*, 132(1), pp. 132–149.

Zhou, X., Hetrick, S.E., Cuijpers, P., Qin, B., Barth, J., Whittington, C.J., Cohen, D., Del Giovane, C., Liu, Y., Michael, K.D., and Zhang, Y., 2015. Comparative efficacy and acceptability of psychotherapies for depression in children and adolescents: a systematic review and network meta-analysis. *World Psychiatry*, 14(2), pp. 207–222.

Chapter 8

Anger

I was dubious I'd be able to make myself angry in session and it was a scary thing to do. It felt dramatic, but it did work to demonstrate to me that I could actually control myself.

(21-year-old male)

Anger is an emotion that is experienced fairly frequently and, while it can last for hours or days, it also often dissipates quickly. It has a similar impact on the body to fear, but is experienced as hot and intense rather than cold. Anger tends to be readily expressed and tends to be expressed outward.

Interestingly, there are few psychiatric diagnoses that link directly to anger. Indeed, many young people frequently request help with anger, to have reflected back that they are 'depressed'. This is deeply frustrating and invalidating and tends to feed problems with anger. At other times, clinicians might be heard to say that anger is 'not a mental health problem', that problems are 'behavioural' or that anger is 'comorbid'. Consistent with this are findings that the majority of people experiencing difficulties with anger have never received interventions targeting their anger (Kessler et al., 2006).

Rapidly increasing rates of diagnosis of ADHD and bipolar disorder (e.g. Moreno et al., 2007; Visser et al., 2014) are potentially due to adolescents and young adults presenting with difficulties with anger. Revised editions of diagnostic manuals are starting to include more specific diagnoses relating to anger; for example, the category of 'Disruptive, Impulse-Control, and Conduct Disorders' in the DSM-V now includes eight separate diagnoses (APA, 2013). Children are given diagnoses such as Conduct Disorder, or Oppositional Defiance Disorder (APA, 2013).

Society tends to have beliefs about anger that perhaps link with this reluctance to include anger in manuals of illness. Anger is often labelled as 'toxic' and 'harmful' and many social scientists have come to view anger as more of a liability than an asset (Izard, 1991). Many authors also appear to conflate aggression and anger, writing as though anger is responsible for the violence in the world and it would be best to get rid of it (e.g. Tucker-Ladd, 1996).

Despite an apparent reluctance to classify anger as a disorder, adolescents and young adults frequently present with anger difficulties (Armbruster et al., 2004). Clinicians also report frequently working with anger difficulties but report less confidence and competence in this work, when compared to fear-based difficulties (Lachmund, DiGiuseppe, and Fuller, 2005).

In the first part of this chapter, we will explore what causes anger, what it is, and what purpose it might serve. In the second section, we go on to the anger trap, which illustrates what happens when adolescents and young adults have difficulties with anger. We then look at the cognitive-behavioural interventions that help move out of the anger trap.

What causes anger?

Anger, in its simplest definition, is a response to threat. Sometimes threat invokes fear, sometimes anger, and sometimes both. Some kinds of threat, however, are more likely to result in anger.

The experience of physical discomfort has been shown to produce anger, even in the absence of other factors (Berkowitz, 1990). This physical discomfort might be the result of pain caused by physical injury, of hunger, or fatigue. Physical discomfort represents a threat to the individual and the body, and a common emotional response is anger. This can be seen in anger directed towards chairs after stubbing toes, or the recently defined concept of 'hangry': the angry feeling that arises from hunger (e.g. MacCormack, 2016). It appears that a threat to the body in physical terms is sufficient, regardless of any cognitive process, to produce anger.

Despite the fact that anger can be produced by physical discomfort alone, it is usually caused by cognitive perceptions of interactions with others. A survey of college students found that the most commonly cited precursor to anger was a sense of being "misled, betrayed, used, disappointed, hurt by others, or treated unjustly" (Izard, 1991: p. 235). Anger has also been described as "developing in response to unwanted, and sometimes unexpected, aversive interpersonal behaviour" (Kassinove and Tafrate, 2002: p 31). Another study defined ten specific causes of anger, including 'self-opinionated people', 'being blamed', and 'being insulted' (Törestad 1990). This definition of anger as a response to the behaviour of others, is consistent with the definition of anger by many people as a response to injustice or wrongdoing.

In summary, the main cause of anger is interpersonal behaviour, i.e. an interpersonal threat. Even when anger arises as a result of life events, for example the loss of a job or physical injury following building collapse, the anger is usually personally attributed to a person or group of people (e.g. the management or the builders) (Kassinove and Tafrate, 2002). Where there is no clear person towards whom anger can be directed, objects are often personalised, for example cars, phones, and video-game consoles.

What is anger?

In Chapter 5 we outlined the five different elements of the emotional experience. We now consider each of these elements in relation to anger. When going through this with adolescents and young adults, it is important to allow space for them to explore these ideas and to spend some time considering anger as an emotion that is often helpful, rather than always harmful.

Feelings

Anger is a relatively frequently experienced emotion. It can last for periods of hours or days, but can also dissipate fairly quickly. It tends to be experienced for longer than fear, but not for as long as sadness or joy. Anger is experienced as hot and intense (Scherer and Wallbott, 1994) and is aversive; the majority of individuals report disliking the feeling of anger (Harmon-Jones, 2004).

Like all emotions, anger can be experienced to different degrees and it is often helpful to encourage adolescents and young adults to notice these variations in intensity. An anger scale, beginning with the least intense, might include words such as: calm, relaxed, tetchy, annoyed, irritated, frustrated, cross, angry, outraged, furious, irate, livid, crazed, 'losing the plot', and 'in a red mist'.

Anger is commonly experienced as an expressive emotion – the urge to express it outwardly is high, and it feels under relatively little control. Indeed, adolescents and young adults especially, often report the sense that anger comes out of nowhere, with no apparent cause, and takes them immediately into a state in which they have relatively little control and sometimes no recollection. It is interesting to note in this list of anger words above that, as the intensity of anger increases, there is an increasing tendency to use labels and terms that imply madness or loss of control. We return to this idea when we think about the function of anger.

Physiology

Anger has a dramatic impact on the body. The characteristics of this impact are very similar to those seen in fear and it is the same sympathetic nervous system that is activated in anger. This is the accelerator pedal system, which gears the body up for action. As we saw in relation to fear, the neurotransmitters epinephrine (or adrenalin) and cortisol result in an increased heart rate and breathing, increasingly dilated pupils, increased muscle tension, an attentional focus on threat, and suppression of other activities, such as digestion and the immune system.

These processes serve to prepare the body for quick, physical activity: muscles are tense and receiving maximum blood flow and energy, the mind is alert and focused on potential threat. While the physiological processes underlying the experience of both anger and fear are similar, the felt sense is almost opposite: anger feels hot, whereas fear feels cold.

Facial expression

Anger is an emotion that tends to be outwardly expressed and is often immediately recognisable on the face.

One of the most dominant facial features of anger is the lowering of the eyebrows and hence a wrinkling of the forehead to produce the characteristic frown. The lowered brows make the eyes appear narrow and more penetrating and the eyes tend to focus hard on the object of the anger. This provides a strong communication as to the cause of the anger. The supposed innate expression of anger reveals the teeth through a hard, angular mouth. Modifications to this expression in which the mouth is tightly shut almost as a signal of restrained anger are thought to be learnt alterations of the innate signal (Izard, 1991).

Appraisals/thoughts

Anger is an emotion that is associated with a great deal of thought; thoughts tend to cluster around two areas.

One area is the cause of the anger: thoughts around the grievance. These thoughts are past-focused and tend to be about what caused or triggered the anger.

The second area is around the desired behaviour as a result; thoughts about action. These thoughts are much more frequent; indeed, in a survey of college students, the majority of thoughts following the incident prompting anger were of revenge, attacking others, and destruction (Izard, 1991). Sometimes these thoughts can develop into fantasies of action and individuals might imagine screaming at people or being aggressive towards others. Sometimes they might even indulge in violent or murderous fantasies. We will say more about this in the behaviour section.

In anger, it can be extremely difficult to direct the attention away from the perceived threat and to attend to other things. Indeed, with increasing intensity of anger, the ability to think rationally decreases and very angry people are often highly irrational and impulsive. This increasing irrationality and a decreased control over the self is encapsulated by the description of the red mist or the expression 'losing it'. The process of dwelling on the anger and ruminating on its cause can lead to an escalation in the intensity of anger and decreasing abilities to manage the emotion.

Behaviours

Anger is an emotion that tends to be outwardly expressed; it is an externalising emotion. The main behavioural impulses associated with anger are therefore approach behaviours. The facial expression signals this sense of approach – the gaze is directed towards others, and often the whole body will move forwards towards the object of anger. Approach behaviours can vary in intensity from a hardening of the body and the words through to extreme aggression and violence.

As outlined above, it is important to note that aggression and anger are not inter-changeable concepts. While aggressive behaviour can sometimes be a component of the emotional experience of anger, anger can be experienced without aggression, and aggression can be displayed in the absence of anger.

Many approach behaviours in anger are expressed and delivered within the face, through gaze, an increase in the volume of the voice, and an increase in the stress given to speech. More intensive verbal approach behaviours might include shouting and screaming, as well as changes to vocabulary (swearing and cursing). Interestingly, the majority of profanities tend to be short and contain hard con-sonants and therefore lend themselves to being delivered in anger. At the more intense end of this spectrum, behaviours might be interpreted by others as verbal aggression.

Other forms of approach behaviours include physical approach behaviours, which vary in intensity. At the more subtle end there might be a hardening, pulling up, and widening of the body. There is often a clenching of the fists and sometimes more volume to the breath. Physical behaviours include banging objects, slamming doors, and throwing things (many mobile phones have gone this way!). At the most intense end, physical approach behaviours are directed towards the object of anger and include punching, kicking, hitting, throwing things, and all-out physical violence. Spitting, and in other cultures throwing particular objects such as shoes, can combine this aggression of anger with a sense of disgust to display contempt.

Many of these behaviours might be outwardly expressed, but commonly they will also develop into fantasies of action. Individuals might spend time thinking and imagining what they might do to others and how they might put them in their place, perhaps verbally having a show down or playing out aggressive behaviour in their minds.

What is the function of anger?

Anger is, like fear, designed to protect. It is the other half of the flight response; the response to fight. Thus, anger is one of the main two alternative responses to threat.

Anger can be caused by physical discomfort but is more often caused by a sense of being mistreated, undermined, betrayed, used, disappointed, or hurt by others. In this context, the threat is interpersonal: another person is threatening to have some sort of negative impact on the individual. The resulting feeling of anger is intense, hot, and energising; the body is geared up and there is a tendency to approach others. The hotter and more intense the anger becomes, the more difficult it is to control and the more impulsive individuals are likely to become.

The result is that anger protects individuals from the threat posed by others by gearing up the individual to counter the initial threat. That is, anger functions to enable the individual to threaten those who pose a threat. In order to represent a threat to others, the body appears bigger and stronger, the eyes appear more menacing, the voice sounds more assertive, and the individual has a tendency to approach, often with more confidence and energy than would ordinarily be the case.

Anger between two people, in this context, often leads to an escalation in threat until the point at which one party has managed to intimidate the other into feeling fear, at which point the other retreats (flight). This is a similar process to that seen in other mammals where, for example, two dominant males will size each other up for a time before deciding whether to engage in battle. During this time, they vocalise their dominance and parade their physical prowess, the aim being to intimidate the other party into backing down so that the individual can have the territory or the mate.

Anger, then, serves to protect individuals from threats, predominantly from interpersonal threats. It serves to gear up the individual to present a counter-threat and to enable the individual to protect themselves. The result might be that the individual gets their own way, that they gain materially, or that they gain power, autonomy, or respect. In this way, anger can be seen as a negotiating tool; it functions to support individuals to look after their interests.

It is interesting, in this context, to think again about the impulsiveness often associated with anger. With increased intensity, there is increased irrationality evident in some of the words used to describe anger, for example 'mad', or 'losing it'. With increased irrationality comes increased unpredictability, and unpredictability in a hostile other is threatening. This means that, as anger intensifies, the individual displaying the anger becomes more and more unpredictable and hence more threatening to those around them, which, in that moment at least, means that they are more likely to win the argument, battle, or stand-off. In this context, even the irrationality and impulsivity of anger can be understood within its function. This is important when discussing anger with adolescents, young adults and their families, as it holds the position that irrationality and unreasonableness is the default state in anger; it takes work and effort to modify.

Anger, then, functions as a negotiating tool and, through gearing up the body to impose a potential threat to others, makes it more likely that the individual will get what they want. While the threat of physical violence in today's society is lesser than it might have been in the past, expressing discontent, indignation, or anger (e.g. through tone of voice, body posture, or verbal threats to make complaints) remains a powerful way in which individuals manage to prioritise themselves over others.

While anger is predominantly an interpersonal emotion, anger is often directed towards inanimate objects. At these times, however, the object is usually per-sonalised during the course of anger. A particular modern example of this is the computer or console, and adolescents and young adults often become angry and smash these things up as if damaging them will somehow bring about positive change.

So far, we have looked at anger at the individual level, but like other emotions, anger also functions to aid social cohesion. A frequently cited cause of anger is injustice and unfairness. Many of the social norms and cultural practices to which members of groups subscribe provide a benefit to the society, but are, at times at least, a burden to the individual. Queuing in the UK, for example, is almost a national pastime, and it would be much better for each individual to go straight to the front of the queue and not to bother with the whole process. However, the threat of anger on the part of others is one of the powerful factors that maintains the behaviour. This is true of many social and cultural norms and this threat of the discontent of others leads to a system which tends more towards fairness and equality than it might do otherwise.

In summary, far from the popular conceptualisation of anger as 'toxic' and best avoided, anger has various important functions at both the individual and the societal level. Indeed, the majority of people, when questioned, report positive interpersonal outcomes from their anger episodes, including greater levels of respect, understanding, and closeness (Kassinove et al., 1997).

Adolescent development and anger

Adolescence is the second period of life that is stereotypically characterised by anger. The first is the 'terrible twos' which is typically the first age at which children experience the thwarting of their desires and wishes by their parents. Adolescence is supposedly the period in which there is conflict and disruption. However, as reviewed in Chapter 2, there is little evidence to support the notion that adolescence is inevitably a time of conflict and strife.

While not all adolescents are invariably angry, problems with anger are significant in adolescence. During the phase in which adolescents are establishing their identities, turning their attentions outside families and towards peers, and facing changes in relationships and allegiance, interpersonal conflict is particularly likely. In addition, difficulties with anger are likely to be viewed in a negative light by peers. Adolescents, young adults, and their families may also start to worry about physical development and resulting increasing strength in light of difficulties with anger problems.

All of this, combined with society's views about anger, as bad, toxic, and dangerous, and a resulting absence of the availability of help and information about anger when compared to other emotions, can isolate adolescents and young adults who struggle with anger.

Anger trap

We have looked at what anger is and what it is for; we know that it is a useful emotion directed towards survival and protecting interests. However, there are times when adolescents and young adults find themselves stuck in intense circular experiences of anger that have a negative impact on those around them and negative consequences for them as individuals. In these cases, the anger trap can illustrate these circular processes and help adolescents and young adults, and their families, think about what might be the best way forward.

The anger trap is a psychological formulation, based on cognitive behavioural therapy, but also informed by more relational models, such as cognitive analytic therapy. Like the other traps in this book, the anger trap aims to illustrate the maintenance of anger as simply as possible. The trap is informed by the understanding of the emotion of anger outlined so far in this chapter. The model of the hand brain further highlights the mechanisms in operation.

The anger trap is illustrated in Figure 8.1. It is made up of two interlinking vicious cycles and the existence of each serves to prevent change in the other. The core of the two cycles is repeated experience of interpersonal conflict, appraisals characterised by an over-estimation of interpersonal threat, and resultant anger.

Interpersonal conflict

As we saw earlier in the chapter, anger is a negotiating tool and arises where there is interpersonal conflict; interpersonal conflict of any sort can be a trigger to the

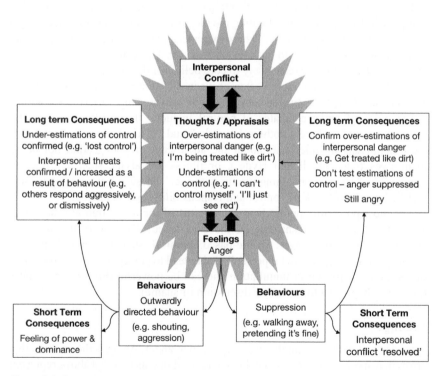

Figure 8.1 Anger trap

anger trap. Interpersonal conflict is most obvious where two people actively disagree about a particular situation. However, situations where there is not an agreed process or usual way forward also potentially represent interpersonal conflict. Examples commonly seen around the home are mealtimes, bedtimes, screen time, home times, and chores. In each of these situations there is the potential for disagreement about whose responsibility it is to do what and when. Examples seen in educational environments include attendance in lessons, arrangements for leaving the classroom, break and lunch times, and consequences (or lack of) for behaviour.

Given that adolescence and early adulthood is a time of rapid change and development, interpersonal conflict is also likely where the expectations of one party have failed to keep pace with the expectations of another. A common situation is where adolescents or young adults believe that they should have more autonomy than do their family or college.

Appraisals/thoughts

There are two groups of thoughts or appraisals that are core to the anger trap: the first are over-estimates of interpersonal threat; the second are under-estimates of control. Both groups tend to be extreme.

Examples of over-estimates of interpersonal threat include: "I am being completely dismissed," "He's treating me like dirt," "I am being humiliated," and "Nobody gives a crap about me." These extreme appraisals about the interpersonal situation are likely to lead to high levels of anger. These appraisals are situation specific, but are often linked closely to core beliefs or dysfunctional assumptions, meaning that similar appraisals often occur in different situations. For example, an appraisal about being treated badly might be activated in a variety of situations.

Examples of under-estimates of control include: "I can't control myself," "I just lash out," "There's nothing I can do," and "It just happens." Sometimes these appraisals include ideas about the adolescent or young adult not being themselves (e.g. 'Jekyll and Hyde'), or illness appraisals, such as "It's my bipolar," or "There's something wrong with me." These are extreme appraisals that fuel a sense of lack of control and responsibility over behaviour.

The most powerful appraisals in the context of the anger trap are those that arise out of a sense of shame, and the experience of shame in interpersonal situations often drives anger. Shame-based appraisals such as "I am worthless," "I am inferior," "I am an awful person" tend to lead to perceptions of interpersonal threat around rejection or humiliation and can be powerful drivers of the anger trap (see Chapter 10 for a further discussion of shame).

Feelings

Appraisals of interpersonal threat quickly lead to anger. Anger is the emotion that arises in response to interpersonal threat and the thoughts outlined above represent a clear perception of an interpersonal threat.

This feeling of anger is powerful and, like all the traps in this book, is central to the trap. Anger is experienced as aversive and so it makes sense that efforts will be made to relieve the feeling. It is these efforts that fuel and drive the anger trap.

Physiology

The physiology of anger is not included separately in the anger trap since it is rarely the cause of distress as it can be in other emotional difficulties. In addition, the trap is already fairly visually complex and so adding in further aspects makes it more difficult for adolescents and young adults to understand. However, the physiology of anger is important and can be included in the broader understanding of anger covered in this chapter so far. Indeed, this is important as some of the interventions outlined later in this chapter focus on the physiology of anger.

Behaviours

At this point in the anger trap, the two cycles diverge. Both are required in the anger trap and anybody stuck in the anger trap will go both ways around the trap, although they may well go around more in one direction than another. Importantly, both types of behaviour are consistent with the appraisal of an extreme inter-personal threat. One cycle is defined by outward expression and the other by suppression.

Outwardly directed behaviours

Outwardly directed behaviours are those that are invited by the experience of anger as outlined above and they are entirely consistent with the feeling, physio-logical response, thoughts, and facial expressions of anger. They are driven by the 'red mist' or the 'boiling blood' of anger. Outwardly directed behaviours are characterised by approach behaviours towards the threatening object. They include shouting, swearing, hitting, punching, and lashing out. For short, we can call these behaviours the 'explode' side of the trap.

As outlined above, these behaviours serve an important function; to represent a potential or actual threat to the object or person that has given rise to anger. These outwardly directed behaviours are potentially more likely where there are lots of appraisals that under-estimate the ability to control anger, for example where anger is believed to be out of the individual's control, or where it is attributed to an illness or deficit.

Sometimes the behaviours might not be overtly expressed, but scenarios in the mind, for example fantasies of screaming at others, verbally humiliating others, physically hurting others, or even torturing and murdering others. At times, the expression of these ideas by adolescents and young adults can lead to panic and fears about a potential criminal trajectory or even psychopathy. However, these ideas can usually be understood in the context of the anger trap and, in the absence of actual past behaviour along these lines, it is usually best to normalise these thoughts and fantasies in this context. Indeed, even where there are risks of actual violence, working with the individual using the anger trap may well be the best way to reduce them in the longer term.

Short term consequences of outwardly directed behaviours

In the short term, outwardly directed behaviour feels really good. It is entirely consistent with the behavioural urges and the feeling of anger, and gives a sense of confidence and authority that provides a welcome relief from the threatened feeling. This response also requires much less effort than the suppression and inhibition usually demanded by society.

In addition, feeling intensely powerful and confident is an almost opposite feeling to that which initially gave rise to the anger, which is usually feeling small and insignificant. For example, if an adolescent or young adult feels forgotten or belittled at a party and responds by jumping onto a table and unleashing a tirade of verbal abuse, suddenly everybody is looking at them and they have the attention and the command of the room. This can lead to feelings of dominance and power; perhaps even invincibility.

As with other traps, it is important to note the positive feelings elicited by this behaviour, as it validates the experience and validates the adolescent or young adult who engages in the behaviour.

Long term consequences of outwardly directed behaviours

Validation, however, is not the usual result of outwardly directed behaviours. Adolescents and young adults caught in the anger trap can experience a variety of responses to their outwardly directed behaviour.

Firstly, the outward expression of angry behaviours can result in a similar response from others, and situations can escalate in which people become angry together. This effectively creates an interpersonal environment characterised by threat that fuels the anger trap.

Secondly, adolescents and young adults might find that they are demeaned, criticised, humiliated, or shamed as a result of their behaviour. This might involve people laughing at their behaviour, or people focusing on their responses and using these to demean and shame them afterwards. Adolescents and young adults frequently feel incredibly remorseful and ashamed of themselves after this kind of behaviour, which can lead to the feelings of shame that then lead to an increased perception of interpersonal threat.

Alternatively, adolescents and young adults might find their behaviour being excused and minimised in light of 'their difficulties' or 'an illness'. This clearly fuels the under-estimation of ability to control anger, but also represents an interpersonal threat in that they are treated as lesser than others as a result of their angry behaviour.

Suppressive behaviours

The other route around the anger trap is via behaviours that are characterised by suppression. These behaviours are often encouraged by society and families and involve activities such as walking away or 'leaving it'. The behaviours involved here importantly involve an almost complete denial of the anger and a pretence that everything is OK; carrying on as normal. For short, we can call these behaviours 'bottling up'.

Short term consequences of suppressive behaviours

In the short term, suppressive behaviours are successful. They lead to the avoidance of conflict and the continuing of life without disruption. The conflict that led to the anger is ignored, the anger that arose is suppressed and pushed away and the interpersonal situation continues with little disruption.

Long term consequences of suppressive behaviours

In the longer term, however, these behaviours tend to be unsuccessful. This is because the adolescent or young adult has not responded to the interpersonal threat and has submitted to the other person without defence. This reinforces the sense of interpersonal threat – being devalued and not taken seriously. Over time this can effectively encourage this behaviour from those around them, with the result that people tend to take advantage or walk over them. This then leads to further experiences that fuel the anger trap.

In addition, suppression behaviours tend not to be sustainable and repeated suppression ('bottling up') is associated with explosion.

Summary of the anger trap

The anger trap begins with the experience of interpersonal conflict and highlights the over-estimation of interpersonal threat as a central component. It then moves through two vicious cycles of behavioural reinforcement ('bottle up or explode'), in which behaviours are reinforced in the short term, but in the longer term maintain the over-estimation of threat.

Anger trap and the hand brain

We saw in Chapter 6 that fear is a response that is located in the old part of the brain; the reptilian brain. Anger, as the other part of the fight or flight response can also be seen to be located within this primitive part of the brain.

As in the fear trap, this helps us to make clear the idea that anger is an emotion based on the over-estimation of threat and that the only way to work with anger is to experience the situations and to demonstrate to the reptilian brain that the threat is not as great as it believes it to be. This is important in the intervention section below.

Drawing the anger trap

Like all traps in this book, it is best to draw the anger trap from scratch on a blank piece of paper. This ensures that the different elements are properly understood, and helps adolescents and young adults feel that the model has been built up with them on the basis of their experience. Despite this, the basic principles and structure of the anger trap should be the same for each individual as it is based on the scientific understanding of human emotion outlined above. Importantly, both sides of the anger trap should always be included, as both will always be present – if adolescents and young adults just used one strategy they would have worked out that it did not work and changed it!

The anger trap illustrates the reasons for sustained anger difficulties so it needs to cover more than a single example. However, it is important to get examples of the kinds of situations and the kinds of appraisals and behaviours in which each individual engages.

The best way to start drawing the trap is to ask about some recent situations in which the adolescent or young adult got angry. Given that anger is an interpersonal emotion, it is important to focus on the interpersonal context, rather than just the geographical one. This means a detailed focus on the exact behaviour of the other people in the situation, including what was said, the way things were said, and how people responded. This can often be a difficult process, particularly where individuals have a great many appraisals about not being able to remember, or anger just springing out of the blue for no reason. In these situations, it can be worth involving the family or other individuals to try to get the detail that is required to understand what was happening. Where this is not possible, it is worth picking a different example, perhaps one where less intense anger was experienced so that the detail is more accessible.

Having spoken about the different examples we can spend some time thinking with the adolescent or young adult about what anger is and how it works. As outlined above, anger is often conceptualised by society as a 'bad emotion' and one that it would be best to be without. To think about it as usually helpful and having a function is unusual and takes some time to explore with adolescents and young adults. This process can also often be particularly helpful to do with families as it is often a new way for them to think about the emotion. The example here (Figure 8.2) is a common one in which an adolescent responds in a particularly angry way to a family argument.

Having identified an example situation, the next step is to identify the appraisals. We are looking specifically for over-estimations of threat and under-estimations of control. If an adolescent or young adult is experiencing difficulties with anger, we will definitely find examples of the first and more than likely

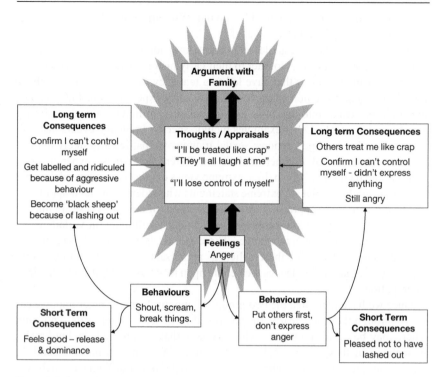

Figure 8.2 Example anger trap

the second as well. However, these appraisals may well be hidden beneath more salient thoughts about planned action (see thoughts section above).

Returning to the examples and the specific detail around the interpersonal situations can help us to think about what the appraisals might be. Keeping in mind that anger is a response to interpersonal threat can also help to guide the exploration towards these appraisals. As in the fear trap, it is important to ensure that the appraisals identified are extreme. They have to be extreme in order to maintain the anger trap – nobody responds by smashing up their room to a mild appraisal! Examples of extreme appraisals include: "They're going to humiliate me!," "They're treating me like dirt!," "Nobody gives a crap about me!," and "They have completely ignored me!"

Adolescents and young adults, as in the fear trap, will often be reluctant to speak of extremes for fear of seeming irrational, but this is precisely the point: appraisals in the anger trap are irrational and are driven by the reptilian and not the rational brain. This idea that we are expecting and looking for extreme kinds of thoughts and appraisals can help them to access these extreme appraisals. It is also important to note that these might be conscious thoughts, or they might be appraisals, a way of making sense of a situation that is not necessarily entirely conscious; these can be explained by saying "You are responding as if . . .," or "Your reptilian brain is behaving as if . . . ."

Another way of helping adolescents and young adults to identify the extreme nature of these appraisals is to refer to their early history. There are often extreme experiences in their pasts that have led to a tendency to over-estimate the threat posed by others. Common examples of these early experiences include ongoing experiences such as bullying in schools or colleges, or highly critical or abusive family environments. Other examples include specific traumatic events that give rise to these kinds of perceptions; sexual traumas are particularly likely to drive an over-estimation of interpersonal threat. Referring to these experiences as extreme and therefore likely to drive extreme views of others can allow adolescents and young adults to relate to extreme statements when identifying their appraisals.

The other group of appraisals are under-estimates of control. These are important to elicit, as many adolescents and young adults will deny, in various ways, that they have control over their anger. These appraisals might also be encouraged by wider family. Including these beliefs as appraisals in the anger trap helps the process of validation, but leaves the beliefs open to scrutiny in the context of later intervention.

Once we have identified the two groups of appraisals in the anger trap, we can move through the rest. Clearly, the emotional response is anger or its synonyms. There may be other emotions, such as sadness that we can include, but bracket or make clear these are secondary to the anger. We can then move around the anger trap one way or the other. It does not make much difference which way around the trap we go, but it is often easiest to head to the left as these behaviours tend to be more noticeable.

There are often plenty of examples of outwardly-directed behaviours, which will include verbal and physical aggression directed towards people or objects. It is also worth asking about and including the fantasies of acting out, as sometimes these can be concerning for individuals or those around them as these are often more extreme than the behaviours themselves (e.g. fantasies of torture, murder, or humiliating others). It can help to suggest that this might be the case as these kinds of thoughts are often not otherwise volunteered.

The next step is to ask about how it feels when they are engaging in these behaviours. Adolescents and young adults will often be reluctant to admit that there is anything positive or pleasurable about these behaviours and will jump to the longer-term consequences. This is often particularly the case where family members may be present. However, it is important to identify the positive reinforcing quality and help adolescents and young adults connect with this feeling; asking how they felt at that moment when they were throwing things, or when they hit the other person etc. can help to elicit this. It is then worth helping them to see that if they get a buzz out of this behaviour it makes sense why they have kept on doing it. It can also help to draw a link between the initial appraisal and the resulting behaviour. For example, an appraisal of "They're treating me like a weakling" might lead to behaviour such as breaking things, which demonstrates power and strength; the situation is then completely opposite to the initial appraisal. Alternatively, initial appraisals about others having power over the individual might be linked to fantasies of possessing extreme power, for example in torturing or murdering others, which is a powerful, albeit temporary, antidote to the initial appraisals of powerlessness.

Next, it is important to include the longer-term consequences of the behaviour, which do not tend to be so positive! There will often be many different consequences, and all can be listed, but it is important to make the link between these consequences and the initial appraisals to make clear the reinforcing nature of the trap. Where others have responded in anger and things have escalated, we can highlight the confirmation of the initial threat appraisal. This threat appraisal is also confirmed by others responding with dismissal or ridicule at the outwardly directed behaviour. Shame and self-criticism can also be seen as confirmation of interpersonal threat. When the adolescent or young adult regrets the behaviour, this can be seen to be confirmation of their lack of control. Other consequences, such as increased isolation or financial cost can also be included.

Next, we need to draw out the other side of the trap. The easiest way to access this is to ask whether there have been times when the individual has not responded in this way to anger, when they have tried to do something else. Often this behaviour has been suggested or encouraged by others – 'just walking away' for example – however it does not often feel particularly positive. In our example, the individual acknowledges the positive sense that they have not lost control, but then also that they have not expressed any anger and so have not tested their ability to control it. They also acknowledge that people have treated them badly as a result, and also that they remain angry. It is important in drawing this section of the trap that the meaning behind each arrow is explained and understood.

The overall trap can be summarised by focusing on the core of the trap in the middle: the interpersonal conflict, the appraisals, and the anger. The two reinforcing behavioural cycles can be summarised as 'bottle up' and 'explode' cycles around the sides.

The anger trap, with its dual-cycle pattern of reinforcing anger, is one of the more complex traps outlined in this book. While it takes some time to draw, however, it powerfully illustrates the interactions between the different elements with an explicit focus on anger.

Breaking the anger trap: intervention

As outlined above, the anger trap begins with the experience of interpersonal conflict and then highlights the importance of two groups of appraisals: over-estimations of interpersonal threat and under-estimations of control. Given that these appraisals maintain the anger trap, interventions following from the anger trap are designed predominantly to target these appraisals.

As we outlined in relation to fear, anger is a response to threat, and as such, can be seen to be a function of the reptilian brain. This means that a package of interventions targeting anger needs to involve exposure to anger-inducing situations and different behavioural responses. It is important to note the parallel with fear, there is no point in talking to a reptile; it has to be shown that the thing it perceives as threatening is not as threatening as it thinks it is. As clinicians, many of us operate under the misconception that while working with fear involves the experience of fear, somehow working with anger should involve its eradication. This may be driven by the popular conflation of anger and aggression (see earlier in this chapter).

The goal of work with anger is therefore not to help adolescents and young adults to remain neutral and calm all of the time (this would effectively be suppression and take them around the right-hand side of the trap). Instead, the aim is to help them to learn to experience tolerable levels of anger and to respond differently. It is important to reiterate here that we are talking about experiencing the emotion – feeling angry and being able to think and tolerate the emotion – we are not talking about lower levels of outwardly directed behaviours or lower levels of aggression. In using these techniques, over time, the situations in which adolescents and young adults feel neutral and calm grows, and those to which they respond with fury and rage reduces.

While there are important theoretical overlaps between work with fear and anger, there are a number of practical differences:

1. **Predictability.** Anger-inducing situations tend to be less predictable than fear-inducing situations. This means it is more difficult to manage the level of exposure to anger than to fear. This is magnified by the fact that anger is an interpersonal emotion and interactions with others increase potential unpredictability.
2. **Short term consequences.** The short-term consequences of going around the anger trap can often be significant, for example damage to property, people, and relationships. As a result, there is often a need for short-term strategies to take the heat out of the situation so that longer-term work can proceed.
3. **Difficulty using different behavioural responses.** Responding to fear differently is relatively simple – don't avoid. Responding to anger differently, however, often requires skills or abilities that adolescents or young adults might not yet possess. As a result, supporting adolescents and young adults to use different behavioural responses often takes more work within the context of anger than it does in fear.

As a result of these differences, it is more difficult to encourage adolescents and young adults into exposure and response prevention without first doing some other work. The intervention section will therefore cover a variety of approaches. First, we will look at environmental interventions that are designed to reduce interpersonal conflict. These tend to be short-term interventions that are likely to help but unlikely to be sufficient alone. The next section covers regulating anger using physiological intervention, which is combined with exposure to increase skills in regulating anger and also challenge appraisals about anger being outside of control. Following this we look at behavioural skills that can support the process of feeling anger, regulating it, and responding differently, before looking at the eventual exposure tasks relating to anger. The evidence base to support this treatment approach is outlined at the end of the chapter.

Environmental intervention: reducing interpersonal conflict

Interpersonal conflict is the beginning of the anger trap; without interpersonal conflict, there would be no experience of anger. Obviously, aspiring for an existence in which everybody gets on all of the time is unrealistic. However, sometimes there are unnecessarily high levels of interpersonal conflict, which can be a major factor in the presentation of anger in adolescents and young adults. In addition, given the negative consequences of going around the anger trap, it often makes sense to start here to take the heat out of the situation to enable other intervention to progress.

Beginning with an environmental intervention requires that we build a clear picture of the kinds of situations that result in interpersonal conflict. A clear, detailed understanding of exactly what happens in particular situations is really important in anger, as in other emotions, and it is worth some time exploring. Given our usual focus in these situations on reducing the consequences of outwardly directed behaviour, the focus of this exploration is specifically on the link between the environment and the behaviour. The A-B-C model is therefore often the best to follow in order to gather information. In this model, the A stands for Antecedent (what was going on before the behaviour), the B stands for Behaviour (what the individual did), and the C for Consequence (what happened as a result of the behaviour).

It may be fairly obvious that particular environments are more likely to result in conflict: adolescents and young adults might experience high levels of anger at home, for example, but much lower levels of anger at school. Alternatively, there may be particular individuals with whom contact is likely to result in interpersonal conflict, or there might be particular times when interpersonal conflict tends to arise (e.g. getting ready for college or bedtime).

These triggers might be fairly obvious and might have been elicited with enough detail when drawing the anger trap. Alternatively, further exploration might be required to highlight where interpersonal conflict is particularly likely.

There are a number of options available here. The first is a retrospective exploration, in which we spend some time exploring the experiences of anger during the course of the past week or two. These can then be explored to build an understanding of the interpersonal context. Imagery can additionally be used to increase the intensity and salience of recall so that the detail might be more readily accessible (for details of how to do this, see the exposure section next). The second option is a prospective exploration in which adolescents, young adults, or their families are asked to record incidents of anger over the next week or two. Basic tools such as diaries, logs, or even the three-column thought record can be useful here (see Chapter 7).

Whichever strategies are used, the guiding principle is that we need a detailed understanding of the interaction between the environment and the individual to properly understand the interpersonal conflict.

Once we have determined the situation(s) that results in conflict, we can proceed with intervention. There are two interventions aimed at reducing interpersonal conflict, one of which is based on individual change and the other on family change. The aim of both is to reduce the likelihood of interpersonal conflict and hence the levels of anger experienced.

Individual work

This technique is known as stimulus control and it involves two basic behavioural strategies: avoidance and escape. The aim is to control contact with the stimuli that result in the experience of anger.

It may be possible to plan, in advance, to avoid contact with such a stimulus. For example, if a brother and sister tend to regularly erupt into anger in the morning when they are both trying to use the bathroom, an intervention that serves to keep them apart during this time (e.g. a timetable or using different bathrooms), will likely lessen the difficulties. Alternatively, if a young adult is frequently in conflict with a particular person at work, reducing the level of contact they have with this person, or changing shift arrangements would reduce levels of conflict. These strategies are short term and will not result in a complete resolution, but they can take the heat out of the situation sufficiently to allow other work to take place.

Where it is not possible to avoid contact in a planned way, escape is another short-term strategy to reduce the negative impact of a trip around the anger trap. The strategy is to encourage adolescents and young adults to leave any situation that is likely to boil over, getting out before engaging in outwardly directed behaviour and therefore avoiding the subsequent reinforcement this involves. Of course, the interpersonal conflict remains and there has been no resolution, but this may well be better than the alternative.

It should be noted that these strategies are short term strategies designed to reduce the frequency of difficulties with anger. They are often the first stage of change, and encouraging adolescents and young adults to override the angry impulse to approach, with instead walking away or avoiding, can be an important step in helping them to feel a little more in control of their anger. This can counter some of the appraisals around their ability to control their behaviour. These strategies are also important to create more opportunities to use other strategies as outlined below. Used alone, however, avoidance and escape will be insufficient to produce meaningful change: they are more likely to take adolescents and young adults around the right-hand side of the trap.

Family work

Another way to reduce interpersonal conflict is to work with the family around the individual. The main technique involved in this process is to reduce uncertainty in the environment using boundaries and limits, thereby reducing situations in which conflict is likely to arise. Alongside this, it is also important to reduce the reinforcement of outwardly directed behaviour and increase the reinforcement of alternative behavioural strategies.

SETTING AND ENFORCING BOUNDARIES

The first task is to develop an understanding of the situations liable to give rise to conflict. From here, the next step is to set some kind of expectation, limit, or boundary, to reduce the uncertainty around this area and hence the interpersonal conflict that arises. With adolescents and young adults, it should be more possible than with children to involve them in the process of setting the expectations ('expectations' is usually a better word than 'boundaries' for this age group too!) Examples include expectations around the times that adolescents and young adults might return home and the kinds of communications that might be expected, or the involvement of adolescents and young adults in tasks around the house. Negotiating, when calm, around what is expected and why, should lead to a sense that the adolescent/young adult is being taken seriously and consulted. Setting expectations in their absence or without their involvement is likely to lead into the anger trap with an interpersonal conflict.

While adolescents and young adults can be involved in negotiating what the expectations might be, they cannot be given sole responsibility for sticking to them. Instead, the aim is to increase behaviour consistent with this expectation, and reduce behaviour that is inconsistent with it. It is helpful for families to think that they should plan only their own behaviour: they should plan their response if the adolescent or young adult does not stick to the expectations.

It is the behavioural principles of positive reinforcement and, to a lesser extent, punishment, that are used by families to manage boundaries and expectations. Positive reinforcement involves rewarding behaviour consistent with expectations, which might involve praise or provision of something desired. Punishment is the removal of something desirable or the provision of something undesirable following a particular behaviour.

REDUCING OUTWARDLY DIRECTED BEHAVIOUR

Many adolescents and young adults who experience and outwardly direct anger in specific environments do so because in these specific environments it serves some kind of function. In behavioural terms, it is likely to result in the provision of something that is desired (positive reinforcement), or the cessation of something that is unwanted (negative reinforcement). Exploration with parents and families (and indeed adolescents and young adults themselves) around recent episodes of outwardly directed behaviour can help to work out exactly what the patterns of reinforcement are. There are then two behavioural techniques that we can use to support the process of modifying these patterns: extinction and positive reinforcement of alternative strategies.

Extinction involves removing the reinforcement from the situation so that the behaviour goes unreinforced; over time it will reduce and eventually cease. Positive reinforcement involves providing reinforcement for alternative and more desirable behaviour so that the adolescent or young adult has an alternative way of getting what they need.

For a detailed outline of methods in this vein that can be used for children, adolescents, and young adults there are some good clinician guides available (e.g. Barkley, 2013; Kazdin, 2008).

EXAMPLE

A 17-year-old girl has been gradually reducing the time she spends at college, because she has worries while she is there. She knows that it would help to attend more, but come the morning she refuses to get up and her mother's encouragements frequently escalate into arguments resulting in less likelihood of attendance. In this case, the difficult behaviour in the morning is unintentionally rewarded by often not going to college, which is a difficult task. This is the case, even though the daughter knows that in the longer term it would be best for her to go to college, as later in the day she feels sad, disappointed, and lonely.

Discussion in-session results in the mutually-agreed target of increasing attendance from around two days to three days per week for the next two weeks. Problem-solving about the helpful things mum can do, and those that are less helpful, and some expectations about what mum expects result in further clear expectations for both mum and daughter. A reward is agreed, which is a weekend activity that daughter would like to do with mum, where the target of three days into college on time is met. This constitutes a meaningful reward, and also further increases the time mother and daughter spend together enjoying themselves. The process of agreeing all of this in advance gives both parties a greater sense of hope and enables them to remain calmer and work better together during the week.

Exposure and physiological intervention: regulating anger in the moment

The interventions outlined to this point have described how to reduce contact with anger-inducing situations. These are only temporary solutions, as the appraisals that maintain the anger trap remain, although they might lessen with reduced interpersonal conflict. In order to directly challenge the appraisals, we need to support adolescents and young adults to experience anger, to tolerate it, and not to respond in the usual behavioural ways. The next step is therefore to support the toleration and regulation of anger.

It is best to begin this in-session. Practically, this involves deliberately bringing angry feelings into the room, increasing their intensity within manageable levels, and then decreasing their intensity again. We might do this on a number of different occasions, building up the anger intensity each time, starting by getting to a 4 out of 10, then up to a 6, and then up to an 8. We rarely need to get all the way up to a 10 out of 10 on any emotion scale, as this usually represents being outside the window of tolerance and so we would encourage emotion regulation before reaching this point. The process of experiencing anger in the room, with the clinician, demonstrates emotion regulation in the moment, teaches regulation skills, and also tests out appraisals about the levels of uncontrollability of anger.

The process is essentially the same as outlined in Chapter 6 on regulating fear, but with anger instead. Using the 0–10 anger scale with some words (examples provided earlier in the chapter) to represent varying levels of anger, we can explore appraisals and beliefs around anger: "Where are you usually on this scale?," "Where are you now?," "At what point do you lose control of your anger?," and "What happens at a six on the anger scale?" We can then set up an experience of increasing the levels of anger in session to a prior agreed point, (e.g. around five or six) and then bring it down. This can be conducted as a formal behavioural experiment, with predictions from the reptilian and rational brains about what might happen (see Chapter 6), or can be conducted more along the lines of an exposure task, where we just launch in.

There are three main aspects of the anger experience we can direct: attention, breathing, and muscle tension (there is more detail about this in Chapter 6). Of course, we also have ourselves and the interpersonal element is a powerful regulating force.

We can start by asking the adolescent or young adult to remember a time when they were angry. Depending on where we are aiming for on the scale, we can support the choice accordingly; an incident of public shame is likely to lead to higher levels of anger than an incident when driving, for example. Our task is to direct attention towards the aspect of the event that resulted in anger. We need to regularly check in with the adolescent or young adult to see where they are on the anger scale and we need to be mindful to stick to the agreed parameters. Once we have built up the levels of anger to the agreed intensity, using attention, muscle tension, and breathing, we can bring it back down again. An example is provided below:

Clinician: "I would like you to remember a time when you felt angry, ideally a situation that remains unresolved." *[unresolved situations tend to elicit more anger]*

Young person:	"OK, there was this time when I was in a rush to go out, I was late, and my dad was supposed to be giving me a lift. He was being really slow putting on his shoes and his coat."
Clinician:	"OK, put yourself back in that situation, see your dad being really slow, what do you notice?" *[inviting an attentional focus on what is going on]*
Young person:	"He is sitting on the chair, really slowly and quietly doing up his laces."
Clinician:	"OK, focus on those laces, how slowly his hands are moving, notice how quiet it is, really focus your attention on that." *[direct the attention narrowly on the aspect of the situation that drives the anger]*
Young person:	"Aaah, that's really frustrating me."
Clinician:	"OK, what do you notice as you do that?"
Young person:	"I'm getting hot, and I can feel my hands tightening."
Clinician:	"Where are you now on the anger scale?" *[check in, making sure that the anger remains in the window of tolerance]*
Young person:	"About a 5."
Clinician:	"Are you OK to go higher?" *[checking in all the time, so that the young person feels in control of the situation]*
Young person:	"OK."
Clinician:	"OK, focus on how slow your dad is doing his laces, feel that heat rising up your body, allow it to get hotter and tense those hands even more, really clench them into fists." *[highlight all of the aspects of the situation consistent with anger and invite an attentional focus on these. Then increase them, encourage them to grow]*
Young person:	"I'm about a 6 now, I can hear my heart beating in my ears."
Clinician:	"What are you thinking, what's going through your mind?" *[important to link all the different parts of the emotional experience, physiology, appraisals/thoughts, environment, emotions etc. This can also provide important information about appraisals that might have been missed; they are much easier to identify in the situation]*
Young person:	"He doesn't give a crap about me, he's being really slow on purpose. Aah, I really feel angry now." *[young person named some clear interpersonal threat appraisals that we can pick up later]*
Clinician:	"OK, where are you on the scale now?" *[repeated checking in, just by pointing to the paper is often sufficient]*
Young person:	"About an 8."
Clinician:	"OK, you said you were OK to get to an 8 but no higher, how does it feel at an 8?" *[ensuring young person feels in*

control, starting to use empathy and naming of emotion to level the intensity off]

Young person: "Well I can still manage, I haven't started breaking things!"

Clinician: "Do you feel like you want to?" *[validating emotional experience but also naming that they are resisting the urge]*

Young person: "Yeah."

Clinician: "OK, shall we come back down now?"

Young person: "Yeah."

Clinician: "What I'd like you to do is to move your attention away from that movement, back into the room with me and look at the ceiling, good, now take a big breath in, and on the breath out let go of some of that tension in your muscles." *[directing process of widening out of attention, decreasing muscle tension, altering posture so that it is less consistent with anger – looking at ceiling and opening up body]*

Clinician: "Good, now wiggle your fingers, loosen your hands, and move your attention to that picture on the wall there. Focus on the different colours, the pattern of light and shade. Good. Now move your attention out of the room, hear the sounds of the music from the waiting room. Where are you now on the anger scale?" *[check in when we are fairly sure there has been a significant drop]*

Young person: "About a 4."

Clinician: "Good, what do we need to do to get it all the way back down to a 2?" *[now there has been a drop, invite a sense of control and self-regulation]*

Young person: "Maybe I'll get up and walk about, and look out the window."

Clinician: "Great, do that, and as you walk, just loosen all those muscles, walk in a way that you normally do when you're calm, and then focus your attention on what's going on outside, see the people walking past." *[encourage self-regulation and enhance it]*

Young person: "I feel OK now."

Clinician: "Great, well done. What was that like?"

During the course of increasing the level of anger intensity, we need to mirror, up to a level just below the level of arousal. We need to tense our muscles, raise our voice, adjust our breathing, and feel the tension ourselves. We also need to avoid empathic connection "Let me try to understand this anger," "I can see the anger in your face" because this will reduce the intensity of the anger; these can be saved for when we are bringing the intensity back down!

To reduce the intensity of anger, we do the opposite of what we have done to increase it. We direct attention away from the anger-inducing stimulus, we encourage and model a loosening of tension, a calming of breath. We use our normal therapeutic skill to ground, soothe, and calm the adolescent or young adult. We can use attention exercises: "Focus on the noise of the traffic outside the room," "Hear the sound of the clock," "Focus on the picture on the wall," we can tense all muscles and then relax (but tense in an open way, stretching open and out rather than forwards and in), we can take deep, slow breaths and allow the tension to subside on the out-breath.

Cautions

Anger is one of the most difficult emotions for clinicians to regulate. The prospect of doing this sort of work is scary and our own reptilian brains run away with all sorts of disastrous situations in which we might land ourselves. There are two important things to remember when working with anger.

The first is to ensure that we are confident in our own ability to contain the situation. The adolescent or young adult has fears about their own anger, arising from appraisals around under-estimates of control. We must be less worried than they are! We should never be complacent, but we should have more confidence than they have that they can manage their anger, otherwise we should not embark on this sort of situation. It takes time to get to know people and we can gradually increase our confidence alongside theirs in increasing the intensity of anger. Adolescents and young adults who present with anger problems will already experience anger in the session, for example when talking about things that have made them angry, and this process is just a development. In this situation, it is better to under-estimate the level of anger that can be tolerated and build from there, rather than the other way around!

The second is to ensure that we never place ourselves into the position in which we represent a direct interpersonal threat. We need to remain in the position of witness to anger and alongside them facing outwards together, towards the object of anger. While we might encourage a focus on things that others have said, or a focus on what they did, we should not repeat the words or model the behaviour but should remain, at all times, emotionally alongside the adolescent or young adult. Also, we should ensure that we manage the situation ourselves through regulating the emotion. We should not tell them to sit down, tell them that they're intimidating us, or tell them to stop swearing. All of these shift the dynamic such that we are now an interpersonal threat, by virtue of our criticism, and the anger is likely to be turned on us. This also feeds an unhelpful process of emotion regulation and represents our blaming adolescents and young adults for the fact that we failed to regulate the emotional content of the session. It is important to remember that the presence of a trusted therapist in the room has a powerful regulatory effect on adolescents and young adults, and we can use this presence to support them to regulate their anger. Throughout the process, we can keep checking in on the anger scale, which becomes a guide to the process and a representation that the situation is managed and contained.

Where clinicians have concerns, it makes sense to practise on individuals without anger difficulties, family members or colleagues, to build confidence in the ability to regulate anger in others. It is much easier than we might think!

Once we have begun to talk and demonstrate how anger can be regulated, the next task is for adolescents and young adults to practise. They can choose a level of anger and practise moving their anger up and down in the same way that we did in session. The experience of feeling anger, labelling its intensity and regulating it in response supports the abilities of adolescents and young adults to do things differently when feeling angry.

Behavioural intervention: improving skills to cope with interpersonal threats

Once adolescents and young adults are better able to regulate their anger, the next task is to support adolescents and young adults to do things differently in response. We can highlight this on the anger trap as an arrow coming out directly underneath the feeling of anger in the middle, which is a balance between outward expression of anger (over-response) and suppression (under-response).

The idea here is to consider specific situations and work towards some practical ideas about what adolescents and young adults might do differently. There are a number of different practical skills that we can consider; the list below is drawn from social skills training and assertiveness training. Social interaction is a complex and difficult business that requires a great many different skills. Deficits in these skills can make it more likely that adolescents and young adults will use the extreme behaviours of the anger trap, which will, in turn, make it more difficult for them to learn the skills. Going through the ideas below with adolescents and young adults and using these to define some areas to practise either within session or without can be a powerful way to support learning of different behavioural responses, that can then be combined with enhanced anger regulation skills to move out of the anger trap.

- **Greetings (and goodbyes)**: first impressions are important and often a source of misunderstandings or awkwardness. Most individuals learn a standard repertoire of greetings that they vary dependent on the situation, and knowing what to do in the initial stages of social interaction aids social interactions. It can also be important to discuss the point of 'small talk' and its role in reducing the awkwardness of the early interactions so that further conversation can continue or can be curtailed. Goodbyes are equally important and again, a standard repertoire of phrases (or even excuses!) can make the whole process much easier. These are good skills to start with as they can be rehearsed and practised in and out of session.
- **Eye contact, distance, and posture**: eye contact is a basic social expectation and is an important aspect of communication. Typical, non-threatening eye contact tends to hold the gaze for a second or so, before shifting away,

and then returning. The absence of eye contact can cause offence, but too much eye contact, or gaze held for too long can feel intimidating and can produce interpersonal tension and conflict. Distance from others and posture adopted towards others are all similar balancing acts, too close or too front-facing being experienced as intimidating, and too distant or turning away often being perceived as dismissive or rude. All of these skills can be practised and experienced in therapy sessions, with feedback from the clinician about how the individual is experienced. This can be really important as this is rarely possible in other situations.

- **Listening and reception**: being able to listen to others, both demonstrating listening, but also taking in the content, are important skills. Allowing others the time and space to speak, and learning to listen and to take on the content can reduce misunderstandings and interpersonal conflict.

- **Giving and accepting compliments**: compliments smooth many social encounters. Many adolescents and young adults caught in the anger trap will brush off compliments because they exist in a threatened state for much of the time, which often results in their receiving fewer of them. Feeling threatened for much of the time also reduces the likelihood of their giving compliments. Giving compliments often results in receiving compliments, and this process can do much to increase the information coming from social encounters that is incompatible with the perception of interpersonal threat.

- **Following instructions**: doing as requested is a skill, and naming it as such can support a move away from interpretation of requests from others as demands or interpersonal threats. Practising following instructions or requests also results in more harmonious social encounters and often leads to compliments!

- **Asking questions and making requests**: the simplest way to increase social connection is to ask questions. Many adolescents and young adults find this idea appealing, as it means that they can increase their social presence without having to turn the attention directly to themselves. It also releases them from the pressure of having profound things to say! Supporting adolescents and young adults to increase the level of social interaction increases the availability of information that is inconsistent with interpersonal threat and can help the reptilian brain to reassess its estimation of threat.

- **Disagreeing, refusing to comply, and discussing displeasure**: for individuals in the anger trap, disagreeing, refusing to comply, or having to challenge somebody is extremely difficult. Situations of this sort are interpreted as interpersonal threats and adolescents and young adults tend to either over-react, or to submissively comply (one way or the other around the anger trap). Learning to disagree in a calm manner is a real skill. The ideas of assertiveness are helpful here. Talking about feelings and keeping statements brief is a really good start, using 'when . . . then' statements: "When you said you didn't want to come out with me, I felt sad and angry."

This avoids labelling and blaming more commonly seen with outwardly directed behaviour: "You must hate me for not wanting to come out with me, you horrible xxxx!" Using 'I' language is also a helpful tool, as it avoids generalising and blaming "I am frustrated because . . ." tends to elicit a better response than "You've made me really angry by . . ."

- **Accepting and giving criticism**: adolescents and young adults are likely to receive greater criticism and feedback than either children or adults, given the numbers of assessments and examinations they face. Learning to give and to receive criticism without experiencing it as interpersonal threat are important skills. Labelling them as skills and naming that they are a normal part of life can be a good start to this process.
- **Apologising**: being able to admit a mistake and apologise is a really important skill and is often the most effective way of diffusing a potentially confrontational situation. There is a balance between the two sides of the trap here, between aggressively blaming others (outwardly directed behaviour) and over-apologising (submission). Simple I statements are a useful template: "I am sorry I spoke to you like that."

Behavioural intervention: exposure and behavioural experiments

Everything that we have outlined so far in the intervention section is designed to support the processes of exposure and behavioural experimentation. The aim is to remain in contact with the stimuli that are appraised as threats to discover that they are not as threatening as the reptilian brain believes them to be. Through the process outlined above, we have challenged appraisals of the under-estimation of ability to control anger, and we have increased the availability of alternative behavioural strategies.

The next step is to encourage adolescents and young adults to use these strategies outside the therapy room in day-to-day situations. It is more difficult to manufacture situations that are likely to produce anger than those that might produce fear. However, it is possible to reduce the avoidance and escape that we might have put in place earlier in the work, or that might have developed prior to the intervention. Using graded exposure or behavioural experiments (see Chapter 6), we can encourage exposure to anger-inducing situations and different behavioural responses. This will challenge the over-estimates of interpersonal threat and move out of the anger trap.

Summary of breaking the anger trap

Breaking the anger trap is based on a number of different stages, which are designed to increase the ability to tolerate and regulate anger, increase the availability of alternative behaviours, and then remain in anger-inducing situations while engaging in different behavioural responses. The process can be challenging for individuals and clinicians alike, but it does work to reduce difficulties with anger for adolescents and young adults and represents one of very few treatment approaches focusing on anger as the primary presenting problem.

Evidence base

As outlined at the beginning of this chapter, anger is an emotion that has received relatively scant attention when compared to fear and sadness. A review in 2007 found 185 references mentioning treatment and anger, compared with 6356 studies mentioning treatment and depression (DiGiuseppe and Tafrate 2007). As a result, the evidence available to inform treatment of anger difficulties is extremely limited and is plagued by methodological issues around such basics as defining what constitutes an anger difficulty (Lee and DiGuiseppe, 2017).

The most recent review of meta-analyses for anger treatments found that there is evidence of a significant treatment effect for a variety of interventions on a variety of anger-related outcomes (Lee and DiGuiseppe, 2017). The research has focused predominantly on cognitive-behavioural interventions, and there is some evidence in support of a stronger treatment effect for behavioural over cognitive approaches. This is particularly the case for children and adolescents. Relaxation also appears to have a fairly strong evidence base. Kassinove and Tafrate (2002) recommend exposure-based techniques for working with anger. Parent Management Training, which informs the section on family work to reduce interpersonal conflict, has a fairly strong evidence base (e.g. Michelson et al., 2013).

This evidence informs the treatment recommendations of this chapter. There is a strong focus on anger regulation skills using skills such as relaxation. There is also a focus on behavioural interventions, including skills development and exposure, which is particularly supported in children and adolescents, as well as adult populations.

References

APA, 2013. *Diagnostic and statistical manual of mental disorders* (5th edn). Washington, DC: Author.

Armbruster, P., Sukhodolsky, D., and Michalsen, R., 2004. The impact of managed care on children's outpatient treatment: a comparison study of treatment outcome before and after managed care. *American Journal of Orthopsychiatry*, *74*(1), pp. 5–13.

Barkley, R.A., 2013. *Defiant children: a clinician's manual for assessment and parent training*. New York: Guilford Press.

Berkowitz, L., 1990. On the formation and regulation of anger and aggression: a cognitive-neoassociationistic analysis. *American Psychologist*, *45*(4), pp. 494–503.

DiGiuseppe, R. and Tafrate, R.C., 2007. *Understanding anger disorders*. Oxford: Oxford University Press.

Harmon-Jones, E., 2004. On the relationship of frontal brain activity and anger: examining the role of attitude toward anger. *Cognition and Emotion*, *18*(3), pp. 337–361.

Izard, C.E., 1991. *The psychology of emotions*. New York: Plenum Press.

Kassinove, H. and Tafrate, R.C., 2002. *Anger management: the complete treatment guidebook for practitioners*. Oakland, CA: Impact Publishers.

Kassinove, H., Sukhodolsky, D.G., Tsytsarev, S.V., and Solovyova, S., 1997. Self-reported anger episodes in Russia and America. *Journal of Social Behavior and Personality*, *12*(2), pp. 301–324.

Kazdin, A.E., 2008. *Parent management training: treatment for oppositional, aggressive, and antisocial behavior in children and adolescents*. Oxford: Oxford University Press.

Kessler, R.C., Coccaro, E.F., Fava, M., Jaeger, S., Jin, R., and Walters, E., 2006. The prevalence and correlates of DSM-IV intermittent explosive disorder in the National Comorbidity Survey Replication. *Archives of General Psychiatry*, *63*(6), pp. 669–678.

Lachmund, E., DiGiuseppe, R., and Fuller, J.R., 2005. Clinicians' diagnosis of a case with anger problems. *Journal of Psychiatric Research*, *39*(4), pp. 439–447.

Lee, A.H. and DiGiuseppe, R., 2017. Anger and aggression treatments: a review of meta-analyses. *Current Opinion in Psychology*, *19*, pp. 65–74.

MacCormack, J.K., 2016. Feeling "hangry": when hunger is conceptualized as emotion, *Doctoral dissertation*, The University of North Carolina at Chapel Hill, NC.

Michelson, D., Davenport, C., Dretzke, J., Barlow, J., and Day, C., 2013. Do evidence-based interventions work when tested in the "real world?" A systematic review and meta-analysis of parent management training for the treatment of child disruptive behavior. *Clinical Child and Family Psychology Review*, *16*(1), pp. 18–34.

Moreno, C., Laje, G., Blanco, C., Jiang, H., Schmidt, A.B., and Olfson, M., 2007. National trends in the outpatient diagnosis and treatment of bipolar disorder in youth. *Archives of General Psychiatry*, *64*(9), pp. 1032–1039.

Scherer, K. R. and Wallbott, H. G., 1994. Evidence for universality and cultural variation of differential emotion response patterning. *Journal of Personality and Social Psychology*, *66*(2), pp. 310–328.

Törestad, B., 1990. What is anger provoking? A psychophysical study of perceived causes of anger. *Aggressive Behavior*, *16*(1), pp. 9–26.

Tucker-Ladd, C., 1996. *Psychological self-help*. Clayton Tucker-Ladd.

Visser, S.N., Danielson, M.L., Bitsko, R.H., Holbrook, J.R., Kogan, M.D., Ghandour, R.M., Perou, R., and Blumberg, S.J., 2014. Trends in the parent-report of health care provider-diagnosed and medicated attention-deficit/hyperactivity disorder: United States, 2003–2011. *Journal of the American Academy of Child & Adolescent Psychiatry*, *53*(1), pp. 34–46.

Chapter 9

Emotion dysregulation

> The understanding is the most important bit. Seeing the cycle of how I interacted with others and having my mum see it too, that was really helpful.
>
> (16-year-old female)

Emotion dysregulation describes an experience characterised by extreme emotional responses, frequent changes in emotional state, and a sense of emotions as unpredictable and out of control. It is often associated with behaviours such as self-harm, substance misuse, and risk-taking, as well as interpersonal difficulties such as frequent conflict and intense, unstable relationships.

For clinicians, working with adolescents and young adults presenting with emotion dysregulation can be a challenging and draining experience. It can be difficult to form a stable therapeutic relationship, to manage the levels of emotion in session, and to maintain a therapeutic focus. We can find ourselves feeling overwhelmed, responsible, working harder than usual, having sessions run over time, or having frequent contact between sessions. We can also find ourselves feeling intimidated, dismissed, belittled, useless, and resentful.

Emotion dysregulation is most commonly understood at the more extreme end of the presentation, where individuals might find themselves with diagnoses such as Borderline or Emotionally Unstable Personality Disorder and Bipolar Disorder (APA, 2013; WHO, 1992). The majority of CBT practitioners will not tend to regularly work with individuals meeting criteria for these diagnoses and will not have received specialist training in this work. However, adolescents and young adults might present with difficulties with emotion dysregulation at lower intensities and it may initially appear that the predominant difficulty is with sadness or fear, for example. Where there are difficulties with emotion dysregulation, the usual models of intervention tend to be insufficient to manage the interpersonal conflicts and tensions that arise both within and without therapy and so a different approach is required. Given that adolescence is a period of rapid development, this can particularly be the case when working with adolescents and young adults.

This chapter does not aim to provide a treatment guide to working routinely with the most severe levels of emotion dysregulation, for which treatment approaches other than CBT have more evidence (see evidence section). It aims instead to support clinicians using CBT in their routine practice to make best use of their skills and abilities when they find themselves working with emotion dysregulation. We begin with an understanding of emotion dysregulation, what causes it, and the interaction between emotion dysregulation and interpersonal difficulty. We then outline the emotion dysregulation trap and look at the interventions available.

What is emotion dysregulation?

Emotion dysregulation is the result of two related processes: a lack of adaptive emotion regulation skills and a presence of unhelpful and often extreme ways of trying to regulate emotions. Emotion dysregulation is therefore not simply an absence of emotion regulation, but a result of emotion regulation processes operating in a dysfunctional manner, causing limitations, restrictions, or difficulties for the individual (Cole et al., 1994).

Emotion dysregulation is a fluctuating, changing, and often overwhelming experience of a collection of different emotional phenomena, few of which feel manageable or understandable. Adolescents and young adults experiencing emotion dysregulation will often speak of feeling overwhelmed, having little control over emotion, switching emotional state regularly and for no apparent reason, and feeling confused and mystified by their emotions.

Emotion dysregulation has been operationalised by referring to six related dimensions (Gratz and Roemer, 2004):

1. lack of awareness of emotional responses;
2. lack of clarity of emotional responses;
3. non-acceptance of emotional responses;
4. limited access to emotion regulation strategies perceived as effective;
5. difficulties controlling impulses when experiencing 'negative' emotions; and
6. difficulties engaging in goal-directed behaviours when experiencing 'negative' emotions.

Emotion dysregulation results in experiences that can be outlined in the same five areas as the other chapters of this book and this is the subject of the next section.

Feelings

The feelings that characterise emotion dysregulation include all those of in this book. They include frequent experience of threat-based emotions: fear and anger, as well as frequent experience of sadness and powerlessness. Happiness and elation are also experienced within this presentation. The aspect of the feelings, though, that characterises emotion dysregulation is the intensity and the rate of change. The simplest way of illustrating the experience of emotion dysregulation is via illustration.

Figure 9.1 outlines a simple way of understanding the regulation of emotion. Each individual has a window of emotional tolerance. Various factors impact on this window of tolerance, including the history and characteristics of the individual, as well as their environmental context, and the particular emotional experience. Within the window of tolerance individuals function well, the different parts of the brain work together well, they can respond and regulate their emotions, and they respond in adaptive ways to their environments (Siegal, 2015). Outside this window of tolerance, rational brain functions are impaired. In conditions of excessive emotional arousal, the reptilian brain is the dominant force, cognitive processes are quick, threat-focused, and disorganised, and the senses are more acute, increasing input into the system and resulting chaos. In conditions of emotional shutdown, there are high levels of parasympathetic nervous system activity, a sense of numbness, lifelessness, and disconnection. Cognitive processes are slowed, senses are dulled, and there is a physical heaviness and apathy. Both of these extreme forms of processing represent states of emotion dysregulation, in which the states are inflexible and, as a result, are not adaptive to the environment (Siegal, 2015).

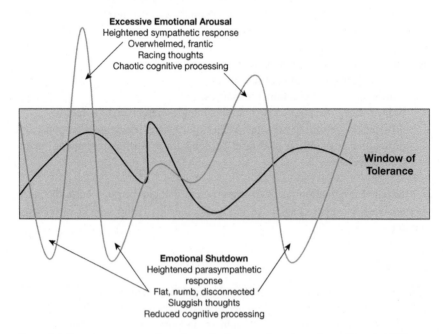

Figure 9.1 Emotion curves and window of tolerance (based on ideas of Siegal, 2015)

In Figure 9.1, the black line represents emotion regulation: the experience of emotion remains within the window of tolerance, a range of emotions are experienced and regulated in terms of intensity and duration, depending on cultural display rules and environmental factors. The grey line represents emotional dysregulation: there are extreme experiences of emotion that frequently move out of the window of tolerance and often trigger regulatory attempts that move straight through the window of tolerance (e.g. from out of the top to out of the bottom). These might include self-harm or substance misuse, for example. The experience of emotions is intense, changeable, and feels out of control. Individuals will talk of emotions as changing for no reason or arriving out of the blue: "I'm happy one minute, sad the next, and there's no reason for it!" As a result, emotions can become phenomena of which to be wary or even afraid. We illustrate this here on paper, but it can be illustrated just as well in session by moving the hand through the air to illustrate the exaggerated and extreme experience of emotion in emotion dysregulation when compared to emotion regulation.

The experiences that tend to lead to emotion dysregulation also tend to lead to interpersonal difficulties (see later section), with the result that interpersonal relationships tend to be unstable and threatening. This potential threat of emotions themselves, combined with interpersonal threat leads to heightened intensity of emotional experience.

In Chapter 2 we noted two of the key skills of emotion regulation: awareness of emotion states and the ability to tolerate emotion. Through the course of healthy emotion regulation development, individuals learn that emotions are tolerable, that emotion states are transient and that there are things that they and others can do to manage these emotion states. Through this learning process, the ability to tolerate emotions grows and so does the window of tolerance. As an example, the toddler who is denied their sweets before dinner may experience an overwhelming anger that they express through beating the legs of their parent. A child of seven or eight, who has developed some ability to regulate emotion is more likely to tolerate this feeling and distract themselves with another activity prior to having their sweets after dinner. This learning effectively means that the ability to tolerate emotions grows; the window of tolerance expands.

Where there have been limitations or disruptions to the development of emotion regulation, the window of tolerance is much narrower. This means that relatively minor fluctuations in emotion are experienced as overwhelming and unmanageable. In addition, the strategies available for regulating emotion are often more crude and more extreme, and are therefore more likely to shoot out the ends of the window of tolerance.

Physiology

As we have outlined in preceding chapters, emotions have a dramatic impact on the body. Depending on the emotion, the physiology of the body responds in a different way. As a result, the experience of emotion dysregulation results in intense and dramatically different physiological experiences. This is highlighted in Figure 9.1 where there are extreme shifts in the activation of the sympathetic and parasympathetic systems. Given that the world, other people, and even emotions themselves, are experienced as overwhelming and potentially threatening, individuals who are emotionally dysregulated tend to have a predominant and often chronic activation of the sympathetic nervous system. As a result, they will often experience ongoing muscle tension and threat focus.

As will be covered in the behaviours section, common strategies that are adopted as attempts to regulate emotions also have a dramatic impact on the body, for example substance use and self-harm.

All of this leads to an intense and rapidly shifting physiological experience in emotion dysregulation.

Facial expression

There is no characteristic facial expression that characterises emotion dysregulation. However, it is worth noting that emotions are often experienced as intense and overwhelming and this heightened experience of emotion will often be expressed on the face. There may well be a resulting tendency for these facial expressions to be too extreme for others to be able to respond to in a helpful or calm manner, or they may be too confusing or difficult to interpret.

Appraisals/thoughts

Thoughts in emotion dysregulation can be driven by the emotion being experienced. For example, in an angry moment, the thoughts will be related to anger, in a sad moment, they will be those of sadness. However, thoughts in emotion dysregulation will often relate to manner in which emotions are experienced.

In Chapter 5 we covered an understanding of the emotional experience as well as the hand brain. We noted that emotions are a response to an environmental stimulus, that decline once the environmental stimulus has changed or has been escaped, these are known as 'primary emotions'. Secondary emotions are driven by appraisals, thoughts, or judgements about the initial emotions that are experienced.

We can use, as an example, an adolescent who believes that they are courageous and strong. One evening they are informed of the death of a grandparent with whom they were close. The initial feeling, the primary emotion, might be sadness, and they might experience a desire to cry and to withdraw. However, given their identity as courageous and strong, they may appraise their experience of sadness as indicating weakness and being something to be ashamed of, which may result in a feeling of shame and then drive a feeling of anger.

The kinds of appraisals individuals make in emotion dysregulation include a non-acceptance of emotion: "I shouldn't get scared," "Crying is for wimps," or "I must always appear fine." Other kinds of appraisals include those around controllability and manageability, for example "If I start crying I'll never stop," "I can't manage how I feel," or "I'm out of control."

The experiences that lead to emotion dysregulation also often lead to interpersonal difficulties, meaning that many of the appraisals seen in emotion dysregulation are interpersonal. Examples include "Nobody cares about me," "I'll be left alone," "They're going to hurt me," and "I'm not safe." We come back to this later, in considering the link between emotion regulation and interpersonal difficulty.

Another way of thinking about the ability to understand and accurately appraise thoughts and feelings is through the concept of 'mentalising'. Mentalising is defined as 'holding mind in mind' or 'attending to mental states in self and others', and can be thought of as a cognitive and emotional representation of the internal state of the individual themselves or somebody else (Allen, Fonagy and Bateman, 2008). In emotion dysregulation, there are significant difficulties with this ability to mentalise the internal state of the self and others.

Behaviours

The behaviours of emotion dysregulation are mostly attempts to manage intolerable levels of feeling. They include self-harm, substance use, and interpersonal behaviours.

Self-harm

Self-harm is defined as the intentional injuring of body tissue without suicidal intention (Klonsky, 2007). Self-harm behaviours include cutting, burning, scratching, banging or hitting body parts, and interfering with wound healing (Klonsky, 2007). There are two main drivers of self-harming behaviour: emotion regulation and interpersonal communication (Scoliers et al., 2009).

EMOTION REGULATION

Self-harm works, at least temporarily, as a form of emotion regulation; the most common reason given for self-harm behaviour in a survey of over 30,000 adolescents was 'to get relief from a terrible state of mind' (Madge et al., 2008). Self-harm can function either to bring down the level of emotional arousal where it is too high, or bring it up where it is too low (Figure 9.1). When the level of emotional arousal is too high, adolescents and young adults feel overwhelmed, flooded, and out of control. Pain signals demand attention and can over-ride these feelings, which effectively removes attention from the initial emotion stimulus and serves as a powerful form of distraction. The deliberate infliction of pain on the self is also a powerful way of asserting control; the individual has total control over the way in which the pain is inflicted, how much and for how long, which is different to the experience of other aspects of the world. In addition, many adolescents and young adults have had experiences that invite perceptions of themselves as to blame or deserving of harm or punishment (see section on what causes emotion dysregulation). In these cases, self-harm can be a familiar experience that feels 'right' given these self-perceptions. Taking on the punishing as well as the victim role can also allow adolescents and young adults to feel more control over their lives. Finally, there is a physiological response to pain in the body (the release of endorphins) that can serve to bring a sense of pleasure after pain. Reviews show that self-harm is usually preceded by high levels of emotion arousal, that individuals frequently cite this as a cause of self-harm, and that self-harm relieves this level of emotion arousal (at least temporarily) (Klonsky, 2007).

When the level of emotion arousal is too low, self-harm can activate emotion centres and make the individual feel 'present' or 'real'. Often the sight of blood, for example when cutting, can be a visual marker of the reality of life. Studies find that this is cited as a reason for self-harm, although less often than bringing down high levels of emotion arousal (Klonsky, 2007).

While self-harm does appear to work in the short term, it is an extreme method of emotion regulation and therefore often overshoots the window of tolerance. For example, while cutting may calm an adolescent or young adult who is feeling overwhelmed, it may well leave them feeling guilty and ashamed for using this strategy and so lead them out the bottom of the window of tolerance to intense guilt and sadness, and a period of withdrawal and isolation.

COMMUNICATION

Self-harm can also be a way of communicating what cannot be seen; can function to provide a visual representation of internal pain. This might be for the individual themselves, but it can also be a powerful communicator to those around them. Self-harm can be a form of communication of distress, or it can be a form of punishment or threat. Examples of these kinds of reasons for self-harm include "I wanted to show how desperate I was feeling," "I wanted to get my own back on someone," "I wanted some attention," which are endorsed by between 20 and 45% of adolescents reporting recent self-harm (Scoliers, et al., 2009).

Self-harm as a form of communication is too extreme and can produce all sorts of unwanted effects. For example, many families are extremely shocked and upset to discover self-harm and it can be difficult for families to tolerate. This can result in extreme forms of response, such as shock and anger, and can often lead to families finding it difficult to cope (Ferrey et al., 2016). Some families may also not respond at all. On other occasions, the ability of self-harm to communicate emotion states is inadvertently encouraged, and families and even professionals use the frequency or intensity of self-harm as a proxy for emotional distress. This is further covered in the intervention section later.

F use

Many adolescents and young adults experiencing emotion dysregulation use substances. Predominantly, substances are used as emotion regulation strategies. Referring back to Figure 9.1, substances can be used to soothe and calm heightened emotional states, or to liven up dull, flat, numb states.

Adolescents and young adults will often use alcohol or cannabis to slow down racing thoughts, to avoid having to think, or to reduce emotional pain. At other times, they might use these substances, or others, such as cocaine, speed, or ecstasy when they are bored, or to increase social confidence.

Substances represent quick, powerful ways of regulating emotion and in the short term they work well. However, they are often too extreme and so, in the longer term they accentuate and magnify problems with emotion regulation. Alcohol use, for example, may lead to an increased sense of calm after a stressful day in a new job (bringing emotion arousal into the window of tolerance), but, during the course of the evening, may lead to a sense of moroseness, pointlessness and worthlessness (coming out the bottom of the window of tolerance).

As with self-harm, in the context of emotion dysregulation, substance use is not considered the primary difficulty, but a response to problems with regulating emotions. In this context, provided the secondary problems with substances do not significantly disrupt the processes of therapy, reduction in substance use need not be a primary goal of therapy. Indeed, substance use is common in adolescents and early adulthood, and many adults use substances, particularly alcohol, to relax or to increase confidence in social situations.

Interpersonal behaviours

Emotion dysregulation is often accompanied by extreme interpersonal behaviour. Individuals with emotion dysregulation can often come across as unpredictable or unreasonable, seeming to suddenly change in the ways in which they interact with others, or to interact differently from one day to the next.

Interpersonal behaviours tend to fall into two broad categories. The first is a tendency to shy away from others, to avoid contact with them altogether, or to manage contact such that it remains superficial, at least on the part of the individual experiencing emotion dysregulation. This includes staying at home, angrily pushing others away, or avoiding getting close to others by not talking about themselves or opening up. The second category of interpersonal behaviour is an opposite tendency to pull towards others in excessive and sometimes controlling ways. This includes clinging to others, desiring continued contact, or becoming angry or scared when others leave. This kind of behaviour can sometimes involve interpersonal threats, such as the threat of self-harm, suicide, or emotional threats such as excessive demonstrations of distress.

These behaviours usually tend to shift around on a fairly regular basis, although sometimes an individual might demonstrate some behaviours with one person, and others with another.

What causes emotion dysregulation?

Emotion dysregulation is caused by two related processes. The first is the failure to develop healthy and adaptive emotion regulation skills. The second is the development of unhelpful and often extreme ways of trying to regulate emotions (Cole et al., 1994).

As outlined in Chapter 2, there are two main influences on the development of emotion regulation. The first is the development of skills such as formal operational thought (the ability to think in the abstract and to think about thinking) and social perspective taking. Difficulties in brain and cognitive development often result in parallel difficulties in emotion regulation. The second influence is environmental. Emotion regulation develops in the context of a responsive interpersonal environment. This environment is required for individuals to develop an awareness of emotions in themselves and others, to learn the language of emotion, and to learn skills to regulate emotion, many of which are interpersonal in nature. Where the interpersonal environment does not provide sufficient opportunities for this process to occur, individuals can develop strategies that are less responsive, more extreme, and are often dysfunctional.

Simplistically, we can consider two kinds of environmental experience that lead to emotion dysregulation: insufficient emotional care and excessive emotional harm. These are different examples of 'invalidating environments', which are defined as environments in which emotional experience is responded to in dismissive, erratic, or inappropriate ways (Linehan, 1993). In reality, most adolescents and young adults with emotion dysregulation will have experienced a combination of both of these experiences.

Insufficient emotional care

The primary task of human infants is to survive. Being forgotten, over-looked, or not attended to, are potentially fatal risks for human infants, given their complete dependence on others for survival at birth. As a result, human infants respond to their environments in ways that elicit care from those around them. Crying, shouting, smiling, and eye gaze, are all behaviours the infant uses to connect to those around them to ensure the continued provision of care. As outlined in Chapter 5, emotions are the mechanism through which infants' responses are coordinated.

As an example, a hungry infant looks to its mother and cries. Tears are in its eyes and its arms and legs move in a manner to indicate distress. The mother notices these signals, talks to the infant and provides food. The infant's emotional response, which has been triggered by hunger, is regulated by the mother meeting the need that triggered the emotional response. The mother's closeness and connection also demonstrates that the emotional signal has been heard, which provides reassurance to the infant that future emotional signals will be heard and responded to in a similar fashion. As the child grows, the emotional signals become regulated by this ongoing interaction between their emotions and those around them. The child gradually learns to become aware of their own emotional states and to speed up the process by communicating more detailed information about their emotions, using labelling, description, more detailed facial expression, and so on. During the course of childhood, this continued dialogue between emotion and interpersonal interaction leads to increasing development of emotion regulation skills.

An absence of care, or a perceived absence of connection on the part of the infant, is a great risk and something that infants, children, and adolescents work hard to avoid. It may be that the parents or the care givers have provided for the infant and the child, but have done so without a great deal of emotional attunement. A parent, for example, might understand the basic needs of children in general and use this abstract knowledge to work out what to do and when, rather than using the emotional signals from their child to inform their response. This can lead to children being apparently well cared for, but struggling with emotion regulation due to this lack of emotional regulation received from the parent. For these children, there remains a fear that their emotions will not be understood or responded to by those around them, and the terror of abandonment and isolation remains. Furthermore, they have not had the dialogue and the practice with others during childhood within which they can learn emotion regulation skills, and rather have had to learn to regulate emotions without much connection with others.

Take the case of an adolescent whose parents have been emotionally distant throughout childhood. This distance might result from the parents' own emotional struggles, parental substance misuse, working patterns, environmental pressures (e.g. lots of other children or children requiring a great deal of attention), or suppressive or dysfunctional emotion regulation strategies on the part of parents. The experience of the child in this environment is that the expression of emotion does not bring about a helpful response from the parent; instead the parents hardly respond to the expressions of the child. The child then faces two options, the first is to manage the emotional situation alone and suppress the associated emotion. The second is to exaggerate the emotional expression in the hope that this might provoke a response. This is the beginning of the development of emotion regulation strategies that tend towards the extreme.

Adolescents and young adults who have difficulties with emotion regulation as a result of these experiences will often feel that they should not have any problems, that they are perhaps exaggerating their difficulties. This can be reinforced by a sense, from others and indeed many professionals, that emotion dysregulation stems from some kind of terrible childhood experience, and that without it, there is nothing to worry about. However, emotion dysregulation is to be expected where there has been inadequate emotional attunement and insufficient opportunity to learn adaptive emotion regulation skills.

When discussing these issues with adolescents and young adults, it is important to proceed with sensitivity. The aim is to support them to understand their own experiences and not to apportion blame or to label parents as ineffectual or not caring. Using the genograms outlined in Chapter 3 can help to bring other information to bear, such as inter-generational difficulties and the struggles of others. Examples of the kinds of language we can use include "Your mother was not able to help you to . . .," "Your father, having had the experiences he had, found it difficult to support you to . . .," "Your family managed well until . . . but then it was much more difficult for them to help you with. . . ."

Excessive emotional harm

The word excessive might seem strange in this context. However, it is important to acknowledge that no environment is perfect and so children and human beings more generally will have experiences of being poorly treated, shouted at, or hurt in their interactions with others. Despite this, the majority of people have a sense that their environment, while not always so, is generally fairly caring, kind, and predictable. As a result, they learn emotion regulation skills appropriate for this environment. Excessive levels of emotional harm can result in emotion dysregulation through the requirement to develop emotion regulation strategies that fit a dysfunctional environment. Children who experience punishment for emotional expression, either physical punishments such as being hit or shut away, or emotional punishments such as being shamed or humiliated, will necessarily learn extreme emotion regulation strategies to cope with their extreme environments.

Children who experience abuse will often find that the expectations in one environment are very different from the expectations in another, for example being abused by one family member and cared for by another. As a result, they will struggle to learn coherent and flexible emotion regulation strategies, resulting in a chaotic and extreme approach to emotions in adolescence and early adulthood. Children who are punished or abused and encouraged to keep quiet about their experiences will learn extreme emotion regulation strategies such as shutting down or dissociation in order to cope with these experiences.

An example might be a child who is sexually abused by a neighbour. This neighbour makes them feel special and wanted, but also hurts and abuses them. They also threaten them if they were to talk to others. As a result, the child learns to distance themselves from their feelings when they are being abused, to suppress their emotions around people who care, and to appear happy and unconcerned to everybody. Underneath, however, the child is likely to feel scared, lonely, and confused, and will have to find ways to regulate these feelings that do not involve opening up to others. This might include self-harm, withdrawal from others, excessive gaming or substance use, or compulsive behaviours.

A child who is abused by a family member, for example an alcoholic parent, can find emotion regulation difficult, as the expectations from the one individual can be so varied. Some of the time the individual appears caring and responds well to their emotional expressions, at other times they ignore or punish their expressions of distress. In this case, the individual will tend to learn to suppress their emotional expression and limit displays of emotion. They may also monitor the emotional state of the parent and attempt to respond to the parents' emotion while disconnecting from their own. Again, they will need to find ways of regulating their own emotions without resorting to the parent, and may rely on connections with other family members, friends, or school work.

Discussing these kinds of experiences with adolescents and young adults can be difficult, and the emphasis should remain on their experience of their early life rather than on blaming or labelling others. In this way, we can hold the position that the experiences they had were unacceptable, without having to go further into what this says about the perpetrators.

What is the relationship between emotion dysregulation and interpersonal difficulty?

Emotions are motivational phenomena; they function to motivate individuals and others around them to various different responses. Emotions also serve important interpersonal functions: keeping groups together and maintaining family bonds. The majority of emotion regulation in childhood occurs through dialogue between a child's emotions and those around them; indeed, in infancy the child is entirely dependent upon others for care and emotion regulation. As a result, there is a close link between emotion regulation and interpersonal function.

To illustrate the link, an individual experiencing insufficient emotional care will not only learn extreme emotion regulation strategies, but will also develop core beliefs consistent with this, for example "Others don't care about me" or "I'm not worth care." Individuals experiencing excessive emotional harm will develop core beliefs consistent with this, for example "Others are dangerous," or "I'm a bad person." Children, adolescents, and young adults will often reason that they are the cause of their experiences. This is often consistent with the messages of those in their environment (abusers will often blame their victims), but even where this is not the case, it is often psychologically safer for children to blame themselves as then they retain a sense of power and control. If they attribute the situation to the other, they become powerless and unable to bring about change.

During the course of childhood, interactions with others become increasingly influenced by children's emotion regulation ability. For example, a child who frequently becomes angry and aggressive with peers as a result of difficulties with emotion regulation will struggle with friends and teachers at school, with the result that the opportunities for developing more adaptive emotion regulation abilities might be limited. As a result, there is interdependence between emotion regulation and interpersonal function that continues throughout life. As noted in

Chapter 2, the well-adjusted individual tends to be emotionally well regulated, and conversely, those experiencing emotional dysregulation also tend to experience interpersonal difficulty.

Emotion regulation and interpersonal function are almost inseparable for these reasons, and it is important to note that an interpersonal strategy has consequences for emotion regulation, and vice-versa. It is these combined experiences of difficulties with emotion regulation and interpersonal relationships that are the main features of diagnoses such as Emotionally Unstable Personality Disorder and Borderline Personality (APA, 2013; WHO, 1992). The link between emotion dysregulation and interpersonal difficulty is highlighted in the emotion dysregulation trap outlined below.

Adolescent development and emotion dysregulation

As outlined in the focal model of development (Chapter 2), there appear to be two reasons for difficulties arising in adolescence. The first is that there were difficulties prior to the period of adolescence. The second is that adolescents face too many changes all at once.

Adolescents and young adults presenting with emotion dysregulation tend to have experienced ongoing difficulties either of inadequate care or excessive harm (or both) during the course of childhood. This has led them to develop emotion regulation strategies that are inflexible or problematic. During adolescence, situations that are emotionally challenging become more frequent and intense (Riediger and Klipker, 2014), and the interpersonal environment also opens up with a broadening friendship and social network (see Chapter 2). These two processes can expose and magnify pre-existing difficulties with emotion regulation, with the result that they often become more apparent during this period. Given the inter-dependence between emotion regulation and interpersonal function, these two difficulties often interact during this period to worsen the situation.

The difficulties managing these situations, combined with pre-existing problems, often then lead to a picture of multiple compounded problems all being faced during adolescence. It is not uncommon to meet adolescents and young adults facing arguments with friends, financial difficulties, ongoing fall-outs with family, and falling educational performance, for example. These difficulties can be further magnified within peer groups where there is a collective struggle with emotion regulation and interpersonal effectiveness.

Emotion dysregulation trap

The emotion dysregulation trap outlines the different aspects that have been covered above, and highlights how they serve to maintain the difficulties. It also highlights the link between the interpersonal and emotion regulation strategies.

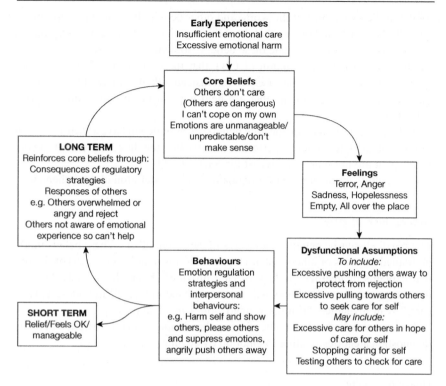

Figure 9.2 Emotion dysregulation trap

This is the most complex trap of this book, but can prove invaluable as other traps do not capture the extreme variability in presentation and interpersonal function that is commonly seen in emotion dysregulation.

Early experiences

The emotion dysregulation trap should always be drawn against a background of a fairly detailed understanding of early life. This can be achieved using the genogram or the timeline, as detailed in Chapter 3. The idea is to get a sense of the various different factors that are likely to drive the emotion dysregulation. When working on the genogram or timeline, it is helpful to keep in mind the two categories of insufficient emotional care and excessive emotional harm, so that we can ensure that we capture the most important experiences that have led into the trap.

Core beliefs

The emotion dysregulation trap is the only trap that explicitly includes core beliefs. The experience of emotion dysregulation, as outlined above, is deeply rooted in the experience of the world and other people. It is these perceptions of the self, the world, and others, that drive the experience of emotion dysregulation and so it is important to include these beliefs. Sometimes, adolescents and young adults will resist the assumption of CBT that these are beliefs held with conviction, and where this is the case, we can instead talk about feared beliefs about the self, the world, or others, that are held with sufficient conviction to drive behaviour.

In the context of this trap, the core beliefs are assumed to have arisen as a result of unusual and uncommon experiences in early life, that have led to a set of core beliefs that are not representative of the wider world.

Core beliefs in the emotion dysregulation trap cluster around three themes:

Others' lack of care

There will always be beliefs about a lack of care from others. These beliefs might be framed in terms of others' intentions, or in terms of a defectiveness of the self that explains or justifies the lack of care provided. Examples include: "Others don't care about me," "Others will reject or abandon me," "I'm undeserving of care," "I'm invisible," "I'm not wanted," or "I'm a bad person."

These core beliefs relate to the 'fear of abandonment' that is included in many diagnostic categories relating to emotion dysregulation.

Unpredictability

There may be beliefs about others' unpredictability or danger. Examples include: "Others are unpredictable," "Anything can happen out of the blue," and "Others are mean and dangerous."

Unmanageability of emotions

There will always be beliefs about the manageability of emotions. These might be explicitly labelled to include emotions, or might be about an inability to cope alone, or feeling overwhelmingly lonely. Examples include: "My emotions are out of control," "I can't cope with my feelings," or "I can't manage on my own."

Feelings

Feelings are important in all the traps in this book. In this trap, there is no specific feeling that is likely to take precedence, and so all feelings can be included. Remember that the threat in the emotion dysregulation trap is abandonment and therefore death; as a result, feelings are likely to be extreme and to include high levels of threat feelings (fear and anger).

Dysfunctional assumptions

This is the only trap that includes dysfunctional assumptions. As we outlined in Chapter 3, dysfunctional assumptions always have two parts, a strategy and an associated aim. The aim should relate back to one of the core beliefs that has already been identified.

In the emotional dysregulation trap, there are core beliefs relating to both the interpersonal and the emotional. Given the interdependence between these two areas, dysfunctional assumptions will necessarily involve both aspects, although one may be more salient and the other inferred.

There are a whole host of different assumptions that might be included in the emotion dysregulation trap and these will be informed by the difficulties with which the adolescent or young adults presents, as well as their history. There are some important considerations to ensure that the trap properly illustrates the process.

Given that there are always core beliefs about a lack of care, there will always be rules about managing this lack of care. There are always at least two rules, one characterised by a pushing away of others, one by a pulling towards others. As in other traps, these are extreme.

Some examples of excessive pushing away of others include:

> "If I hide all my feelings from others and don't ask for any help or care, then I won't have to feel they don't care for me and I'll be safe."

> "If I angrily push others away, then I won't get hurt by their rejection (and they may come back, proving that they care)."

Some examples of excessive pulling towards others include:

> "If I exaggerate how I feel and 'scream' out for help, then people will hear me and I'll get the care I need."

> "If I spend all my time with one person, tell and show them everything about me, then they'll understand me and I'll get the care I need."

It is important that there is at least one pushing away, and one pulling towards. The point is that adolescents and young adults will flip between these different strategies; if they only had one, they would have worked out that it did not work!

Other assumptions that might be important include those about self-care or those about working hard for others:

> "Nobody else cares about me, so I won't bother to care about myself."

> "If I work hard to provide really good care to others, then they'll value me and care for me in return."

> "If I can make other people feel important, then they might do the same for me."

Behaviours and their consequences

Each of the rules or assumptions is associated with particular behaviours. These will include both interpersonal behaviours and emotion regulation behaviours.

Each behaviour is then associated with short-term and long-term consequences that should be included in the trap. The short-term consequences are reinforcing: they tend to feel pleasant (or at least less unpleasant). The long-term consequences reinforce the core beliefs.

Common behaviours that are used to suppress feelings and avoid expressing them to others include 'wearing a mask' when mixing with others and focusing on others and adapting the self to fit what others seem to want. These behaviours are also associated with behaviours such as self-harm and substance use to try to suppress feelings. The short-term consequences of these behaviours are that there is a degree of interpersonal success, sometimes appreciation and gratitude from others, and an avoidance of potential conflict. In the longer term, however, these kinds of behaviours reinforce core beliefs about others not caring and the individual not being worth care, because others tend to ignore their needs and wants, primarily because they are not aware of them. Sometimes others might take the individual for granted and even begin to walk over them or abuse them because they learn that the individual does not protest. This can lead to exhaustion, resentment, and anger towards others, or avoidance of them. Finally, others often do not particularly notice or like individuals who do not have a strong sense of identity and who shift about in the way that they behave, meaning that they are unlikely to care or to seek them out, reinforcing the initial beliefs.

Common behaviours associated with magnification of emotion or over-reliance on others include clinginess or neediness for example in seeking constant reassurance of love of affection, displays of helplessness of overwhelming emotion, and 'loud' self-harm behaviours such as scratches to the face or threats of self-harm when in conflict with others. These behaviours are associated with an up-regulating of emotion to the point of feeling overwhelmed, and many adolescents and young adults displaying these behaviours will cry uncontrollably or become extremely distressed in the company of others, for example family members, teachers, friends, or professionals. In the short term, these behaviours can elicit care and helpful responses from others, which feels good and positive. In the longer term, however, others have a tendency to feel overwhelmed or to burnout from the overwhelming need that is placed upon them. This can lead to rejection or struggles on the part of the others, which leads to a reinforcing of beliefs that others will reject or abandon.

There are other behaviours, such as substance misuse and self-harm that can be associated with this presentation. In the short term, these kinds of behaviours tend to lead to temporary feelings of relief, confidence, happiness, or even elation. However, in the longer term, they lead to further difficulties in emotion regulation (e.g. from come-downs), and interpersonal difficulties and conflicts.

Summary of the emotion dysregulation trap

The emotion dysregulation trap is a combination of vicious cycles, which operate simultaneously on emotion regulation and interpersonal dynamics. It is a blend of the longitudinal CBT formulation and the maintenance cycle, and this is important as difficulties with emotion dysregulation are characterised by a frequent playing out of deep-seated assumptions about the self, the world and others.

The assumptions, associated behaviours, and short- and long-term consequences are more unique for this trap than for others in the book. While these paths around the trap can be more idiosyncratic, there are a number of principles. Each path should follow from a core belief, and end up, in the longer term, reinforcing a core belief. Each path should include each element in a way that fits together and makes sense. Each path should also include both and interpersonal and an emotion regulation element. Finally, the trap as a whole should be based on core beliefs relating to an absence of care, and should include at least one path that covers an extreme of emotion suppression and pushing others away, and another path that covers an extreme of emotion magnification or feeling overwhelmed and drawing others in.

Emotion dysregulation trap and the hand brain

In emotion dysregulation, the different parts of the brain do not work well together. There is a high level of activation of the reptilian brain's threat systems as a result of the continued threat of abandonment and therefore death. This activation interferes with the operation of the rational brain such that the different elements of emotions, including the thoughts and behaviours often tend to appear chaotic, unreasonable, and irrational. The reptilian brain's threat system can be sent into threat mode with a single trigger, and the rational brain does not have the abilities to regulate this activation, so the 'flipped lid' is a common phenomenon in emotion dysregulation.

The aim of the work is therefore to support the rational brain to understand these processes, hence the explanations about emotions, emotion regulation and the emotion dysregulation trap, and to learn to regulate emotions and the threat systems of the brain. In this way, the rational brain can be seen as holding the ability to soothe and calm the reptilian brain. This metaphor can be a powerfully simple one to support the processes of intervention.

Drawing the emotion dysregulation trap

Unlike the other traps in this book, drawing the emotion dysregulation trap is not always an early aim of therapy. This is because the difficulties of emotion dysregulation and associated interpersonal problems are likely to be active in the context of therapy. It is important for us, as clinicians, to have a sense of what the trap might look like and to respond accordingly (see intervention section), but this need not involve drawing the trap together, right at the beginning of therapy. The risk is that, for adolescents and young adults who find themselves feeling overwhelmed and struggling to regulate their emotions and relate to others, illustrating and highlighting their difficulties too early in therapy can be overwhelming and can escalate the difficulties before there are structures in place to support this process.

Drawing the emotion dysregulation trap also needs to be thought about relative to the developmental stage of the adolescent or young adult. Firstly, understanding the trap requires abilities such as formal operational thought: the ability to think about thinking, think about feeling, and think about relating to others. These are abilities that are likely to develop more slowly in the context of emotion dysregulation. Secondly, the trap highlights the environmental factors that have led to the difficulties faced by adolescents and young adults. Children and adolescents are likely to attribute the difficulties to themselves and work hard at altering their behaviour as a result. This means they retain a sense of power and control. The emotion dysregulation trap highlights the environment as a greater influence on the situation than the adolescent or young adult themselves. This is important as it reduces the sense of self-deficiency. However, if the adolescent or young adult has little ability to influence the environment (e.g. because they are too young) then it can increase the sense of powerlessness and make things worse. In this situation, it can make sense to focus more on the emotion and emotion regulation aspects of intervention, rather than the interpersonal aspects so heavily.

Having said all of this, we have been clear throughout this book that it is important to have a clear understanding of what is going on, and so even where the totality of the trap is not shared with the adolescent or young adult, it is important that we, as clinicians, have a copy for our own reference and to direct our work.

There are times where the trap, or aspects of it, need to be drawn out very early on in sessions. This is particularly the case where interpersonal assumptions and regulatory strategies are interfering in the process of establishing a therapeutic relationship. This can be the case where there is an impact on attendance at sessions, or where the interpersonal behaviours within session are so disruptive as to prevent sufficient collaboration to work on the presenting issues. In these cases, we do not need to highlight the historical elements immediately, but to begin with the fears of being rejected or not cared for or abandoned, and draw the strategies from here.

As an example, we can take a 19-year-old whose parents argued a great deal during her childhood, struggled with alcohol use, and were sometimes violent; from the age of 8 her uncle sexually abused her (example trap in Figure 9.3). She presented to therapy because there were times when she was extremely distressed and nobody knew what to do, and there were also concerns around self-harm, which was superficial but increasing. In the initial appointment she was guarded and, at times, quite difficult, saying that she had tried everything, nothing had worked, and asking what this therapy was going to offer that was any different.

In this case, it is important to draw a basic trap fairly early on in the work, as the interpersonal strategies that it highlights are already evident in the therapeutic relationship. The aim is to name the processes as understandable responses to difficult experiences. In this way, the understanding of the responses needs to be based in an understanding of history and so we have to refer to the history in order to come forward to the present situation. This does not necessarily need to involve a lengthy history taking or genogram immediately, but a shared understanding that there were some bad experiences in early life, focusing in particular on insufficient emotional care and excessive emotional harm. In our example, we have highlighted the unpredictability of the parents and the sexual abuse from the uncle. From this, we can move through to the core beliefs, which should also focus on beliefs about care or harm in relation to others. While we may identify a variety of core beliefs, to keep the trap simple, we have highlighted the two most powerful core beliefs: "Nobody cares about me" and "Others are dangerous." We have also captured the extreme nature of these beliefs by highlighting that they were developed in early life.

These core beliefs are likely to give rise to intense emotions. It is better to over-emphasise the emotions rather than under-emphasise and risk invalidating them. In the emotion dysregulation trap, all emotions may well be present and it is important to highlight the range of emotions that may be experienced. In our example, we have emphasised terror, hopelessness, and anger.

All of the trap so far can be done fairly quickly and fairly early on in sessions, perhaps even in the first one, where we have some awareness of the history. Naming, accurately, the dysfunctional assumptions is far more difficult. Sometimes, where we are looking to draw something to highlight processes in session, we can skip this bit entirely and focus on the behaviours. Where we do this, though, we, as clinicians, need to have a sense of what these dysfunctional assumptions are, otherwise we can miss important parts of the trap.

The important dysfunctional assumptions in our example are focused on the core beliefs about others and capture the extreme nature of the push and pull responses. The first is a strategy of excessive pulling towards others "If I try really hard with some people, they'll like me and love me." The other is a strategy of excessive pushing away of others "If I hate others they can't hurt me." Both of these are extreme and opposite and capture the different approaches that are adopted with different people or at different times. The behaviours that follow from these strategies are working hard for others and suppressing her own feelings, or being difficult and uncooperative with others and being angry with them (Figure 9.3).

It is useful, as in other traps, to regularly review progress with drawing the trap. This reinforces the idea that the processes of the trap are understandable and make sense. In the case of the emotion dysregulation trap this is particularly important, as it demonstrates that we, as clinicians, understand the behaviour of the individual in the context of their early experiences. In this case, we can say something like:

> So, when you were little, your parents were unpredictable and sometimes violent, your uncle also sexually abused you. As a result, you grew up with the sense that nobody cared for you and other people were dangerous. Experiencing the world in this way is really frightening and also makes you feel angry and hopeless. You have to find some way to cope with this, to continue to live. What you have found yourself doing is working really hard to try to get others to care for you, and this is often at the expense of yourself and your feelings. At other times you find yourself pushing others away and keeping them at a distance to try to make sure they can't hurt you.

Regular summarising is an important part of CBT, and it helps to ensure that we are on the right track and working through things together. Referring back to feelings is also important and can ensure that we keep connected emotionally: "How does it feel to see it drawn like that?," "How does that look to you?." Often, the process of drawing this trap is really difficult and emotionally challenging, and we can recognise this:

> This is really hard, we're focusing on all the most difficult stuff right now, you're doing really well. It's important, because if we can understand exactly what's going on, then we're in a position to think about what to do about it.

Next, we need to consider the consequences of the behaviours. In relation to working hard for others, it is important to acknowledge that this often works, she has friends, connections with others, and at times, feels that she receives care from others. However, the long-term consequences are not always so positive. Sometimes adolescents and young adults are aware of the consequences of these kinds of behaviours, but other times they need a little prompting:

Clinician: "What happened in your last relationship with your ex?"
Young person: "He really treated me badly."
Clinician: "What kind of things did he do?"
Young person: "He didn't listen to me, when I used to say 'no' [referring to sex] he would carry on anyway."
Clinician: "So trying to please him all the time didn't work, he took advantage and didn't listen to you."
Young person: "Yes."
Clinician: "And how did you cope with that, what did you do afterwards?"
Young person: "I used to go into the bathroom and cut myself."

Clinician:	"That sounds really hard, really difficult, what did those experiences make you think about yourself and the world?" [looking at trap so far]
Young person:	"Well, it's those again [pointing to trap], nobody cares and people are horrible."

These kinds of conversations are not unusual when drawing the emotion dysregulation trap and it is important to use the experiences of the past to draw the trap, so that the trap can help understand the processes of relating. It is also important to validate the difficulty of the experiences but also to keep the process moving and not to get stuck back in the past with the difficult experiences. The trap, like all traps in the book (and indeed all formulations), serves to validate the experiences by providing an understanding.

The next step is to look at the consequences of the behaviour of getting angry with others. There is an important element of feeling safe and protected from others, which might link back to the previous conversation, at least she is not being harmed by others. However, other people might get angry back, or at least will refrain from providing care, which leaves her on her own and feeling that nobody cares.

The complete trap is shown in Figure 9.3.

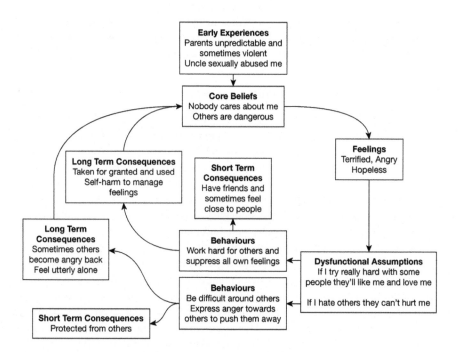

Figure 9.3 Example emotion dysregulation trap

Breaking the emotion dysregulation trap: intervention

Breaking the emotion dysregulation trap is theoretically no different from breaking the other traps in this book. From a behavioural point of view, the aim is to tolerate the emotion and to remain with it while not engaging in the usual behaviour. From a cognitive point of view, the aim is to understand the processes and then to question the thoughts and beliefs to better determine their accuracy.

Despite this theoretical similarity with other traps in this book, in practice, the nature of the difficulties in emotion dysregulation interacts directly with the processes of therapy. Individuals with emotion dysregulation find it difficult to regulate their emotions; experiencing emotion is a central tenet of the therapeutic process. They also tend to have interpersonal difficulties, and therapy, by its nature, is an intense interpersonal interaction.

As a result, there is often more work required to provide a therapeutic environment in which emotion regulation can develop and there is sufficient interpersonal connection to allow for therapy. The provision of this environment is not just a precondition for therapy, but is an important part of the process of therapy itself. The level of work required to provide this environment for adolescents and young adults will vary dramatically depending on the presentation and the degree and type of emotion dysregulation.

The intervention section is separated into two parts: the first is about emotion regulation. This section includes the education and modelling of emotion regulation, and includes regulatory strategies in the areas of cognition, physiology, behaviour, and environment. The second part covers interventions directed at interpersonal patterns, and focuses on cognitive work and behavioural experiments.

Modelling and teaching emotion regulation

The emotion regulation strategies outlined in the trap are based on two broad themes: under-regulation or suppression, and over-regulation or magnification. In our example (Figure 9.3), these two strategies are clear: suppression by not expressing any outward feeling and managing instead through self-harm, and magnification by over-expression of anger. Adolescents and young adults with emotion dysregulation difficulties will tend to exhibit both of these strategies at different times and in different ways. These strategies will tend to result in a frequent overshooting of the window of tolerance and a limited ability to tolerate emotion.

The task, from an emotion regulation point of view, is to support adolescents and young adults to tolerate emotion to a greater extent and to widen this window of tolerance. This requires the development of more subtle strategies to regulate emotions. In order to properly do this, we need to understand the processes of healthy or adaptive emotion regulation. We can consider four: awareness, naming, contextualising, and responding. These principles of emotion regulation can be taught, in much the same way as other skills are taught in CBT. The four principles are outlined in detail next, following by an example of them in action.

Awareness of the self

The first process is to bring the awareness to the self; to attend to the different aspects of emotional experience: feelings, physiology, facial expression, thoughts, and behaviours. Adolescents and young adults presenting with emotional dysregulation will tend to avoid attending in a calm way to themselves and will tend to shut off or run away from feelings, or become consumed by one aspect of them.

Inviting an attentional focus on the different aspects of the body while adolescents and young adults are experiencing emotion can help them to stand back from the experience and perceive it in a calmer manner. With the information in other chapters of this book, we can model and support this process by guessing what is going on, for example where somebody looks scared we can guess what else might be going on in their bodies and what kind of behavioural urges they might be experiencing. This ability to model emotional attunement is a powerful way of demonstrating that emotions are phenomena that can be understood and inferred, which already challenges some of the appraisals about emotions highlighted in the trap.

Naming the emotion

The next process is to use this information about what is going on in each of these domains to infer an emotion state. There are various different tools that can be used for this purpose. Examples include emotion wheels, the emotion scales in the chapters relating to specific emotions, or more simple lists of emotions available online.

The information in other chapters of this book about the way in which emotion states work and how this relates to a purposeful function can be powerful ideas to present to adolescents and young adults. This might include the general awareness of emotion science (Chapter 5) or more specific emotions such as fear (Chapter 6) or sadness (Chapter 7). The hand brain model can also help them to understand that they can be experiencing an emotion while simultaneously having a sense that the emotion is exaggerated or over-the-top; "The rational brain has a sense of what is going on, but the reptilian brain is in charge."

Contextualising the emotion

A central premise of this book is that feelings are reasonable, purposeful phenomena. Helping adolescents and young adults to understand that each feeling they have is an understandable response to some kind of environmental (or perhaps internal) stimulus is an important part of the work. This does not mean that the emotional response is always based on an accurate reading of the situation or cannot be modified or regulated in some way, but there is always a reason for it; emotions do not arise of their own accord without trigger.

Through this stage of the process we are inviting and developing the premise that emotions are understandable phenomena, that serve an important purpose, and that the best way to respond is to stop and to think about what is going on; to engage the rational brain.

Responding to the Emotion

Next is to invite adolescents and young adults to consider their options to respond to the feeling. In phrasing it in this way, we are maintaining the value of emotion states and are inviting a response to emotion states, instead of a denial or an ignoring of them. We are not suggesting that there is a solution, not asking what do they need to do to feel 'better' or 'cheer themselves up', merely inviting some kind of response. This is a challenge to the usual perception of emotions seen in this presentation, where there is a fear of emotion and hence a tendency to suppress, distract from, avoid, or desperately alter the emotional state.

In CBT terms, there are five areas in which regulatory strategies can operate: environment, physiology, facial expression, thoughts, and behaviours.

ENVIRONMENTAL RESPONSES

Emotions function to aid individuals' adaptation to their environments; hence the most common emotion regulation strategies involve some kind of interaction with the environment. The most obvious environmental examples are proximity to threat: moving closer to a threat will intensify fear or anger, and moving away will diminish these emotional states.

Environmental change such as changing job, changing college, adjusting friendship group, spending more time out of the bedroom or going to stay with relatives are all important ways of regulating emotions and can regulate many different emotions. Often these environmental options are forgotten or overlooked as a result of a tendency to individualise difficulties rather than remain aware of the broader context.

Other environmental strategies might include adjusting the environment and problem solving particular relationships, as outlined in the sections on behavioural activation (Chapter 7) or stimulus control (Chapter 8).

Within the therapy room, there are environmental ways to regulate emotion, for example the level of light, the position and height of the chairs, or the position of a table all regulate emotion. Direct front-on positioning of chairs with no barrier can increase a sense of openness and connection, or might increase a sense of interpersonal threat. A darkened room might intensify feelings of sadness or might reduce feelings of fear and anger. Getting up and moving about, providing materials to fiddle with or draw on are also basic environmental strategies that can support the regulation of emotion.

It is important to consider environmental strategies first, as emotions are responses to the environment and so there should be a good reason for regulating in other ways. A common example is where individuals are feeling sad in an environment that is providing few opportunities for fulfilment or happiness. It makes most sense to encourage environmental change, rather than trying to help adolescents and young adults feel happier in environments they dislike.

PHYSIOLOGICAL/FACIAL RESPONSES

Responses in the physiological domain include the three main aspects of the autonomic nervous system over which there is also conscious control: breathing, muscle tension, and the direction of attention. Regulating these three aspects of the physiology will adjust the balance in activation of the sympathetic and the parasympathetic nervous systems. To increase the activation of the sympathetic nervous system, we can encourage increased muscle tension, increase the rate and depth of breathing, and increase the attentional focus on threat. This will increase the intensity of emotions such as fear or anger. To decrease the activation of the sympathetic nervous system and stimulate the parasympathetic nervous system, we can decrease muscle tension, we can move the attention away from the source of threat, and we can slow down the rate of breathing and focus on the out breath. Altering the facial expression can also mediate emotions: loosening a frown, for example will tend to decrease feelings of frustration, and given the importance of facial expressions in communication with others may also result in an interpersonal environmental shift. Examples of physiological regulation are available in Chapters 6 and 8.

COGNITIVE RESPONSES

Thoughts and appraisals are another important part of the emotional experience and many of the interventions in CBT focus on challenging cognitions to regulate emotion. Examples include the thought records or continuums outlined in Chapter 7.

Essentially, we can use changes in the pattern of thoughts or we can use changes in the content of thoughts to regulate emotion.

Certain thoughts or appraisals are likely to drive particular emotion responses. For example, "I am out of control," "I am going mad," or "I am falling apart" would all likely elicit fear or anger. Focusing on these thoughts can intensify these feelings. At other times thoughts or images can represent emotional stimuli and bringing these to mind can intensify all kinds of emotion. Bringing the thought closer or focusing in on the image can intensify the emotion, whereas allowing the thought to move away or the image to fade or change to black and white can all reduce the intensity of the emotion.

Circular patterns of thought also have a tendency to intensify emotion, sadness and anger are particularly characterised by repetitive circular processes of thought and inviting this tends to intensify the emotion. Moving away from this and inviting the thoughts to proceed or move through tends to reduce the emotion.

Shifting perspective or decentring from thoughts (see Chapter 7) can reduce the intensity of emotion and can invite different thoughts or different appraisals which can have a powerful regulatory effect. This is the central premise behind many cognitive interventions.

BEHAVIOURAL RESPONSES

Behavioural emotion regulation strategies can follow straight from the urge relating to the emotion. Running away from threat is a powerful way to regulate fear, attacking a threat regulates anger. However, these are not always the 'best' ways to behaviourally regulate emotion.

One of the most powerful regulatory strategies is communication. Talking about emotions and having somebody else hear and understand the emotion regulates the emotion as the emotion is heard and responded to. Remember, outlined earlier, the fear and terror that can arise from a sense that nobody is picking up the emotion signals and the sense of isolation that can result. Naming and demonstrating an understanding of emotion states is a powerful regulator. It can intensify emotion where the emotion tends to be suppressed, or it can diminish it where the emotion is highly intense or overwhelming. The communication of emotion does not only occur verbally, but through posture. Mirroring and similar displays of emotion on the part of others can equally reduce emotion, as the emotion does not need to intensify in order to be heard.

'Successful' emotion regulation

It is important to remember that successful emotion regulation tends to result in the ability to:

• experience of the full range of emotions;
• modulate the intensity and duration of emotions;
• make fluid changes between emotions;
• conform to cultural display rules, and;
• use words to regulate emotion processes (Thompson, 1994).

When working with individuals with emotion dysregulation, we need to keep in mind these five principles and organise our work around them.

In-session emotion regulation

Working with emotion dysregulation requires the clinician, more so than in other presentations, to help individuals regulate their emotions during the session. Those with emotion dysregulation are likely to find the process of discussing difficulties, naming problems, and interacting with somebody in a caring role, to be an intense and unusual experience. They are likely to use their usual extreme forms of regulation, either complete suppression or over-powering intensity. Our task, as clinicians, is to embody the principles of emotion regulation; to act in accordance with them, use them, and talk about them during the session.

We need to be confident in our own abilities to regulate emotions, and our own abilities to regulate others' emotions, as this involves:

- encouraging awareness of emotion, for example, noticing and asking about physiological changes, thoughts, behaviours, and facial expressions;
- encouraging the use of emotional language to label these different states, and guessing or trying to read emotions where adolescents or young adults are struggling;
- assisting with techniques to regulate emotion, for example direction of attention, physiological emotion management, and perspective taking;
- modelling the value of emotion and not reacting in fearful or angry ways to expressions of emotion;
- modelling the complexity of emotion: noting the presence of more than one emotion at once, noting the changing intensity of emotion, and shifts between emotion states.

The task for clinicians in working with this population is to be active in session, modelling and assisting in regulating the emotion experience, but simultaneously teaching and describing the process in which we are engaging. Importantly, clinicians need to be willing to increase the intensity of emotion in session, to encourage the expression of emotion and to enhance and intensify it, as well as to decrease its intensity and regulate it downwards.

Example

As an example, we can consider the girl whose trap we outlined above, who comes into session having had an argument with her boyfriend. She launches in to a fast-paced description of what happened and starts to whizz through a 'I said ... he said' narrative. We can slow down the process, checking that we are understanding and naming that we really want to make sure we are getting things right. Instead of allowing the narrative to whizz along a cognitive plane, we can ask questions to develop awareness of other aspects of the situation, the physiology, the emotion, or the environment.

Clinician:	"How did you feel when you found that out?" *[slowing down the narrative]*
Young person:	"I was really angry, I thought 'how dare he do that!'"
Clinician:	"Where did you feel that in your body?" *[encouraging awareness on the self]*
Young person:	"It was just here, a tightness in my chest."

Clinician:	"Can you feel that now, there, when you're telling me about it?" *[moving into the present, noting present awareness of emotion]*
Young person:	"Yes, and I'm starting to get hot." *[legs start to jiggle]*
Clinician:	"So you can feel that tightness in your chest, and you're getting hot. Anything else you're aware of, maybe your heart rate, or in your muscles – your legs look like they're tense." *[modelling emotions being understandable and predictable, also modelling attending to their internal state]*
Young person:	"I'm getting angry thinking about it."
Clinician:	"How angry are you, right now, 0 being not at all and 10 being the most possible?" *[encouraging links between awareness of internal state and intensity of emotion]*
Young person:	"About a 6."
Clinician:	"OK, you're doing well, just take a deep breath, sit back in your chair a little." *[modelling and directing in-the-moment emotion regulation using breathing and posture – mirror the directions towards posture by sitting back too]*
Young person:	"OK."
Clinician:	"OK, what happened next?" *[moving on through the narrative as a way of regulating emotion]*
Young person:	"He said he was fed up with me and he didn't want to go out with me later on." *[shifts in seat and tears spring into eyes]*
Clinician:	"OK, how did that feel, it looks as though that's a different feeling." *[noting emotional shift and naming it]*
Young person:	"Yes, I was really upset."
Clinician:	"What kind of upset? Sad, scared. . ." *[encouraging naming of specific emotion, rather than broad vague terms]*
Young person:	"Really sad, like I was all alone, and really scared too."
Clinician:	"Can you feel that now? Where do you feel that?"
Young person:	"It feels awful, like a big weight." *[starting to cry, leaning forwards in chair]*
Clinician:	"Yes, it looks really heavy, you've sat forwards like its pushing you down." *[validating, encouraging attention and making links between emotions and aspects of experience]*
Young person:	*[sobbing]*
Clinician:	"What do you usually do, when you feel like this?"
Young person:	"I can't stop thinking about cutting myself."
Clinician:	"OK. You're doing well. What I'd like you to do is take a deep breath in, and feel the breath pulling you upwards. Good, notice the light in the room, the sun outside the window, and stretch your shoulders back. Well done, good. What happened next?" *[noting closeness to window of tolerance, not eradicating emotion but regulating it to keep in window of tolerance,*

directing emotion regulation, decreasing intensity of sadness by adjusting posture, giving clear direction and modelling the behaviours too]

Young person:	"He left and I was all on my own. I thought that he didn't love me, that nobody loved me and I was going to cut."
Clinician:	"So you were about to cut?" *[using summarising to keep the narrative moving]*
Young person:	"But I messaged him to say sorry, and he messaged back."
Clinician:	"And how did that feel?" *[returning to emotion]*
Young person:	"I started to feel better, like it was going to be OK. I was pleased I hadn't cut."

While we progress through the narrative, we can model regulation of emotion. We might want to increase the emotional content as she tells the story, by focusing on a particular aspect of the situation, for example the words that her boyfriend used, or the feeling she had in her chest when he said that, or the thought that nobody would ever love her. Equally, we might want to decrease the level of emotional arousal, by suggesting a slowing down of breathing, or a moving through to what happened next when she is stuck on a part of the narrative. Our aim, through this process, is to slow down the narrative, to encourage an awareness of the different and changing emotional states in the different domains of experience, and, in the process, to encourage adolescents and young adults to tolerate the emotion that they feel while telling us about what happened. We can support them to tolerate it by using techniques to support them to regulate emotional intensity and keep them going. In the room, we value the emotion experience, we are curious about it, we respect it and don't try to eradicate it. Our aim is to enable the adolescent or young adult to connect with the emotion of the situation but not feel overwhelmed by it.

A narrative of this sort, told in this way, should feel intense, it should feel uncomfortable; we should feel that we are working hard to help the adolescent or young adult to regulate their emotions. Too often, we behave in ways that reinforce the fear felt by adolescents or young adults about their feelings. We might pass the tissues, get a parent, or start to try to make them feel better. A common issue for those of us doing CBT is that we rush into using intervention strategies, such as cognitive restructuring, part way through a narrative of this sort which invalidates the emotional experience and represents a suppressive emotion regulation strategy. One of the particular fears for us clinicians is around regulating anger and there is a section in Chapter 8 that covers anger in session.

Risk management

Risk behaviour commonly arises as a consequence of emotion dysregulation, and the best way to manage risk is to use and embody the principles of emotion regulation in order to reduce the risk. Exactly how risk is managed will depend on a variety of factors, including the level of risk, the clinical setting, and the role of the clinician. Despite these variations, however, the principles of risk management in emotion dysregulation remain the same.

As outlined in the trap, self-harming behaviour, or threats of risk behaviour are attempts at emotion regulation. In the short term, they can be effective, but the longer-term consequences maintain the difficulty. In order for adolescents and young adults to begin the process of change, they need to experience the dysfunction of these regulatory strategies and need to be supported to develop alternatives. From a clinician's point of view, this means that we aim to reinforce behaviours consistent with adaptive emotion regulation and ignore (or at least reduce our focus on) behaviours consistent with emotion dysregulation strategies.

Unfortunately, the risk management behaviour of many services inadvertently reinforces these behaviours through a number of different routes. Firstly, risk behaviour tends to elicit an increase in response from services, reinforcing the communicative power of the behaviour. Secondly, an excessive focus on risk behaviours can result in their becoming a proxy for emotional communication. This can include an excessive focus on managing the risk so adolescents and young adults are asked about frequency of self-harm, rather than how they have been feeling during the period between appointments. It can also include a 'ban' on self-harm, in which adolescents or young adults are 'forbidden' from self-harm, meaning that self-harm remains a powerful communicative tool and a way of punishing those in services, the family, or the individual themselves. Thirdly, services may use levels of risk to make decisions about who receives services, which services they receive, and how quickly they are delivered. All of these factors inadvertently reinforce the risk behaviours of adolescents and young adults.

Obviously, there are pragmatic concerns to be addressed, as risk behaviours represent a potential for serious harm, and it is important to take steps to reduce this likelihood. However, it is also important to acknowledge that a reduction in likelihood of serious harm in the longer term will occur through increasing functional emotion regulation strategies. The principle should be that dysfunctional regulation strategies should be experienced as such.

Within therapy, there are a number of ways in which this can be achieved. Self-harm in and of itself should not be treated as a communication, it should not be taken to mean that the adolescent or young adult is struggling, or that they cannot do something or that somebody has done or said something wrong. Self-harm should only elicit a deep curiosity about what is going on: the context around the self-harm, the environment, and the thoughts, feelings, physiology, and behaviours of what must have been an intense emotional experience. When hearing about an incident of self-harm, we can take adolescents and young adults through the emotional journey of their experience (like the example outlined earlier), so that self-harm becomes a smaller part of a larger, more important experience. This sense of our being interested not in their behaviour and the resultant impact on their body, but in their emotional experience and the choices they made during the course of this experience, is a powerful way of increasing a tendency towards emotion regulation and away from emotion dysregulation. Demonstrating the same degree of interest in an event that resulted in self-harm and one that did not will also help to reduce the communicative power of self-harm and increase reliance on other, more adaptive emotion regulation strategies.

Our response to self-harm more generally can also follow similar lines. Upon ensuring that adolescents and young adults are unlikely to bring about irreversible harm through their behaviour, we can maintain only as much interest in the behaviour as they desire. If, for the time being, they are OK with the behaviour, then we can reduce our focus on it and instead work on the other aspects of the presentation. The expectation being, with successful work, the behaviour will reduce in favour of more adaptive emotion regulation practise. When adolescents and young adults more actively desire a reduction in self-harm behaviour, we can support this process. The important principle is that self-harm is not seen, in and of itself, as a problem we need to address; the problem is the broader issue of emotion dysregulation and interpersonal difficulty.

Summary

The aim for us, as clinicians, is to work with adolescents and young adults to encourage a different response to their emotions. We do this by simultaneously discouraging emotion dysregulation, such as self-harm, substance misuse, and threatening interpersonal behaviour, and encouraging emotion regulation.

Behavioural experiments: interpersonal change

So far, we have focused on considering the skills of emotion regulation and the development of skills, within session and without, that can support more adaptive emotion regulation ability. Throughout the chapter, we have noted the close link between emotion regulation and interpersonal function and there are specific interventions that can be targeted towards testing interpersonal strategies.

Many of the interpersonal strategies that are employed in emotion dysregulation have discrete aims and hopes attached to them. For example, working hard to care for other people can be associated with a sense that this will mitigate against rejection, or that it can bring care and attention from others. Alternatively, avoiding asking others for help will protect against rejection and there may be a hope that others will figure out what is wrong without having to be told. The core of the emotion dysregulation trap is that these strategies tend to backfire and instead reinforce the difficulty and the underlying core beliefs. During the course of our conversations with adolescents and young adults about things that are emotionally salient, we will probably have developed a sense of the kinds of interpersonal relationships they tend to form and the kinds of difficulties they experience as a result.

Behavioural experiments, as we have outlined in other chapters of this book (e.g. Chapter 6) can be used to test out these dysfunctional assumptions, to see whether the fears are confirmed or whether something different happens.

As in emotion regulation, interpersonal strategies in the context of this trap tend to be extreme, often in both directions. However, adolescents and young adults tend to relate more to one strategy and work harder at it than another. For example, some individuals will work really hard for other people, putting on a mask, putting up a front, and moulding themselves to the ways in which they believe other people want them to be. Others will be pushy, demanding, and controlling of others.

Behavioural experiments in emotion dysregulation are the same as with other presentations. The first task is to define, exactly, the belief that we are aiming to test. Tying the experiment to the core belief increases the power of the experiment and increases the likelihood of generalisation. This belief then flows through to make a prediction about what might happen in a given situation (which will often be consistent with the dysfunctional assumption). The reptilian brain can make a prediction about what might happen and we can rate the degree of conviction in this scenario, and the rational brain can also make a prediction. Finally, we define the experiment. Figure 9.4 outlines an example behavioural experiment designed to test the degree to which the adolescent avoids asking others for help. This example includes three different tests, which should ordinarily be written out as three different experiments, but are amalgamated here.

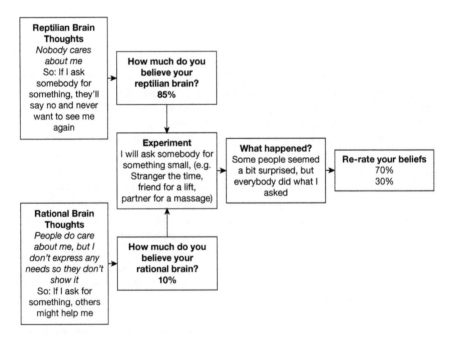

Figure 9.4 Example behavioural experiment

Behavioural experiments can also be used to test:

- expressing own opinions or making suggestions;
- expressing feelings to others;
- disagreeing with others (calmly);
- reducing avoidance of others;
- making eye contact with others;
- sending notes/texts/letters to others.

An important premise of this trap and this work is that the environment that gave rise to the emotion dysregulation is not representative of the wider environment as a whole. Stated another way, the core beliefs we are testing are generalisations from an extreme situation to a less extreme reality. Behavioural experiments are designed to highlight this discrepancy. As such, it is important that adolescents and young adults are encouraged to try things out in different environments to those in which they grew up; otherwise the likelihood is that their fears and expectations will be confirmed!

A clear interpersonal opportunity which will be different from the usual interpersonal environment is that of therapy. One of the main tasks of therapy is to create an interpersonal space which facilitates the expression of emotion, and offers interpersonal acceptance. These two qualities of the therapy are already markedly different to the kinds of environments that are likely to lead to emotion dysregulation. One of the tasks of therapy is to use this space in this way and support adolescents and young adults to begin to express their emotions, and relate to others in a different way, and the easiest and most obvious place to begin this process is in therapy. This will usually begin right from the start of therapy, but we can also encourage a reflection on this process, naming that it must be strange to sit in a room and be asked questions about feelings, or asking how each session has gone and what it has been like to talk or to feel in the presence of another. Sometimes this will need to be much more explicit, for example where the therapy space is experienced as so different as to feel threatening, and this needs to be named using the trap outlined above. The trap can be continually referred to in order to illustrate the interpersonal processes as they happen.

At other times, the therapeutic space can be used to model and teach interpersonal strategies and to test out these strategies, perhaps using behavioural experiments. This is particularly useful for unusual experiments, such as those around making eye contact, or practicing making requests, for example.

Summary

There are two broad areas of intervention in emotion dysregulation and these map onto the difficulties previously outlined in the chapter. The first aim is to model and teach emotion regulation strategies that are more flexible and less extreme than those associated with emotion dysregulation. The second aim is to model, teach, and encourage experimentation with interpersonal behaviours that are more flexible, less extreme, and less like to result in conflict and difficulty.

While these interventions have been separated, for ease of understanding, they are intertwined and often co-occur. Indeed, both are often necessary in order for therapy to continue and will occur throughout the course of intervention. It is important, though, that they are explicitly addressed and named so that adolescents and young adults are aware of the changes that they are making and aware of how to continue them.

This trap is the most complex in the book, and working with this presentation requires the most skill on the part of the clinician. The skills are not fundamentally different from those in the other presentations covered in the book, but the clinician needs to be able to use the skills flexibly and in the moment, while also being able to invite reflection on the process to support the learning of the adolescent or young adult. Those presenting with emotion dysregulation often represent the most challenge to clinicians, and being able to recognise where this is the main difficulty and having a framework within which to work is an important pre-requisite for offering interventions that are likely to help.

Evidence base

The evidence base for emotion dysregulation focuses on the more difficult end of the spectrum, those that might meet criteria for Borderline or Emotionally Unstable Personality Disorder. It also tends to look at models of therapy besides CBT (e.g. Dialectical Behavioural Therapy, Cognitive Analytic Therapy, and Mentalisation-Based Therapy).

A recent review concluded that there was some evidence for each of these different types of therapy in adolescents with presentations consistent with Borderline Personality Disorder diagnoses, but also noted that this was preliminary evidence, not least because of different views about the use of this diagnosis in an adolescent population (Sharp and Fonagy, 2015). Another review looked at interventions for self-harm in adolescence and concluded that there was a paucity of evidence overall, but that Therapeutic Assessment, Mentalisation, and Dialectical Behaviour Therapy all warranted further investigation (Hawton et al., 2016).

For adults who meet criteria for Borderline or Emotionally Unstable Personality Disorder, evidence suggests that treatment should proceed within a strong theoretical framework in which clinician and those seeking help are aware of the model (NICE, 2009). There is also evidence that interventions focusing on emotion regulation have stronger support (Klonsky, 2007). One of the interventions often cited as having a strong evidence base is Dialectical Behaviour Therapy, which has a focus on improving capabilities such as distress tolerance, emotion regulation, and interpersonal skills. There is one strong trial supporting its efficacy for suicidal women with a diagnosis of Borderline Personality

Disorder (Linehan et al., 2006), but other evidence does not sufficiently distinguish this treatment from others (NICE, 2009). Indeed, there appears to be a lack of evidence in this area, represented by insufficient further evidence relating to this presentation to warrant an update of the UK guideline for treatment (NICE, 2015).

The relative lack of strong evidence for what to do when adolescents and young adults present in this way, however, does not prevent them from asking for help, and we, as clinicians, need to find some way of supporting them. The treatment outlined in this chapter therefore draws upon the best available evidence: principles of emotion science that inform the whole book, the strong evidence base for CBT across a range of presentations, and the evidence that focusing on emotion regulation and interpersonal function is likely to be most beneficial. For regular work with high levels of emotion dysregulation, evidence suggests supplementary training in another therapeutic approach would most likely be the best way forward.

References

Allen, J.G., Fonagy, P., and Bateman, A.W., 2008. *Mentalizing in clinical practice.* Washington DC: American Psychiatric Publishing.

APA, 2013. *Diagnostic and statistical manual of mental disorders* (5th edn). Washington, DC: Author.

Cole, P.M., Michel, M.K., and Teti, L.O.D., 1994. The development of emotion regulation and dysregulation: a clinical perspective. *Monographs of the Society for Research in Child Development, 59*(2–3), pp. 73–102.

Ferrey, A.E., Hughes, N.D., Simkin, S., Locock, L., Stewart, A., Kapur, N., Gunnell, D., and Hawton, K., 2016. The impact of self-harm by young people on parents and families: a qualitative study. *BMJ Open, 6*(1), p.e009631.

Gratz, K.L. and Roemer, L., 2004. Multidimensional assessment of emotion regulation and dysregulation: development, factor structure, and initial validation of the difficulties in emotion regulation scale. *Journal of Psychopathology and Behavioral Assessment, 26*(1), pp. 41–54.

Hawton, K., Witt, K.G., Salisbury, T.L.T., Arensman, E., Gunnell, D., Townsend, E., van Heeringen, K., and Hazell, P., 2016. Interventions for self-harm in children and adolescents. *BJPsych Advances, 22*(5), pp. 286–286.

Klonsky, E.D., 2007. The functions of deliberate self-injury: a review of the evidence. *Clinical Psychology Review, 27*(2), pp. 226–239.

Linehan, M.M., 1993. *Cognitive behavioral therapy of borderline personality disorder.* New York: Guilford Press.

Linehan, M.M., Comtois, K.A., Murray, A.M., Brown, M.Z., Gallop, R.J., Heard, H.L., Korslund, K.E., Tutek, D.A., Reynolds, S.K., and Lindenboim, N., 2006. Two-year randomized controlled trial and follow-up of dialectical behavior therapy vs therapy by experts for suicidal behaviors and borderline personality disorder. *Archives of General Psychiatry, 63*(7), pp. 757–766.

Madge, N., Hewitt, A., Hawton, K., Wilde, E.J.D., Corcoran, P., Fekete, S., Heeringen, K.V., Leo, D.D., and Ystgaard, M., 2008. Deliberate self-harm within an international community sample of young people: comparative findings from the Child & Adolescent Self-harm in Europe (CASE) Study. *Journal of child Psychology and Psychiatry*, *49*(6), pp. 667–677.

NICE, 2009. *Borderline Personality Disorder: the NICE guideline on treatment and management*. London: The British Psychological Society.

NICE, 2015. *Clinical guideline CG78: Borderline Personality Disorder: treatment and management, centre for clinical practice – surveillance programme, recommendation for guidance executive*. London: The British Psychological Society.

Riediger, M. and Klipker, K., 2014. Emotion regulation in adolescence. In J.J. Gross (ed.) *Handbook of emotion regulation*. New York: Guilford Press, pp. 187–202.

Scoliers, G., Portzky, G., Madge, N., Hewitt, A., Hawton, K., De Wilde, E.J., Ystgaard, M., Arensman, E., De Leo, D., Fekete, S., and Van Heeringen, K., 2009. Reasons for adolescent deliberate self-harm: a cry of pain and/or a cry for help?. *Social Psychiatry and Psychiatric Epidemiology*, *44*(8), pp. 601–607.

Sharp, C. and Fonagy, P., 2015. Practitioner review: borderline personality disorder in adolescence–recent conceptualization, intervention, and implications for clinical practice. *Journal of Child Psychology and Psychiatry*, *56*(12), pp. 1266–1288.

Siegel, D.J., 2015. *The developing mind: how relationships and the brain interact to shape who we are*. London: Guilford Press.

Thompson, R.A., 1994. Emotion regulation: a theme in search of definition. *Monographs of the Society for Research in Child Development*, *59*(2–3), pp. 25–52.

World Health Organization (WHO), 1992. *The ICD-10 classification of mental and behavioural disorders: clinical descriptions and diagnostic guidelines* (Vol. 1). Geneva, Switzerland: World Health Organization.

Chapter 10

Disgust

Basing our practice in emotion science invites us to consider the broad range of emotions rather than the discrete few that have been the focus of the diagnostic model. Disgust is included in many different theories of emotion as a primary emotion. Indeed, the power of disgust to elicit a wide array of bodily responses for the individual's protection is often used as an example of the function of emotions (Izard, 1991).

Despite this, disgust has been relatively under-researched, particularly in the context of emotional difficulties (McNally, 2002). Recently however, it has been implicated in a variety of different presentations, most specifically fears around spiders, blood injury, and contamination based obsessive compulsive problems (Davey, 2011). While these difficulties also involve fear, disgust sometimes represents the primary difficulty, and there is evidence that treatment using traditional fear-based protocols is not always sufficient (Mason and Richardson, 2012). Disgust is also often seen following abuse, particularly sexual abuse (Badour et al., 2013), and can represent a powerful barrier to treatment progression.

In this chapter we will cover what causes disgust, what it is, and its function. We will then cover the difficulties sometimes seen with disgust and look at how treatment approaches can be adapted to better tackle feelings of disgust.

What causes disgust?

The predominant cause of disgust is often considered to be offensive food; anything that 'tastes bad' (Rozin and Fallon, 1987). Disgust is elicited by revulsion stemming from a potential oral inception, a sense of offensiveness, and potential contamination.

Despite this, food related disgust represented only 25% of the reasons cited in one study for the experience of disgust: others included inappropriate sexual acts, poor hygiene, death, and violations of the 'ideal' body (e.g. deformity, obesity) (Haidt et al., 1997).

It seems that disgust is caused by anything perceived by the individual to be offensive, be this food, a behaviour, or another individual.

What is disgust?

In this section, we will explore the impact of disgust on the five areas of emotion experience.

Feelings

The feeling of disgust is of relatively short duration and relatively low intensity; it is experienced fairly frequently and not associated with a particular felt temperature (Scherer and Wallbott, 1994). Synonyms for disgust include revulsion, repugnance, distaste, horror, and repellence.

Physiology

Disgust has an interesting impact on the physiology and one that is not entirely understood. It seems that disgust is associated with fairly low arousal of both the parasympathetic and sympathetic nervous systems (Scherer and Wallbott, 1994). However, many studies have found a decreased heart rate, certainly when compared to fear, but also when compared to neutral stimuli. In examining this phenomenon, Cisler et al. (2009) conclude that the physiological response to disgust is not merely a reduced form of that for fear, but a response unique to disgust. It is theorised that this unique slowing of the heart rate might relate to the fainting sometimes seen where individuals have difficulties with blood or needles.

Facial expression

The facial expression of disgust involves a screwing up of the face and a sticking out of the tongue. It is powerfully observed in infants who have been given a distasteful substance (e.g. a lemon). Over time, the facial expression becomes moderated and it is interesting to consider the child's sticking out of the tongue at others as a socially-symbolic gesture of distaste or rejection (Izard, 1991).

Appraisals/thoughts

Thoughts do not tend to be particularly extensive in the case of disgust. They are often simple labels of the emotion or perception of the stimulus: "yuck," "gross." Appraisals, however, are often the eliciting stimulus for the emotion, as disgust is often experienced in the absence of a bad taste, but merely in the presence of something that is believed to have a bad taste (Woody and Teachman, 2000). Two appraisals are particularly important in disgust: contagion and similarity.

Contagion is a belief that things that have come into contact with disgusting stimuli become disgusting in themselves. Examples include a drink that is perceived as distasteful because it has come into contact with a dead, sterilised cockroach, and a subsequently laundered jumper that is less desirable after being worn by a disliked rather than a neutral person (Rozin, Millman, and Nemeroff, 1986).

Similarity is the process through which something is perceived as disgusting because it resembles something disgusting. People reject acceptable foods (chocolate bars) after they have been shaped to look like faeces rather than if they have been shaped into a disc (Rozin, Millman, and Nemeroff, 1986).

Behaviours

Behaviours in disgust involve creating distance between the stimulus and the individual. For the most basic situation, in which something disgusting has ended up in the mouth, the behaviour is to spit out. For disgusting smells, the face is screwed up and efforts made to avoid smelling it and to avoid fumes in the eyes.

For other situations, behaviours tend primarily to involve avoiding and creating distance between the individual and the stimulus.

Summary

Disgust is a fairly low-intensity emotion that is frequently felt and dissipates fairly rapidly. It has a unique impact on the body and is primarily associated with expulsion and avoidance.

What is the function of disgust?

Disgust, in its most primitive form, is a threat-based emotion that serves to protect individuals from the threat of disease-causing organisms potentially present in food (Rozin and Fallon, 1987). It motivates expulsion of the offending food and avoidance of food that might be similar or might have come into contact with this food in future, and therefore reduces the likelihood that the individual will contract disease.

It is theorised that this clear evolutionary function has been co-opted, through evolutionary history, so that the emotion of disgust has come to protect not just the body of individuals, but their souls and social order (Rozin, Haidt, McCauley, 2008). Disgust can be seen to protect individuals from three separate threats to survival: pathogen disgust, sexual disgust, and moral disgust (Tybur et al., 2013). Pathogen disgust serves to protect the individual from disease, sexual disgust helps to avoid contact with individuals jeopardising fitness, and moral disgust serves to uphold social structures and condemn those violating social norms.

When disgust becomes a problem

Disgust is a predominantly helpful emotion that serves to protect the individual from disease and other potentially harmful situations. However, like all emotions, there are times when disgust can lead to problems. Research has focused on three areas of difficulty in which disgust appears to be an important factor: spider phobia, blood injection injury phobia, and contamination based obsessive compulsive problems (Davey, 2011). These three areas relate to the presentation of disgust combined with fear. Disgust can of course be combined with other emotions. Where disgust is combined with anger, the resulting emotion is contempt. Where disgust is directed towards the self rather than an external stimulus or individual, the resultant feeling is more akin to shame.

Disgust, with its relation to food, sexual, and moral contamination, is often seen following trauma and sexual trauma is particularly likely to result in feelings of disgust, often towards the self and/or the perpetrator of the abuse (Badour et al., 2013).

The next section will cover the treatment of disgust combined with fear, for which there is some evidence (see evidence section).

Interventions for disgust and fear

Where adolescents and young adults present with combined difficulties of disgust and fear, it makes most sense to use the fear trap, outlined in Chapter 6. Disgust, is, like fear, a threat-based emotion in which the predominant behaviour is avoidance and so both can be included on the same trap.

The main adjustment to the fear trap in these cases is the explicit inclusion and discussion of disgust as a factor in the trap. As outlined in the fear chapter, effective treatment is based on specificity of intervention, and the same is true of disgust. Naming disgust, including appraisals of disgust, the physical sensations of disgust, and behaviours associated with disgust are all important parts of targeting these areas in intervention.

For example, for a young person with obsessive hand washing, we might include an appraisal of the filthiness of their hands, a feeling of disgust, and the associated physical response of a desire for distance from their hands. Behaviours will include the obvious hand washing, but also potentially some of the facial expressions of disgust such as an upturned nose or a holding of the hands away from the body, which are behaviours potentially more consistent with the emotion of disgust than fear.

For another young person who avoids spiders, we might include an appraisal of spiders as disgusting, as well as potentially harmful, include a feeling of crawling on their skin and a walk around spiders on tiptoe with as much of their bodies away from the spider as possible, which again, is a behaviour more consistent with disgust rather than fear.

Once disgust has been included in the trap and we have discussed the emotion of disgust, what it is for, and how it can interact with fear, we need to include disgust in intervention.

Behavioural interventions: graded exposure to disgust

The evidence about treating problems with disgust is in its infancy (see evidence section), however it suggests that disgust does respond to extinction and hence to graded exposure (covered in Chapter 6), although this might take longer than in fear. This means that where disgust is a component within the fear trap, it will potentially need a heavier focus and more targeted work than some of the fear-based appraisals. There is evidence that targeting exposure specifically to disgust has a more beneficial effect (Hirai et al., 2008; Olatunji et al., 2009).

Graded exposure to disgust should explicitly include ratings of disgust and should be designed to reduce disgust rather than fear. Practically, this involves using a hierarchy of disgust rather than fear, and using ratings of disgust to test for extinction rather than ratings of fear. Of course, for some situations we may well use both. Incorporating disgust into the treatment will most probably alter the particular interventions we might use in therapy. For example, an image of a spider might elicit feelings of fear but not such high levels of disgust, whereas a plastic spider might elicit feelings of disgust but not such high levels of fear. The appraisals in disgust are also different to those in fear, and so the experiments will need to be targeted specifically towards the disgust-based appraisals.

The second group of appraisals in the fear trap relate to appraisals about an ability to cope and to tolerate the feeling of fear. There may well be appraisals about the ability to cope with disgust: "I can't cope with this feeling of disgust," "This feeling will make me sick," "If I touch that I'll never feel clean again." Some authors (Teachman, 2006) suggest that the best way to target difficulties with disgust is to target these appraisals and to focus on reducing fears relating to the feelings of disgust. This involves a very similar process to the graded exposure above, but involves explicitly inducing feelings of disgust and testing the feared beliefs about these feelings.

Cognitive intervention: conceptual reorientation

While there is little cognitive processing present in disgust, the emotion is largely dependent upon the way in which objects are perceived. Studies have demonstrated that drinks coming into contact with sterilised cockroaches are disgusting (Rozin, Millman, and Nemeroff, 1986). Individuals know that there is no risk of contamination and yet they still feel disgust: the feeling of disgust is dependent on their perception of the object.

Conceptual reorientation, in which individuals are invited to alter their perception of the stimulus, for example to understand that the meat they are negatively perceiving is not horse meat, but beef, can significantly reduce the disgust response when faced with the stimulus.

There has been some success in altering the perception of an amputation to that of the perspective of the surgeon, in reducing sensations of disgust (Gross, 1998). This perspective taking is also likely to reduce some of the subtle behaviours of disgust, such as the moving back of the body, which might facilitate exposure as well. Conceptual reorientation might involve teaching adolescents and young adults about the different types of spider, so that rather than perceiving the similarities between spiders and eliciting the disgust response, they are focused on the differences between spiders, eliciting an interest response.

Despite the intuitive appeal of these ideas, there is little empirical evidence in their support.

Evidence base

There is, as outlined above, little evidence for the efficacy of different interventions in the context of disgust. A recent clinically-focused review (Mason and Richardson, 2012), provides a good overview of the research and some useful clinical ideas, with associated evidence. The recommendations above follow primarily from this source.

Two studies show preliminary evidence that interventions targeting disgust rather than fear alone are more effective in reducing disgust (Hirai et al., 2008; Olatunji et al., 2009). Another study looked at adding in disgust-specific information to enhance the extinction effect and found that this enhanced the rate of extinction (Bosman, Borg, and de Jong, 2016).

Recommendations relating to extending treatment sessions for disgust are consistent with a variety of different studies, summarised in Mason and Richardson (2012). Recommendations about targeting secondary appraisals about disgust follow from Teachman (2006).

References

Badour, C.L., Feldner, M.T., Blumenthal, H., and Bujarski, S.J., 2013. Examination of increased mental contamination as a potential mechanism in the association between disgust sensitivity and sexual assault-related posttraumatic stress. *Cognitive Therapy and Research*, *37*(4), pp. 697–703.

Bosman, R.C., Borg, C., and de Jong, P.J., 2016. Optimising extinction of conditioned disgust. *PloS ONE*, *11*(2), p.e0148626.

Cisler, J.M., Olatunji, B.O., and Lohr, J.M., 2009. Disgust, fear, and the anxiety disorders: a critical review. *Clinical Psychology Review*, *29*(1), pp. 34–46.

Davey, G.C., 2011. Disgust: the disease-avoidance emotion and its dysfunctions. *Philosophical Transactions of the Royal Society of London B: Biological Sciences*, *366*(1583), pp. 3453–3465.

Gross, J.J., 1998. Antecedent- and response-focused emotion regulation: divergent consequences for experience, expression, and physiology. *Journal of Personality and Social Psychology*, *74*, pp. 224–237.

Haidt, J., Rozin, P., McCauley, C., and Imada, S., 1997. Body, psyche, and culture: the relationship between disgust and morality. *Psychology and Developing Societies*, *9*(1), pp. 107–131.

Hirai, M., Cochran, H.M., Meyer, J.S., Butcher, J.L., Vernon, L.L., and Meadows, E.A., 2008. A preliminary investigation of the efficacy of disgust exposure techniques in a subclinical population with blood and injection fears. *Behaviour Change, 25*(3), pp. 129–148.

Izard, C.E., 1991. *The psychology of emotions.* New York: Plenum Press.

McNally, R.J., 2002. Disgust has arrived. *Journal of Anxiety Disorders, 16*(5), pp. 561–566.

Mason, E.C. and Richardson, R., 2012. Treating disgust in anxiety disorders. *Clinical Psychology: Science and Practice, 19*(2), pp. 180–194.

Olatunji, B.O., Wolitzky-Taylor, K.B., Willems, J., Lohr, J.M., and Armstrong, T., 2009. Differential habituation of fear and disgust during repeated exposure to threat-relevant stimuli in contamination-based OCD: an analogue study. *Journal of Anxiety Disorders, 23*(1), pp. 118–123.

Rozin, P. and Fallon, A.E., 1987. A perspective on disgust. *Psychological Review, 94*(1), pp. 23–41.

Rozin, P., Haidt, J., and McCauley, C. R., 2008. Disgust. In M. Lewis, J.M. Haviland-Jones and L.F. Barrett (eds) *Handbook of emotions* (3rd edn). New York: Guilford Press, pp. 757–776.

Rozin, P., Millman, L., and Nemeroff, C., 1986. Operation of the laws of sympathetic magic in disgust and other domains. *Journal of Personality and Social Psychology, 50*(4), pp. 703–712.

Scherer, K. R. and Wallbott, H. G. 1994. Evidence for universality and cultural variation of differential emotion response patterning. *Journal of Personality and Social Psychology, 66*(2), pp. 310–328.

Teachman, B.A., 2006. Pathological disgust: in the thoughts, not the eye, of the beholder. *Anxiety, Stress, and Coping, 19*(4), pp. 335–351.

Tybur, J.M., Lieberman, D., Kurzban, R., and DeScioli, P., 2013. Disgust: evolved function and structure. *Psychological Review, 120*(1), pp. 65–84.

Woody, S.R. and Teachman, B.A., 2000. Intersection of disgust and fear: normative and pathological views. *Clinical Psychology: Science and Practice, 7*(3), pp. 291–311.

Chapter 11

Guilt and shame

Guilt and shame are considered 'social emotions', which arise from an under-standing of the social environment. They are often considered together, as both follow from similar causes, but there are important differences between the two.

In this chapter we explore the emotions, what they are, and their function. We then cover difficulties with guilt and shame. The aim is to consider what adjustments we might make to our usual practice where there are difficulties with guilt and shame, not to provide a comprehensive outline for presentations dom-inated by these emotions. As outlined in the evidence section at the end, there are other approaches with substantial evidential support that have been specifically developed for working with high levels of shame-based difficulty (e.g. Compassion-Focused Therapy).

What causes guilt and shame?

Both shame and guilt tend to be caused by a sense of wrongdoing, erring, or making a mistake. However, there are differences between the eliciting stimuli of each emotion.

Guilt appears to be based on three psychological conditions: acceptance of moral values, behavioural internalisation of these moral values, and ability to perceive discrepancies between these values and behaviour (Ausubel, 1955). Guilt results from behaviour that is perceived by the individual to represent a violation of their own standards or beliefs. Guilt is activated predominantly by an individual's own actions, or a failure to act. Simply, it is an individual's perception of their own wrongdoing, whether this is through a moral transgression, a failure to act, or a betrayal of trust (Izard, 1991).

Shame can be caused by similar events to guilt: a perception of having done wrong. However, shame results from an interpretation of the event as representing a global deficiency of the self and a perception of the self as inferior, inept, or wrong (Lewis, 1995). While shame can follow a moral or value transgression, it can also be experienced in the absence of any such action; indeed, it can be produced solely by the actions of others. Another's focus on an aspect of the body can produce shame without any action on the part of the individual, for example. Shame is characterised by a sudden shift in perception of the self, to a focus on the self as inferior, powerless, or bad (Gilbert, 2009). Many authors have noted that shame often arises within the context of a previously pleasant emotional state, such as interest or happiness, which enhances the sudden nature of the shift (Tomkins, 1963).

What are guilt and shame?

Guilt and shame have differential impacts on the body and this is important in distinguishing between the two emotions.

Feelings

Guilt and shame feel relatively similar and are often confused. Other words that are often used to describe the emotion of shame include disgrace, embarrassment, humiliation, and indignity. Other words used to describe guilt include regret, remorse, and responsibility.

Shame is an emotion associated with a felt sense of heat, for example in the experience of blushing or the phrase 'burning with shame'. Guilt has a fairly neutral felt temperature. Shame also tends to be experienced for relatively less duration than guilt (Scherer and Wallbott, 1994).

Both guilt and shame are experienced as aversive, but shame is more potent, being experienced as a highly negative and painful state (Lewis, 1995).

Physiology

Shame is associated with fairly high levels of activation of the sympathetic nervous system, next only to fear and anger (Scherer and Wallbott, 1994). Guilt, on the other hand, is not associated with activation of either the sympathetic nor the parasympathetic nervous system.

Shame often results in an almost complete disruption to ongoing processing: a sense of confusion, and an inability to sustain behaviour or speech (Lewis, 1995).

Facial expressions

The facial expression of shame typically involves an aversion of eye gaze and a turning away of the face. In the face and also in the body, the effect is to make the individual appear smaller and less significant.

The most powerful facial indicator of shame is the blush. Blushing appears to be controlled by the autonomic nervous system and is not under voluntary control (Izard, 1991). As individuals age, however, it does appear that they blush less often; children and adolescents are more liable to blushing than adults. This may be due to learning to control the response, a lowering of the blushing threshold, or perhaps to an increased ability to avoid or escape shame-inducing situations (Izard, 1991).

While shame has a relatively distinct facial expression, the same is not true of guilt; there are no known reliable external or internal indicators of guilt (Izard, 1991).

Appraisals/thoughts

Both guilt and shame are associated with significant cognitive processing. This cognitive processing focuses on the mistake or error that led to the feeling of either guilt or shame. It is in the appraisal of this situation in which guilt and shame can be most clearly distinguished, and this appraisal explains the different responses in the other domains of experience.

In guilt, there is an appraisal of having done a bad thing, of having made a mistake. This is an appraisal specific to the situation and sits against a background of a concept of the self as generally OK (Lewis, 1995).

In shame, there is an appraisal of being a bad person, of being defective, useless, or incompetent. Tomkins (1963) states that in shame the individual 'feels himself naked, defeated, alienated, lacking in dignity and worth' (p.185). In guilt, the focus of attention is on the other and the harm done to them through the behaviour. In shame, the focus of attention is on the self and that aspect of the self perceived as indecorous or inadequate. It is as though something hidden from others is suddenly under a burning light in public view.

A commonly used measure of shame and guilt illustrates the different cognitions in the two emotions (TOSCA 3; Tangney et al., 2000). For example, one item relates to forgetting to meet a friend; the guilt cognition is: "I should make it up to my friend as soon as possible," the shame cognition is "I'm inconsiderate." Another item relates to an exam which didn't go as well as hoped; the guilt cognition is "I should have studied harder," the shame cognition is "I'm stupid."

In summary, appraisals in shame and guilt are very different: shame is focused on the self and the self as incompetent, bad or defective; guilt appraisals are based on the self as being relatively OK but having done something bad or made a mistake and are focused on the other.

Behaviours

The behavioural urges associated with guilt and shame are also very different.

In guilt, the motivations are reparative, to try to make amends or to restore the situation. In shame, the motivations are to avoid and to hide away.

The TOSCA 3 again illustrates the distinction well. One item relates to spilling red wine on a cream carpet and nobody noticing: the guilt-driven behaviour is to stay late and help clean the stain, the shame-driven behaviour is to leave the party as soon as possible. Another example relates to making a mistake and seeing somebody else blamed: the guilt-driven behaviour is to make efforts to correct the situation, the shame-driven behaviour to keep quiet and avoid the person blamed.

Behaviours in shame are attempts to avoid, to hide. In shame, the appraisal is of an inadequate or defective self and the associated behaviour is to attempt to conceal this from others. In guilt, the appraisal is of an adequate or good enough self that has erred, and the aim is to repair the damage done to the other through the initial action.

Summary

Guilt and shame are 'social emotions', arise from similar situations, and are often confused. However, they differ significantly, primarily as a result of the appraisal of the self in the situation. In guilt, the self is appraised as adequate and good enough and the situation giving rise to the emotion seen as a mistake inconsistent with this adequate self. As a result, the behavioural urge to is make amends and repair the connection with the other. In shame, the self is appraised as inadequate or defective and the situation giving rise to the emotion as evidence of this inadequacy and potentially exposing the inadequate self to the view of the world. As a result, shame is a more threatened emotion than guilt, and the behavioural urge is to protect the self through avoidance and hiding away.

What are the functions of guilt and shame?

Guilt is clearly an emotion that motivates individuals to behave in ways consistent with moral and ethical values. That 'doing wrong' is associated with an unpleasant feeling of guilt decreases the likelihood of wrongdoing. This has evolutionary benefits for the population as a whole. Guilt, however, is more specific than this, and is associated with a motivation towards behaviour that repairs or puts things right with the individual who has been wronged (Izard, 1991). This motivating power increases the sense of social cohesion and bonds with others.

Shame is a powerfully aversive emotion from an individual point of view. Avoiding the experience of this emotion is a powerful motivating force to uphold social and cultural norms. Given the association between shame and ineptness or incompetence, the threat of shame is also a powerful motivating force for individuals to develop skills and competence in a variety of different domains (Izard, 1991).

We outlined earlier that guilt and shame are the 'social emotions'. Their eliciting stimuli tend to be in the social domain, the behaviours associated with the emotions tend to be in the social domain, and both emotions function to enhance social cohesion and adherence to social norms.

Difficulties with guilt

Guilt, as we have seen, tends to arise from specific situations and motivates behaviours associated with these specific situations. Most often, guilt serves to motivate individuals to interact in socially-harmonious ways and it is an emotion that is easily regulated by putting right the initial wrong.

There are two situations in which guilt can produce difficulties. The first is where motivation to act is impeded such that individuals become stuck with guilt feelings that they find hard to shift. The second is where individuals feel responsibility, and therefore guilt, over things for which they do not have control and cannot be responsible for. The first we can include in the sadness trap, the second in the fear trap.

Guilt and the sadness trap

When adolescents and young adults are stuck in the sadness trap (see Chapter 7), they experience decreased motivation, decreased energy levels and often respond with a reduction in activity. This, combined with negative thoughts about the self, is likely to result in feelings such as sadness, powerlessness, and hopelessness. Adolescents and young adults also frequently feel guilty for their lack of activity and the negative impact that they have in terms of their environment and those around them.

Work with guilt in this context can be incorporated relatively easily into the behavioural activation programme outlined in Chapter 7. The aim of this programme is to support change in the way adolescents and young adults behave and interact with their environments. Specifically measuring levels of guilt, exploring the thoughts and appraisals around guilt, and designing behavioural activation programmes to target not just sadness and powerlessness, but also feelings of guilt are also likely to support change and progress.

A good example of this is where a young adult feels guilty and is criticised for not helping around the house. While doing the washing up might not particularly fit with an achievement, connection, or enjoyment task, it might be an important part of reducing some of the feelings of guilt tied up in the sadness trap. Indeed, engaging in behaviours that reduces feelings of guilt might be important in order for the young adult to feel that they 'deserve' to engage in another activity that might be targeted towards increasing enjoyment, for example.

Guilt and the fear trap

Adolescents and young adults will often feel guilt or responsibility for things over which they do not have control. In this case, guilt tends to present alongside fear. This is most obviously evident in the case of obsessive-compulsive difficulties, which can be understood in the context of the fear trap (Chapter 6). In these cases, adolescents and young adults will perform behaviours in order to reduce feelings of fear and guilt, which, in the short term provide relief, but in the longer term sustain the beliefs about fears and responsibilities.

Work with guilt in this context can proceed along the lines outlined in Chapter 6, but again, it is important to measure levels of guilt alongside levels of fear and to target graded exposure or behavioural experiments to both fear and guilt. Reduction in both emotions will be required to support adolescents and young adults in their efforts to bring about change.

The second example of obsessive-compulsive difficulties outlined in Chapter 6 includes the emotions of both fear and guilt. These feelings arise as a result of sexual intrusive thoughts. Guilt, driving reparative behaviour, may well be an important component maintaining the cycle, as outlined in this example. Interventions can proceed on the usual basis, but it may be important to measure guilt as well as fear during the course of intervention; reducing just fear may be insufficient to break the trap. It may also be important to consider the appraisals around the feelings, as these may be specific to guilt: "This guilty feeling will last forever," "I can't function with this level of guilt."

Difficulties with shame

The majority of adolescents and young adults presenting with significant difficulties with shame will have experienced some form of trauma. This might include sexual, physical, or emotional abuse. Bullying is also particularly likely to result in an experience of shame at the time and subsequent global negative self-evaluation. Other forms of early experience, such as feeling forgotten, ignored, or unimportant, might also be significant (Gilbert, 2009). In addition to these experiences, adolescents and young adults will have appraised these experiences in a self-focused manner; they will have attributed the experience to a flaw, deficit, or deficiency on their part, which results in the core belief or global negative self-evaluation (Lewis, 1995).

Where there appear to be difficulties with shame, we need to ensure that we undertake a detailed early history, including a genogram and timeline. This enables us to support adolescents and young adults to make the links between their early experiences and their core beliefs. In shame, these core beliefs will include global negative self-evaluations, such as "I'm worthless," "I'm an awful person," or "I'm a piece of dog poo." This is the first step in questioning the core belief: to show that the core belief might be associated with the experiences of the adolescent or young adult, rather than a statement of truth about the individual themselves.

One option here is to do some work focusing on the early experiences that are linked to the core belief. Another option is to focus on the factors that maintain this self-belief and prevent its disconfirmation. The former option will involve predominantly cognitive work, although trauma focused work might be more effective (not covered in this book), whereas the latter will move us back into the traps outlined in other areas of this book and the associated treatment programmes.

Shame is an extremely unpleasant and aversive emotion. The way in which the adolescent or young adult tries to manage the shame experience, informs the decision about the best way to help them to understand their difficulties. Ideas about the three ways of managing schema are helpful here: submission, over-compensation, and avoidance (Young, Klosko, and Weishaar, 2003).

Submission: where adolescents and young adults submit to negative self-evaluations, they are likely to present with difficulties most consistent with those outlined in the sadness trap. They are likely to tend to withdraw, isolate themselves, and spend long periods ruminating on these negative self-perceptions. In line with the consistency of the sadness trap, this is entirely consistent with emotion of shame: "I am inferior and so should be excluded from society."

Over-compensation: where they attempt to manage these beliefs through over-compensation and attack, their difficulties are best understood in the context of the anger trap. In these situations, shame will enhance the feelings of anger and impulsivity given the powerfully aversive nature of shame. Attempts will be made to devalue others, particularly those seen as the originators of the experience of shame.

Avoidance: where adolescents and young adults present with attempts at avoidance of these core beliefs and attempts to hide the self from others, they are most likely to present with difficulties consistent with the fear trap. In the social fears trap (Chapter 6), there is often a combined sense that the individual is somehow flawed and that others are extremely judgemental. With shame, the negative self-concept is extremely potent and encouragements to open up to others, to talk more, be more open, connect more, are likely to produce feelings of shame and then immediate withdrawal.

All of the above: If adolescents and young adults switch between different ways of managing the feelings of shame, they are likely to relate best to the emotion dysregulation trap.

In each of these cases, shame, as a highly aversive and disarming experience, is likely to significantly intensify the difficulty and to make treatment more difficult.

The most important point in each of these cases is to ensure that we have identified that high levels of shame are present. We can use the descriptions at the beginning of this chapter to support its identification. The next important point it to ensure that the core beliefs identified through the early history and genogram are included, explicitly, in the treatment protocol.

Behavioural interventions for shame

Behavioural interventions, such as graded exposure (Chapter 6), behavioural activation (Chapter 7), or behavioural experiments (Chapters 6 and 9) can all be used where there are difficulties with shame. In each case, the work will involve adolescents and young adults gradually allowing others to 'see' those aspects of themselves they appraise as shameful, in environments that are unlikely to result in a shaming experience. Given the powerfully aversive nature of shame, this work, in all contexts, will be difficult and challenging.

The obvious environment in which to begin this process is the therapeutic environment, and adolescents and young adults can be encouraged to talk about aspects of their lives in sessions to experience empathy rather than the humiliation they might expect. It is often useful to highlight that the process of therapy has already involved some significant change in the way that adolescents and young adults relate to others, for example in relation to openness or honesty or emotional expression.

More formal behavioural work can be undertaken using the behavioural protocols outlined in the relevant chapters, for example graded exposure (Chapter 6) or behavioural activation (Chapter 7). In these cases, it is important to ensure that the cognitions, appraisals, or core beliefs that are the subject of any work are clearly linked with shame. This will usually mean ensuring that we have identified a core belief that represents a global negative self-perception.

Finally, given that shame is associated with a sudden shift of attention onto those aspects of the self perceived as inferior or inadequate, it is important to work on attentional focus and its manipulation, as outlined in Chapter 6 (regulating fear in the moment). This should support adolescents and young adults to manage the behavioural tasks and to reduce the likelihood of feeling shame and the associated confusion, which might lead to further shame-based appraisals.

Cognitive interventions for shame

For cognitive interventions, for example thought records or continuum methods (Chapter 7), we need to ensure we target core beliefs that drive shame. A thought record targeting the belief "I'm worthless" is more likely to have an impact on shame than one targeting "I should have done more" (which is more consistent with a feeling of guilt). Equally, in continuum work, we need to ensure that the core belief and alternative schema relate directly to shame, and that the alternative belief is inconsistent with the emotion of shame. Statements such as "I work hard" might not be inconsistent with the global negative self-perception of shame; "I'm a valuable person" is likely to be better.

Evidence base

As noted by Gilbert (2009), while concerns with self-evaluation are central to many therapeutic approaches, few incorporate an understanding of shame into their framework. Compassion-Focused Therapy (Gilbert, 2009) is a notable exception that has been designed specifically for individuals who experience high levels of shame or self-criticism and who have difficulty expressing warmth and kindness towards themselves and others. There is some evidence in support of this approach (for review see Leaviss and Uttley, 2015).

For clinicians using CBT, the evidence base for working with shame is subsumed within the evidence base for the other presentations that also involve shame, and covered in the relevant chapters on fear, sadness, and anger.

References

Ausubel, D.P., 1955. Relationships between shame and guilt in the socializing process. *Psychological Review*, *62*(5), pp. 378–390.

Gilbert, P., 2009. Introducing compassion-focused therapy. *Advances in Psychiatric Treatment*, *15*(3), pp. 199–208.

Izard, C.E., 1991. *The psychology of emotions*. New York: Plenum Press.

Leaviss, J. and Uttley, L., 2015. Psychotherapeutic benefits of compassion-focused therapy: an early systematic review. *Psychological Medicine*, *45*(5), pp. 927–945.

Lewis, M., 1995. *Shame: the exposed self*. New York: Simon and Schuster.

Scherer, K.R. and Wallbott, H.G., 1994. Evidence for universality and cultural variation of differential emotion response patterning. *Journal of Personality and Social Psychology*, *66*(2), pp. 310–328.

Tangney, J.P., Drearing, R., Wagner, P.E., and Gramzow, R., 2000. *The Test of Self-Conscious Affect – 3 (TOSCA-3)*. Fairfax, VA: George Mason University.

Tomkins, S.S., 1963. *Affect imagery consciousness, 2: the negative affects*. New York: Springer.

Young, J.E., Klosko, J.S., and Weishaar, M.E., 2003. *Schema therapy: a practitioner's guide*. New York: Guilford Press.

Chapter 12

Happiness

Happiness is an emotion rarely, if ever, included in treatment manuals. This is despite the fact that the majority of people presenting for treatment would consider an increase in happiness an important treatment goal. Indeed, many of the emotions often considered as pleasant or sought after are rarely included in treatment manuals; often they are not even known about. For example, the emotion of interest, the tendency to seek out new experiences and explore novel environments, often included as one of the basic emotions and of massive importance to the survival of the human species, is rarely mentioned outside the field. Love, an emotion that occurs within the context of a closeness with another is also rarely discussed in psychology and yet is clearly of huge importance for human beings across the globe.

It is this situation that brought about the discipline of positive psychology, as an attempt to rebalance the focus away from aversive and difficult emotions towards pleasant emotions and a fulfilling life.

In this chapter, we focus on the most obvious of the pleasant emotions: happiness. We look at what causes happiness, what happiness is, and what it is for. We then cover the happiness wheel, a tool to help us to support adolescents and young adults to increase their levels of happiness. While this chapter is separate from the others in the book, we would not normally use the happiness wheel alone, but, as treatment progresses, the work often shifts away from how to get out of the other traps in the book, and towards how to increase and sustain the improvements and the happiness achieved. The interventions included in this chapter therefore overlap significantly with the other interventions in this book. The foundation of this book in emotion and emotion regulation means that the same interventions that help to move away from difficulty will also help to move towards happiness and wellbeing.

What causes happiness?

Babies around 4 to 5 weeks of age will begin to smile during social interaction. The human face and contact with others is the most effective stimulus in eliciting this smile. Many young infants will often laugh and smile with abandon in interactive games between parent and child, for example making facial expressions or moving around eye gaze (Izard, 1991). It is this same interaction and closeness with others that is usually the cause of happiness in adulthood as well: a closeness and intimacy and enjoyment of another's company (Scherer, Wallbot, and Summerfield, 1986).

While happiness is often focused around the interpersonal, it can also arise as a result of satisfaction and achievement. This is based on a sense of satisfaction with what has been achieved (Argyle, 2013). Interestingly, the happiness resulting from achievement is often enhanced or particularly expressed in social situations (Kraut and Johnson, 1979).

What is happiness?

Happiness is an emotion that is experienced in the five areas that we have outlined in relation to other emotions. There are links between happiness and sensory pleasure, for example eating or sexual activity; indeed, some authors have confused or conflated these phenomena (e.g. Argyle, 2013). However, happiness is different to pleasure. Emotions are coordinating phenomena occurring across the domains of human experience (see Chapter 5), whereas sensory pleasure can be experienced in a single area. A pleasurable taste need not be accompanied by experiences in the cognitive or behavioural domains for example. Sensations of pleasure can also be induced through the effects of alcohol and other substances, and this alone does not constitute an emotional experience, although it might be a contributing factor (Izard, 1991).

Feelings

Happiness is a pleasant emotion, which is desirous and rewarding. It is relatively intense, long lasting, and is hardly controlled or regulated in its expression (Scherer and Walbott, 1994). Happiness is experienced to different degrees and in varying intensities. Descriptive words for feelings of happiness, in increasing intensity include: content, cheerful, joyful, delighted, ecstatic, elated, blissful, jubilant, and 'over the moon'.

Happiness, like other emotions is transient. Nobody can be happy all of the time. However, it is common to have a tendency towards particular emotions: a great deal of sadness would indicate being caught in the sadness trap, a great deal of fear being stuck in the fear trap. There is not exactly a happiness trap, but there are ways of being that bring about a tendency to happiness. This does not preclude the experience of other emotions, such as fear, sadness, or anger.

While there have been confusions between the emotion of happiness and the tendency towards happiness and contentment, terms such as wellbeing or flourishing now tend to be used to define the ongoing experience of life in comparison to the transient emotional experience (see later in this chapter). In this chapter, happiness refers to the emotional experience, and the happiness wheel illustrates how to increase the frequency and intensity of happiness.

Physiology

Happiness feels warm or hot. The parasympathetic nervous system, whose dominant activity characterises sadness, is hardly activated at all. Likewise, the sympathetic nervous system which is highly activated in the threat emotions (fear and anger) is also fairly low in activation (Scherer and Wallbott, 1994).

Happiness and joy are associated with increased heart rate, increased sense of vigour, energy, and strength; the body's internal systems also function more smoothly and more easily (Izard, 1991).

Facial expression

Happiness tends to be signified by a smile. The simplest smile involves a single pair of muscles; the zygomatic major on each side of the face pulls the corners of the mouth backward and upward (Izard, 1991). Most smiles also involve the eyes: the muscles next to the eyes pull the eye lids closer together, lift the cheeks, and create small wrinkles (crow's feet) next to the eyes. Interestingly, 'false' smiles tend not to involve the eye muscles and also tend to differ in terms of timing relative to the eliciting event (Ekman and Friesen, 1982).

Happy faces tend to invite approach from others (Scherer and Wallbott, 1994). Happy faces also tend to be perceived as more attractive (Golle, Mast, and Lobmaier, 2014) and happiness is easier to recognize than other facial expressions (Calvo and Beltrán, 2013).

Appraisals/thoughts

Happiness is not characterised by complex thought processes, unlike other emotions such as sadness, which usually trigger a search for meaning. Happiness tends to produce an attentional focus on the present and an absorption in the present moment. It tends to be associated with a broadening of attentional focus, an appreciation of the whole, rather than a focus on dissecting, analysing, or altering (Meadows, 1968). We return to this idea in considering the function of happiness, later in the chapter.

Appraisals of situations in happiness are likely to be positive, based on confidence and strength and there is likely to be a sense that things are possible, that the future is bright, and that things are going to be OK (Izard, 1991).

Behaviours

As noted above, happy faces tend to invite approach behaviours in others, and happiness is associated with pro-social and approach behaviour in the individual themselves. Approach behaviours include physical displays of affection such as embracing, hugging, and kissing, as well as more subtle signs of affection such as proximity, touch, or eye gaze. Pro-social behaviours include giving, sharing, and conversing. There is a clear interdependence here, as happiness tends to be caused by interactions with others, and leads to further interaction with others (Aknin et al., 2012).

Another common behaviour in happiness is laughter. Laughter is often a sign of happiness and tends to increase the subjective experience of happiness; laughing also increases social bonding and cooperation between strangers (Van Vugt et al., 2014).

A common behaviour in happiness, and also in interest, is that of play. Play is a creative process, often based on experimenting, trying out, and investigating the novel. Play can occur in relation to objects, for example with toys (or kitchen implements!), but a great deal of play is also interpersonal, often known as pretend-play. Children's play has been linked with their cognitive and emotional development (Singer, 1979).

What is the function of happiness?

Many authors have struggled to define the purpose of happiness in evolutionary terms. Happiness does not follow the profile of other emotions in coordinating different systems to narrow the focus of attention and respond to immediate threat. Fredrickson (e.g. 2004) argues that the role of happiness is instead to broaden and widen the repertoire of thoughts and actions. In this way happiness produces the urge to play, to interact, to create, and to cooperate with others to experiment and push the limits. Consistent with this idea, there is evidence that the physical activities practised in play are later used in more threatened situations (Dolhinow, 1987). This is also evidence that social play serves to deepen social bonds and the subsequent availability of social support, as well as developing the intellectual capacity and the brain (see Frederickson, 2004).

Happiness, with its broadening of attention and focus has also been shown to be an 'antidote' to other emotions, such as sadness or fear. While the emotions are not necessarily opposite or fundamentally incompatible with each other, happiness has been shown to reduce feelings of sadness or fear (Frederickson et al., 2000).

Happiness has also been associated with a variety of different outcomes in an extensive review by Lyubomirsky, Sheldon, and Schkade (2005), who conclude that 'happy people' (defined as those experiencing more 'positive affect'):

- are more productive at work and more creative;
- make more money and have better jobs;
- are better leaders and negotiators;
- are more likely to marry, have fulfilling marriages, and less likely to divorce;

- have more friends and social support;
- have stronger immune systems, are physically healthier and live longer;
- are more helpful and philanthropic;
- cope better with stress and difficulty.

The variety of these conclusions supports this overlapping and inter-dependent idea that happiness breeds success and successful interpersonal connection, which in turn fuels further happiness.

Happiness, wellbeing, and flourishing

The word 'happiness' describes a transient emotion. However, it is also a word that has been used to describe a character trait, or a more longstanding pre-disposition to emotion: 'a happy person'. More recently, with the development of positive psychology and a move towards researching and developing what are commonly referred to as 'positive emotions', there has been a trend to measure the happiness of populations and even nations (Huppert and So, 2013). To differentiate between the emotion of happiness and longer-term tendency towards happiness, other terms such as 'wellbeing' and 'flourishing' have been adopted.

The normal curve, outlined in Figure 12.1 is commonly referred to in positive psychology. This graph is used to illustrate the criticism of a problem-focused narrative, by highlighting a tendency to support individuals on the far left of the curve to move from 'emotional difficulty' into 'languishing'. This is where interventions commonly stop and the argument goes that the rest of the curve has been relatively neglected. Positive psychology argues for a re-focus on wellbeing and flourishing, which is on the far right of the curve. In fact, the aim of positive

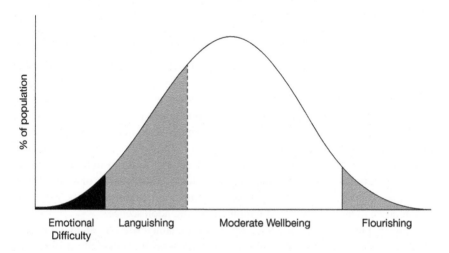

Figure 12.1 Positive psychology normal curve

psychology is often defined as an attempt to move the whole of the curve towards the right; to support the population as a whole to improve in terms of wellbeing and happiness.

Martin Seligman (e.g. 2012) is a key proponent of the positive psychology movement and has written books such as 'Authentic Happiness' and 'Flourish', which are arguments and evidence for a shift into positive psychology. His current model of wellbeing includes five areas theorized to contribute to the over-arching concept of wellbeing. The five are: positive emotion, engagement, meaning, accomplishment, and positive relationships. Seligman (2012) argues that each of these five relate directly to wellbeing, are pursued for their own sake, and do not relate to the other dimensions. Another theory of flourishing includes these five plus a further five areas (Huppert and So, 2013). Interestingly, these ten dimensions have been measured across European nations, with the result that Denmark and other Scandinavian countries come out on top, the UK in the middle, and the Eastern European nations towards the bottom. An earlier theory included 14 different fundamentals in order to work towards happiness and wellbeing (Fordyce, 1981).

These theories help to clarify the distinction between emotions and the under-lying constructs of wellbeing or flourishing. All include frequent experience of the emotion of happiness, but all include it alongside other aspects of life: frequent experience of joy, pleasure, and happiness is necessary but not sufficient for wellbeing and flourishing.

Adolescent development and happiness

In Chapter 2 we dispelled myths that adolescence was inevitably a time of misery and strife. Perhaps in accordance with these myths, there is not a great deal of research studying adolescent happiness. One study found that, between the ages of 12 and 15 years, there is a decrease in happiness, both globally and school-related happiness; where respondents advanced reasons for this, they tended to mention difficulties with peers and confidence relating to others (Uusitalo-Malmivaara, 2012). Another study in America found that younger adolescents (12–14 years) were more likely to flourish, whereas older ones (15–18 years) were more likely to experience moderate mental health (Keyes, 2006). The study concludes that there is a 10% loss in flourishing between middle-school and high-school.

Adolescence, characterised by a shifting of social priority from family to peers represents a time of risk for connecting with others. The demands of adolescence, in terms of study, changing cognitive and emotional experience also represent potential challenges to levels of happiness during adolescence.

Despite these challenges, adolescence is not characterised by an evitable lack of happiness nor are the determinants of happiness fundamentally different to other stages of life.

Happiness wheel

There is no happiness trap, as the word 'trap' has negative connotations, so this section is called the happiness wheel. The happiness wheel outlines the broad factors that are associated with happiness and wellbeing. The happiness wheel is designed to be as simple as possible and includes four different ideas, which are drawn from other models of wellbeing and linked to the evidence-base.

Valuing emotion

All models of wellbeing include an element of pleasurable or 'positive' emotion; many also include emotion regulation as a component. Given the emphasis of this book, this element is defined as valuing emotion: the entire emotional experience. Wellbeing and flourishing are seen to involve embracing the emotional experience and using it in order to live a whole and fulfilling life. This component also includes the related construct of emotion regulation, which follows from valuing

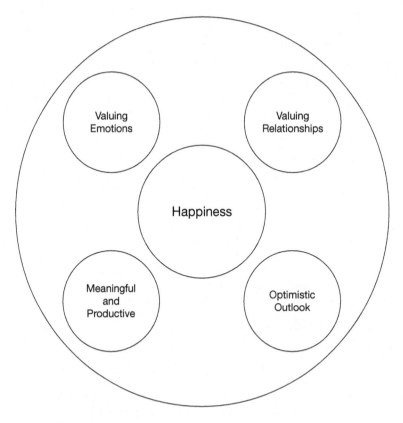

Figure 12.2 Happiness wheel

emotion and responding to emotions (both the individuals' own and others') with kindness, empathy, and understanding. Emotion regulation ability has been associated with higher levels of happiness and wellbeing (Quoidback, Mikolajczak, and Gross, 2015). The perceived ability to cope with difficult feelings has also been explicitly linked with happiness in adolescents (Suldo and Huebner, 2006).

The final aspect of this component is high level of value placed on happiness itself and a willingness to engage in activities that are likely to bring it about, as well as a desire to savour the experience. Both of these aspects have been linked with levels of happiness (Fordyce, 1981; Lyubomirsky et al., 2011).

So, the first component of wellbeing is valuing emotion, with resulting emotion regulation skills and value placed on happiness and wellbeing.

Valuing relationships

A rewarding social life has been linked with happiness and wellbeing more strongly than success, wealth, or indeed any other factors studied by psychologists (Fordyce, 1981). Connection with others is a factor included in all models of wellbeing and flourishing and is a simple testament to our nature as social beings. As we outlined above, happiness is bound up with interpersonal experience and as we saw in Chapter 9, interpersonal relationships are also crucial in emotion regulation. Simply put, socialising with others is the most happiness-inducing of human activities and happy people tend to be highly social. Conversely, we have seen how difficulties in relationships or absences of connection with others are implicated in the difficulties we have covered in this book.

Valuing relationships involves spending time with others. Social contact alone, however, is not sufficient. Close relations have a greater impact on wellbeing than do distal relationships and so a relationship structure in which there is a mix of close and distal relationships, and in which the relationships that are most highly valued are those with the closest people is linked most strongly with happiness (Fordyce, 1981).

In adolescence, there are a variety of different environments in which close relationships can exist, and adolescent happiness has been associated with parents, school, friends, and communities (Lambert et al., 2014). This of particular importance for adolescents and young adults, where close people will involve a variety of different people: family, friends, classmates, colleagues etc.

Meaningful and productive activity

The way individuals spend their time has a significant impact on how they feel: emotions are heavily influenced by activity. Spending time doing things that are engaging, that are likely to maintain and sustain attention and that are perceived as meaningful is strongly associated with happiness (Seligman, 2012). This element relates to the message, throughout this book, that the behaviours in which adolescents and young adults engage are a really important aspect of their lives.

This component also includes physical activity, which has been strongly linked with happiness in both adults and adolescents (Holder, Coleman, and Sehn, 2009).

Optimistic outlook

The way in which adolescents and young adults see the world, their thought processes (and thought biases) have an important impact on their levels of happiness and wellbeing. We have seen negative thoughts and appraisals implicated in many of the difficulties in this book. It is perhaps unsurprising that the reverse also holds: happy people tend to think in more optimistic ways (Argyle, 2013). Indeed, people who undertake exercises to improve their outlooks tend to increase in levels of happiness (Lyubomirsky et al., 2011).

Summary of the happiness wheel

The happiness wheel has just four spokes: valuing emotions, valuing relationships, meaningful and productive activity, and an optimistic outlook. Each of these spokes is important, but there are also dependencies between the spokes (as there are in any wheel!). The simplicity of the wheel and the invitation to move from the more complex traps in this book towards a simple wheel, can illustrate the progress within therapy. The overlap between the constructs of the wheel and the progress already made to move away from other traps also cements the progress made in therapy. The happiness wheel frames the processes for adolescents and young adults as they move out of therapy and on with their lives, highlighting the areas upon which they might want to focus their energies.

Happiness and the brain

Unlike the other traps in this book, in happiness, the different parts of the brain work together in harmony. The rational brain has awareness and an understanding of how the whole brain works and can regulate and respond to the other parts of the brain, such that there is a connection and a unity that is evident in an enhanced level of function throughout.

Happiness wheel: intervention

There are a number of different interventions to boost happiness and wellbeing. Many of these interventions clearly overlap with earlier interventions designed to support adolescents and young adults out of traps, in line with the normalising premise of this book. However, there are some which are more specific to happiness. They are grouped into emotion regulation, behavioural interventions, and cognitive interventions.

Emotion regulation

Therapeutic work as outlined throughout this book will increase the awareness, the labelling, the acceptance, and the regulation of emotion, and will avoid devaluing emotion by trying to push it away or regarding it as an illness or disorder. Emotion regulation was covered in detail in chapters 2 and 9, and a better ability to regulate emotion will result in a movement towards happiness.

The next step, which often follows naturally from improved emotion regulation, is to start to broaden the experience of emotion, to notice and to value emotional shifts and changes, and to use this awareness to inform decisions about life. Many adolescents and young adults will emerge from work targeted towards specific traps in this book and start to become aware of other emotions, often including happiness. It is important to spend time talking about what happiness is, how it works as an emotion, and what kinds of strategies are available to regulate happiness.

Regulating happiness ordinarily means prolonging or intensifying the experience, rather than curtailing it or reducing its intensity. The simplest way to prolong and intensify happiness is to notice, to label, and to savour the experience in the present moment. As we have noted, happiness involves connection, whether with an activity or with another. The ability to protect these moments from distraction or worry and to savour them, to immerse in them, is likely to prolong, intensify, and deepen these experiences.

Adolescents and young adults can be asked to notice and record these happy moments, to support their ability to notice them. Mindfulness exercises are also likely to support them to remain in the present moment.

Behavioural interventions

Behavioural interventions relate most specifically to the second and third elements of the happiness wheel: valuing relationships and meaningful and productive activity. There are a number of different interventions that can support adolescents and young adults to adjust their behaviour to bring about significant changes to how they feel and increase their levels of happiness and wellbeing.

Behavioural activation

Behavioural activation was covered in detail in Chapter 7, where we covered three important qualities of different activities: achievement, connection, and enjoyment. Enjoyment maps onto the first of our components of wellbeing, connection onto the second, and achievement onto the third. This means that a balance of these three types of activity is not only important in moving out of the sadness trap, but is equally important in the happiness wheel and moving towards wellbeing and flourishing.

Behavioural activation can be delivered in the same way in the context of the happiness wheel as in the sadness trap. However, it is not usually necessary to go into the same level of detail and depth, as those moving towards happiness and flourishing are more likely to have a greater sense of agency and higher levels of motivation than those moving out of the sadness trap. Instead of detailed diaries and schedules, it is often sufficient to move into comparing how adolescents and young adults are spending their time, with the principles of behavioural activation and the happiness wheel. This can lead to clear actions that relate to adjusting the balance of activity, or problem solving particular aspects of their lives to increase their levels of connection, achievement, enjoyment, and meaning.

Where fear gets in the way of making these changes, we can use the ideas from the fear trap to support the process. The circles from the fear chapter, for example, can be a really helpful way of illustrating the processes of building confidence by gently pushing into the uncomfortable zone.

With regards to socialising with others, it is important to also consider the quality of interaction. Many adolescents and young adults have not yet found the balance of meeting their own needs versus meeting the needs of others. Where they are socialising with others, but in ways that are not fulfilling for them, we can use the ideas from the emotion dysregulation trap (Chapter 9) to illustrate the patterns of interaction and help them to move towards more healthy, balanced relating.

Organisation, planning, and problem-solving

Productivity, which is linked so closely with achievement and meaning, does not arise by itself; it is based on a set of skills and abilities that can be learned. Adolescents and young adults spend a great deal of their time engaged in learning and study, as well as balancing competing demands on their time. The demands of learning shift throughout education and it becomes increasingly important to use organisational skills. Teaching adolescents and young adults these organisational skills can support them to increase their levels of productivity and resultant happiness.

Some key skills include: how to prioritise, how to break things down, how to maximise thinking space, how to manage time, and how to overcome blocks.

Acts of kindness

Practicing acts of kindness is a discrete positive psychology intervention, which is linked with increasing the immediate levels of happiness, but also developing and valuing relationships with others.

Adolescents and young adults are given a relatively simple task: to undertake a given number of acts of kindness (often three) during the course of the week and to record these acts to be discussed later. Behavioural tasks of this sort are based in the interpersonal nature of happiness and are designed specifically to alter the way in which individuals relate to those around them. They commonly result in an increase in wellbeing for the individual themselves, and also often result in gratitude, displays of warmth or affect, or reciprocal acts of kindness from others.

Using strengths

A final specific positive psychology intervention is using strengths, which relates to the meaning and productivity element of the happiness wheel. In this task, adolescents and young adults are asked to identify their 'signature' strengths. They are then asked to use these strengths in novel ways and to do this regularly. An example is a young adult who identifies critical thinking as a key strength based on their performance at work, who could use this skill in the novel situation of supporting a friend who is facing a social dilemma.

The invitation to identify and broaden the use of strengths is a behavioural intervention that develops individuals' behavioural repertoire, beginning from a positive self-image. This task can follow relatively easily from other behavioural work that might have been undertaken in relation to other traps in this book.

Cognitive interventions

Cognitive interventions target the fourth element of the happiness wheel: optimistic outlook. Previous sections on cognitive interventions have focused on reducing the tendency to negative thought biases and challenging negative thoughts, appraisals, and beliefs. In previous sections on cognitive interventions, however, we have already noted the importance in identifying alternative and more positive beliefs with which to challenge the negative ones. We have also noted that work often progresses better when the focus is on increasing conviction in a positive self-belief versus reducing conviction in a negative self-belief. Cognitive interventions in happiness follow directly from these interventions and aim to develop and expand an optimistic outlook. They often involve the development of the cognitive techniques already covered but there are a number of specific ways in which we can further encourage a positive outlook.

Positive data logs

Positive data logs are based on the same principles as those covered in Chapter 7 on thought challenging and evidence gathering. However, the aim is to explicitly favour the positive and gather only evidence in support of a positive belief. Adolescents and young adults can be asked to write down all the times when they did or said things that were consistent with a positive self-belief, for example "I'm intelligent," "I'm a caring person," or "Other people are caring."

Counting blessings/gratitude exercises

Other common methods used in positive psychology are counting blessings or gratitude exercises. Again, the process is relatively simple: adolescents and young adults are asked, on a fairly regular basis to think about things that for which they are grateful or thankful. This invites an attentional focus on the positive aspects of life and invites a 'glass half full' perspective. Over time, this can correct and overtake the opposite tendency.

These kinds of exercises often also have the knock-on effect of encouraging behaviours, such as saying thank you or demonstrating appreciation for others, that results in a reinforcing loop.

Summary

The interventions outlined to support the happiness wheel are core CBT interventions we have covered throughout this book. They include emotion regulation, behavioural change, and cognitive challenge. Our core CBT interventions often tend towards the positive, but the happiness wheel provides an invitation to extend this and to explicitly work with our clients not just to support a reduction in distress, but to support an increase in their levels of happiness and wellbeing. These kinds of tasks can be undertaken towards the end of therapy, without much more work, but with significant shift in terms of outlook and a real sense of cementing and building on the progress already made.

Evidence base

As outlined in the introduction, happiness and positive psychology are relatively new areas of investigation. Despite this, there has been a recent upsurge in interest and research in the area and there is a fair degree of evidence to support the interventions outlined in this section.

Many studies have compared, on a cross-sectional basis, individuals who tend to be happy, versus those who do not. These studies often include relatively large samples, and support the model outlined in the happiness wheel above. A selection of the studies supporting the model are cited in the text about the happiness wheel above.

Many of the interventions outlined in relation to the happiness wheel are drawn from studies that have demonstrated efficacy in reducing distress. However, there is a fair degree of evidence in support of specific positive psychology interventions. Seligman et al. (2005) investigated five different tasks that were designed to increase levels of happiness. They found strong evidence in support of two of them (counting blessings and using strengths), which are included above. A later meta-analysis has provided strong support for a variety of interventions which have been shown to both decrease scores on depression measures and increase scores on wellbeing measures (Sin and Lyubomirsky, 2009). Acts of kindness have been investigated in younger age groups and there have been strong links found with increases in prosocial behaviour and peer relationships (Layous et al., 2012; Pressman, Kraft and Cross, 2015). In a large study, gratitude exercises were found to be particularly helpful for those tending towards self-criticism (Sergeant and Mongrain, 2011).

Overall, the evidence for CBT in happiness is consistent with the evidence for CBT in other emotions: explicitly and clearly encouraging particular types of behaviour or particular patterns of thought reliably results in significant emotional changes.

References

Aknin, L.B., Dunn, E.W., and Norton, M.I., 2012. Happiness runs in a circular motion: evidence for a positive feedback loop between prosocial spending and happiness. *Journal of Happiness Studies*, *13*(2), pp. 347–355.

Argyle, M., 2013. *The psychology of happiness*. London: Routledge.

Calvo, M.G. and Beltrán, D., 2013. Recognition advantage of happy faces: tracing the neurocognitive processes. *Neuropsychologia*, *51*(11), pp. 2051–2061.

Dolhinow, P.J., 1987. At play in the fields. In H.R. Topoff, *The natural history reader in animal behavior*. New York: Columbia University Press, pp. 229–237.

Ekman, P. and Friesen, W.V., 1982. Felt, false, and miserable smiles. *Journal of Nonverbal Behavior*, *6*(4), pp. 238–252.

Fordyce, M.W., 1981. *The psychology of happiness: a brief version of the fourteen fundamentals*. Fort Myers, FL: Cyprus Lake Media.

Fredrickson, B.L., 2004. The broaden-and-build theory of positive emotions. *Philosophical Transactions of the Royal Society B: Biological Sciences*, *359*(1449), pp. 1367–1377.

Fredrickson, B.L., Mancuso, R.A., Branigan, C., and Tugade, M.M., 2000. The undoing effect of positive emotions. *Motivation and Emotion*, *24*(4), pp. 237–258.

Golle, J., Mast, F.W., and Lobmaier, J.S., 2014. Something to smile about: the interrelationship between attractiveness and emotional expression. *Cognition and Emotion*, *28*(2), pp. 298–310.

Holder, M.D., Coleman, B., and Sehn, Z.L., 2009. The contribution of active and passive leisure to children's well-being. *Journal of Health Psychology*, *14*(3), pp. 378–386.

Huppert, F.A. and So, T.T., 2013. Flourishing across Europe: application of a new conceptual framework for defining well-being. *Social Indicators Research*, *110*(3), pp. 837–861.

Izard, C.E., 1991. *The psychology of emotions*. New York: Plenum Press.

Keyes, C.L., 2006. Mental health in adolescence: is America's youth flourishing? *American Journal of Orthopsychiatry*, *76*(3), pp. 395–402.

Kraut, R.E. and Johnston, R.E., 1979. Social and emotional messages of smiling: an ethological approach. *Journal of Personality and Social Psychology*, *37*(9), pp. 1539–1553.

Lambert, M., Fleming, T., Ameratunga, S., Robinson, E., Crengle, S., Sheridan, J., Denny, S., Clark, T., and Merry, S., 2014. Looking on the bright side: an assessment of factors associated with adolescents' happiness. *Advances in Mental Health*, *12*(2), pp. 101–109.

Layous, K., Nelson, S.K., Oberle, E., Schonert-Reichl, K.A., and Lyubomirsky, S., 2012. Kindness counts: prompting prosocial behavior in preadolescents boosts peer acceptance and well-being. *PloS ONE*, *7*(12), p.e51380.

Lyubomirsky, S., Dickerhoof, R., Boehm, J.K., and Sheldon, K.M., 2011. Becoming happier takes both a will and a proper way: an experimental longitudinal intervention to boost well-being. *Emotion, 11*(2), pp. 391–402.

Lyubomirsky, S., Sheldon, K.M., and Schkade, D., 2005. Pursuing happiness: the architecture of sustainable change. *Review of General Psychology, 9*(2), pp. 111–131.

Meadows, C.M., 1968. *Joy in psychological and theological perspective: a constructive approach.* Unpublished doctoral dissertation, Princeton Theological Seminary, Princeton, NJ.

Pressman, S.D., Kraft, T.L., and Cross, M.P., 2015. It's good to do good and receive good: The impact of a 'pay it forward' style kindness intervention on giver and receiver well-being. The *Journal of Positive Psychology, 10*(4), pp. 293–302.

Quoidbach, J., Mikolajczak, M., and Gross, J.J., 2015. Positive interventions: an emotion regulation perspective. *Psychological Bulletin, 141*(3), pp. 655–693.

Scherer, K.R. and Wallbott, H.G., 1994. Evidence for universality and cultural variation of differential emotion response patterning. *Journal of Personality and Social Psychology, 66*(2), 310–328.

Scherer, K.R., Wallbott, H.G., and Summerfield, A.B. (eds), 1986. *Experiencing emotion: a cross-cultural study.* Cambridge, UK: Cambridge University Press.

Seligman, M.E., 2012. *Flourish: a visionary new understanding of happiness and well-being.* New York: Simon and Schuster.

Seligman, M.E., Steen, T.A., Park, N., and Peterson, C., 2005. Positive psychology progress: empirical validation of interventions. *American Psychologist, 60*(5), pp. 410–421.

Sergeant, S. and Mongrain, M., 2011. Are positive psychology exercises helpful for people with depressive personality styles? *The Journal of Positive Psychology, 6*(4), pp. 260–272.

Sin, N.L. and Lyubomirsky, S., 2009. Enhancing well-being and alleviating depressive symptoms with positive psychology interventions: a practice-friendly meta-analysis. *Journal of Clinical Psychology, 65*(5), pp. 467–487.

Singer, J.L., 1979. Affect and imagination in play and fantasy. In: C.E. Izard (ed.) *Emotions in personality and psychopathology.* New York: Springer, pp. 13–34.

Suldo, S.M. and Huebner, E.S., 2006. Is extremely high life satisfaction during adolescence advantageous? *Social Indicators Research, 78*(2), pp. 179–203.

Uusitalo-Malmivaara, L., 2012. Global and school-related happiness in Finnish children. *Journal of Happiness Studies, 13*(4), pp. 601–619.

Van Vugt, M., Hardy, C., Stow, J., and Dunbar, R., 2014. *Laughter as social lubricant: a biosocial hypothesis about the pro-social functions of laughter and humor.* Centre for the Study of Group Processes Working Paper, University of Kent, UK.

Index

abandonment (fears of) 185, 190, 193, 194

A-B-C (antecedent – behaviour – consequence) model 163

abstract thought *see* formal operational thought

abuse *see* excessive emotional harm; sexual abuse

ACE (achievement, connection, enjoyment) 127, 128, 129

acetylcholine 59–60

activity monitoring 127–128, 129, 130, 131

activity scheduling 129–130, 131

acts of kindness 239–240

adaptive beliefs 36, 140; *see also* maladaptive beliefs

adaptiveness (in evolution) 30, 38, 61, 62, 73, 178

ADHD 146

adolescence 5–27, 63–66; age range 1, 6, 22, 64; and anger 152; and 'angst'/emotional difficulty 14, 64; brain development 6, 7–8, 15; cognitive development during 8–9; delayed 6; developmental process of 3, 63–66; and emotion dysregulation 188; and emotion regulation 12–16; and fear 74; and happiness 234; identity development 10; levels of wellbeing during 3; negative perceptions of 5; parental perceptions of 3; positive experience 3; relationships with adults 3; and sadness 116; social cognitive development 9–10; societal views 5, 20; stereotypes 5; theories of 17, 20, 63; transitions in 6, 22, 63–66

adrenalin 59, 68, 148

aggression 16, 146, 149–150, 153, 155, 160, 162

agoraphobia *see* fear; panic attacks

alcohol *see* substance use/misuse

all or nothing thinking 133

alternative predictions/thoughts/beliefs 91, 136–139, 140–141, 227, 240

anger 55, 62, 146–175, 197; adolescence and 152; appraisals/thoughts in 149; behaviours of 149–150; causes of 147; cautions 170; facial expression of 149; feelings in 148; function of 150–152; physiology of 148; regulating in moment 166–171

anger trap 152–161; appraisals/thoughts in 154; behaviours 155–157; drawing 158–161; evidence for 174; feelings 154–155; hand brain and 157–158; intervention 161–174; physiology 155

antecedent 163

anti-social behaviour 19

anti-stigma campaigns 46

anxiety 29, 40, 45, 58, 71, 75; *see also* fear

apathy 121, 178

apologising 173

appraisals 30, 60–61; in anger 149; in anger trap 154, 158–161, 167, 173; in disgust 214–215, 217–218; in emotion dysregulation 180–181; in fear 72–73; in fear trap 76–77, 81–82, 89, 96, 98, 101–102, 103, 104, 106; in guilt and shame 222, 224–225, 227; in happiness 231, 237; in sadness 113; in sadness trap 118–120

approach behaviour 149–150, 155, 231–232

Arnett, J. 5, 14, 15, 19, 20